Booker T. Washington **in Perspective**

α

BOOKER T. WASHINGTON
in Perspective

Essays of Louis R. Harlan

Edited by Raymond W. Smock

University Press of Mississippi
JACKSON AND LONDON

91 90 89 88   4 3 2 1

The paper in this book meets the guidelines for permanence and
durability of the Committee on Production Guidelines for Book
Longevity of the Council on Library Resources.

Designed by John A. Langston

All illustrations are from the Library of Congress, unless otherwise noted.

Library of Congress Cataloging-in-Publication Data

Harlan, Louis R.
    Booker T. Washington in perspective : essays of Louis R. Harlan /
edited by Raymond Smock.
        p.   cm.
    Includes index.
    ISBN 0-87805-374-3 (alk. paper)
    1. Washington, Booker T., 1856-1915.   2. Afro-Americans—Civil
rights.   3. Afro-Americans—Biography.   4. Educators—United States-
-Biography.   I. Smock, Raymond.   II. Title.
E185.97.W4H36 1988
378'.111—dc19
    [B]   88-17338
                                                                  CIP

The University Press of Mississippi thanks all publishers for
granting permission to reprint these essays.

The essays in this volume were originally published as follows:

"Booker T. Washington in Biographical Perspective." *American Historical Review*, LXXV (October
1970), 1581-99. Copyright, American Historical Association, 1970.

"Booker T. Washington's West Virginia Boyhood." *West Virginia History*, XXXII (January 1971),
63-85. Copyright, The State of West Virginia, Department of Culture and History, 1971.

"Booker T. Washington and the Kanawha Valley, 1875-1879." *West Virginia History*, XXXIII
(January 1972), 124-41. Copyright, The State of West Virginia, Department of Culture and
History, 1972.

"Booker T. Washington and the White Man's Burden." *American Historical Review*, LXI (January
1966), 441-67. Copyright, Louis R. Harlan, 1966.

"Booker T. Washington and the National Negro Business League." In William G. Shade and Roy
C. Herrenkohl, eds., *Seven on Black: Reflections on the Negro Experience in America*.
Philadelphia/New York: J.B. Lippincott Company, 1969. (pp. 73-91). Copyright, Harper &
Row Publishers, Inc., 1969.

"The Secret Life of Booker T. Washington." *Journal of Southern History*, XXXVII (August 1971),
393-416. Copyright, Southern Historical Association, 1971.

"Booker T. Washington and the *Voice of the Negro*, 1904-1907." *Journal of Southern History*, XLV
(February 1979), 45-62. Copyright, Southern Historical Association, 1979.

"Booker T. Washington's Discovery of Jews." In J. Morgan Kousser and James M. McPherson,
eds., *Region, Race and Reconstruction: Essays in Honor of C. Vann Woodward*. New York:
Oxford University Press, 1982. (pp. 267-79). Copyright, Oxford University Press, 1982.

"Booker T. Washington and the Politics of Accommodation." In John Hope Franklin and August
Meier, eds., *Black Leaders of the Twentieth Century*. Urbana: University of Illinois Press, 1982.
(pp. 1-18). Copyright, University of Illinois Press, 1982.

"The Booker T. Washington Papers." (With Raymond W. Smock), *Maryland Historian*, 6 (1975),
55-59. Copyright, *Maryland Historian*, 1975.

"Sympathy and Detachment: Dilemmas of a Biographer." In Dwight W. Hoover and John T. A.
Koumoulides, eds., *Conspectus of History*, 1 (1974), 29-36. [Ball State University History
Department, Muncie, Indiana] Copyright, Ball State University, 1974.

"Booker T. Washington: The Labyrinth and the Thread." *ADE Newsletter*, 5 (December 1983),
5-9. [Now titled *Documentary Editing*, a publication of the Association for Documentary
Editing]. Copyright, Association for Documentary Editing, 1983.

CONTENTS

PREFACE

Louis R. Harlan first saw the Booker T. Washington Papers almost forty years ago, when they were still a vast unsorted collection of more than a million items stored in the bowels of the Manuscript Division at the Library of Congress. This vast collection represented the most voluminous historical record of any individual black American in our history, with the possible exception of the Papers of Martin Luther King, Jr., which are now being edited for publication.

Since that first contact with Washington's amazing documentary legacy, Louis Harlan has devoted a large portion of his professional career to the study of the enigmatic and controversial educator and race leader. Harlan's study of Booker T. Washington resulted in the publication of the articles collected in this volume, a fourteen-volume documentary edition of Washington's papers, and a two-volume biography of Washington, which won two Bancroft Prizes and the Pulitzer Prize for Biography in 1984.

The essays in this collection span more than twenty-five years of research and writing on the life and times of Booker T. Washington. They represent a scholarly odyssey to understand Washington from several perspectives, all necessary to explain the motives and actions of a man who was the most powerful black man in America at the opening of the twentieth century and the last national race leader who was born in slavery. Many of the articles in this volume originally appeared in major scholarly journals and books, while others, such as "Booker T. Washington: The Labyrinth and the Thread," appeared in small circulation publications which are difficult to locate.

To reveal Washington in all his complexity Harlan had to understand not only the man but his times and the lives of his contemporaries, both black and white, who shaped Washington's philosophy and his actions. The essays often cover in greater narrative detail the subjects presented in **ix** the biography and the documentary edition. In "Booker T. Washington and the *Voice of the Negro*," for example, Harlan presents a remarkable case study of how relentless Washington could be toward his black critics. Furthermore, several of the selections in this volume explain the craft of biographical and historical writing. The reader will not only learn about Booker T. Washington, but will come to understand the problems faced by historians as they work. Three of the essays, "Booker T. Washington in Biographical Perspective," "Sympathy and Detachment: Dilemmas of a Biographer," and "Booker T. Washington: The Labyrinth and the Thread," address the relationship of history and biography and the use of Washington's voluminous private papers.

Washington, as Harlan states in "Sympathy and Detachment: Dilemmas of a Biographer," is "among the less lovable major figures in American black history." Readers of these essays will, however, come to realize that this seemingly harsh judgment is tempered with great sensitivity and a remarkable blend of sympathy and detachment, as the title of the essay suggests. In a career rich in irony, probably the most ironic element of all was that Washington became powerful and famous in an era that Rayford Logan called the "nadir of Negro life in America." Washington's personal power was rising while the fortunes of black Americans were at their lowest ebb. Lynchings, disfranchisement, racial segregation, pseudo-scientific theories of black racial inferiority, racist demagogues in state legislatures and the national Congress, were all at their peak when Booker T. Washington was gathering his forces. To know Washington we must understand the Age of Accommodation which lasted through much of the late nineteenth and early twentieth centuries.

Washington saw himself as an axis between the races, as the only leader who could keep the peace by holding the extremists on both sides in check. His popularity among blacks and whites was based on his conservative program of economic and educational advancement. He accommodated to white America by playing down the importance of political agitation for civil rights. Looking back from the perspective of the 1980s this program of economic and educational striving and the eschewal of politics and agitation for civil rights seems timid and unheroic. The purpose of these essays, however, is not to defend Washington's outmoded social philosophy and program for race advancement, but to explain the world in which Washington operated and to understand what it meant to be a black leader in such times. Students of history who ignore the career of this important American will never be able to fully grasp the meaning of racism in America nor will they be able to appreciate the profound changes that have taken place in America since Booker T. Washington's time.

When the great Civil Rights Movement of the 1950s and 1960s occurred, Booker T. Washington was swept under the rug. More militant black leaders and their white allies found Washington to be an "Uncle Tom," a lackey of white America, rather than a champion of black freedom. The Civil Rights Movement needed heroes who had spoken out eloquently for the race, such as Frederick Douglass and W. E. B. DuBois, who were harbingers of things to come rather than reminders of the way things had been. But a careful look at Washington's career shows him to be far more complex than his stereotyped public image. Professor Harlan goes beyond the conventional wisdom about Washington and reveals the remarkable contrast between Washington's carefully cultivated public image and his fascinating secret life behind the scenes.

Thanks to the work of Louis Harlan in the areas of narrative history, documentary history, and biography, and the brilliant pioneering work in intellectual history by August Meier in *Negro Thought in America, 1880-1915: Racial Ideologies in the Age of Booker T. Washington* (Ann Arbor, 1963), we have important scholarly tools at our disposal to help us evaluate the life and times of Booker T. Washington. Students should be familiar with the results of the past quarter century of research if they hope to improve their understanding of the black experience in the United States. This volume of essays will contribute to that goal.

The essays in this volume have been organized to reflect the development of Booker T. Washington's life and career, rather than according to the date of publication. They appear in full as they were originally published. A few minor editorial changes have ben made for clarity and consistency for this new edition. In a few of the essays published in the late 1960s and early 1970s the use of the word "Negro" has been changed to "black" or "black American." Footnote style has been left as it was in the original except to use "BTW" for Booker T. Washington, and to eliminate cross references to the author's own works now that they have been assembled in one volume. Several of the essays originally appeared without footnotes.

Raymond W. Smock
Lanham, Maryland

ACKNOWLEDGMENTS

I am grateful to Seetha Srinivasan, associate director of the University Press of Mississippi, for originally suggesting that Louis Harlan's scholarly essays on Booker T. Washington be brought together in one volume. I worked with Louis Harlan for twenty years, first as a graduate student and later as coeditor of the *Booker T. Washington Papers*, so preparing these essays for publication was truly a labor of love. Professor Harlan's enthusiasm for the project has made the task a genuine pleasure.

Permission to reprint the articles was graciously provided by the original publishers or their assignees. I would like to thank the American Historical Association, the Southern Historical Association, the Association for Documentary Editing, Harper and Row Publishers, Inc., Oxford University Press, the University of Illinois Press, the History Department of Ball State University, the University of Maryland, and the West Virginia Department of Culture and History for their generous cooperation.

Booker T. Washington **in Perspective**

Booker T. Washington in Biographical Perspective

In the current vogue of black history Booker T. Washington has been a figure to ignore rather than to grapple with, an anomaly, an embarrassment. This is partly because his methods were too compromising and unheroic to win him a place in the black pantheon, but it is also because he was so complex and enigmatic that historians do not know what to make of him. We have lost the thread we used to believe would guide us through his labyrinth. When his rich private collection of papers was opened to scholars two decades ago, historians had to abandon the simpler picture of Washington presented in his autobiography. They generally seized upon the concept that Washington was a symbol of his age in race relations, a representative figure whose actions and philosophy were pragmatically adjusted to the demands of an era of sharply worsening race relations. He was the type of black leader that the age of Jim Crow would throw to the top. There is something to be said for this view, and certainly Washington was delicately attuned to his age. From the biographical perspective, however, Washington seems thoroughly consistent throughout a life that spanned from the slavery era into the twentieth century. In the period of his leadership after 1895 he followed the lessons he had learned at Hampton Institute in the seventies and practiced at Tuskegee in the eighties.

In his mature years Washington's life became extremely complex. There was first of all the public image, that of a race leader who told his people to accommodate themselves to the realities of white power, and whose own personal success illustrated that such a course could be personally rewarding. In the Atlanta Address in 1895, the year the old militant leader Frederick Douglass died, Washington stated the formula: "In all things that are purely social we can be as separate as the fingers, yet one as the hand in all things essential to mutual progress." Put down your buckets where they are, make peace and common cause with your white neighbor, **3** seek a white patron, but also improve yourself slowly through education and property, through "severe and constant struggle rather than . . . artificial forcing."[1] A few years later Washington's success story, *Up from Slavery*, a worldwide best seller, further buttressed the accommodation formula. It described, somewhat mythically, his rise from a slave cabin to the middle class, the inculcation at Hampton Institute of Puritan virtues, and their practice through a useful and successful life. It was a comforting witness that even the American race system could not keep a good man down. Tuskegee Institute, which he founded in a black church and a henhouse and built into one of the largest and best-endowed schools in the South, was a monument to the effectiveness of his approach.

Though Washington never made another speech of the significance of the Atlanta Address nor wrote another book equal to *Up from Slavery*, he remained throughout his life a popular platform speaker and magazine article writer. He expressed what John Kenneth Galbraith calls "the conventional wisdom" of his day in race relations and social thought. He was the apostle of things as they were. He had to employ a series of ghost writers to meet the demand for books and articles. Unfortunately, however, under his instructions the ghost writers merely paraphrased Washington's earlier utterances, thus freezing his public thought in outmoded patterns. His mind as revealed in formal public expression became a bag of clichés.

Washington's mind or psyche as the directing force of his private actions, on the other hand, was kaleidoscopic in its changing patterns and apparent lack of a central design. The source of this complexity, no doubt, was being a black man in white America, with the attendant dualism and ambivalence that black people feel. Washington's life and thought were layered into public, private, and secret and also segmented according to which subgroup of black or white he confronted. For each group he played a different role, wore a different mask. Like the proverbial cat, Washington lived nine lives, but he lived them all at once. Yet there were so few slips of the mask that it is no wonder his intimates called him "the wizard."

One of Washington's private roles was that of master of the Tuskegee plantation. From his big house, "The Oaks," Washington ran his school without delegation of authority and with infinite attention to detail. Even during his absences in the North, he continued to direct affairs closely through the confidential reports of his brother, private secretary, and other informers. He saw the sparrow's fall. Faculty members dreaded the crunch of carriage wheels that signaled his return, for each morning he toured the campus on horseback and noted every scrap of trash, every stray chicken, every dirty plate, every evidence of student waste or neglect. It all went into his little red notebook,[2] from which flowed a thousand memoranda reminding errant faculty members of their high duty to make of Tuskegee a black utopia, a proof that blacks were capable of the petit bourgeois life.

In the radically different world of the white philanthropists Washington showed his appealing mask, deferential but dignified. At first, following the example of Hampton Institute, he made Boston his Northern head-quarters and the church and Sunday-school philanthropy of New England small towns his principal philanthropic target. At the turn of the century, however, he began spending his winters and summers in New York, center of the new wealth of industry and finance. Showing that there can be a subtlety even in platitudes, Washington gradually modified his rhetoric from the style of Puritan homiletics to that of the "gospel of wealth." His principal appeal to businessmen, however, was that he seemed so much like them, not only in his attitude toward labor, property, public order, and other questions but in the earnestness, diligence, and energy with which he conducted his school. What struck Andrew Carnegie, when he gave Tuskegee a library, was Washington's ability, through the cheap labor of students, to get so much building for so little money. He was a safe, sane, self-made man who could be trusted with one's money. Moving freely in the offices, homes, and summer resorts of the wealthy, Washington constantly crossed the color line in the North, riding first-class cars and staying at first-class hotels. Though he had dinner at the White House only once, that was no measure of his dining habits among the Northern elite, who accepted him on perhaps more completely equal terms than any other black American in history.

Among Southern whites Washington was more circumspect. He made a point of not crossing the color line while in the South. He sought to reduce social friction by what Southerners called keeping his place. Washington divided white Southerners into two classes: employers who were the benefactors of blacks and fit allies of Northern philanthropists, and poor whites, who were enemies of the black people and of a harmonious social order. Washington's strategy of partnership with the Southern white elite was notably unsuccessful in halting the tide of white racial aggression, violence, disfranchisement, discrimination, and segregation in his day. The white planters and businessmen turned out to be not as benevolent as expected and nowhere near as powerful, and the Southern political system and to some extent its economy fell into the hands of whites in whose lives of hardship and disappointment in a depressed Southern economy the Negro served as a convenient scapegoat. Washington refused to face this worsening of race relations realistically, refused to doubt the viability of his Atlanta Compromise. In 1908, after a tour of Mississippi, then in the throes of Vardaman's demagoguery, he wrote to Oswald Garrison Villard: "I was surprised to find a large number of white men and women who, close down in their hearts, I am sure are all right, but only need encouragement and help to lead them to the point where they will speak out and act more bravely." When a white mob at Lula, Mississippi, hanged two blacks where Washington could see them as his train passed, he assured Villard that this episode was not significant "outside of the ordinary disgraceful lynchings that so frequently occur in that state."[3]

Among Southern blacks Washington presented a fatherly image. He was of the same rural Southern peasant origins and could speak to them in their own language. They responded also to the peasant conservatism of his economic program, with its emphasis on the basic needs of a rural people—small property accumulation, education of a practical sort, recognition of the dignity of toil, doing the common, everyday things of life "uncommonly without a murmur," Washington conceived of Tuskegee as "a school built around a social problem." He thought that all his compromises would be justified if his industrial school, located like a settlement house in the middle of a rural slum, could transform the lives of the black sharecroppers of Macon County, Alabama, and the surrounding Black Belt. So he not only trained teachers and skilled farmers and tradesmen to return to these communities, but he offered them schemes to improve their lives. The Jesup Wagon, an agricultural classroom on wheels, toured the back roads; an annual Negro Conference brought farmers from Alabama and neighboring states for lessons in scientific agriculture and the economics of land ownership. Tuskegee managed several loan funds to aid local farmers to buy their land.[4] It is easy to see now that Washington's plan for economic progress was bound to fail because he sought to build through small business institutions in a day when big business was sweeping all before it. Worse yet, it was in agriculture, the sickest industry in America, and in the South, the nation's sickest region, and in certain obsolescent trades such as blacksmithing that Washington sought to work his economic wonders. All that was less clear in his day, however, and besides he had an emotional commitment to "keep them down on the farm," for he hated and feared the city.

Despite his Southern rural distrust of the city and particularly the black intellectuals and professional men of the Northern cities, Washington used the power that white approval and financing gave him to dominate also the Northern black ghetto-dwellers. As August Meier has shown so convincingly, he even bound a large segment of the "talented tenth," the professional-class elite, to him by patronage and mutual interest rather than common ideology.[5] He was the founder and president of the National Negro Business League, an organization he shrewdly used to create a nucleus of conservative blacks in all the Northern cities. He could not completely control black journalistic expression, but he did dominate it by a combination of ownership of some newspapers and advertising subsidies to others, and by paying a black syndicated columnist to follow the Tuskegee line. Black professors were kept under control by college presidents who recognized that Washington could reward or punish them when philanthropists asked his advice. His smile or frown could govern the fate of a college library, and he personally dispensed much of the black philanthropy of Carnegie, Schiff, and Rosenwald. His white friends patronized the black painters, singers, and writers whom he favored. His friends infiltrated the leading black church denominations and even the black Odd Fellows and Prince Hall Masons in his interest. In all the activity of this Tuskegee Machine was a determination to crush rash militants who were more and more openly denouncing him as a traitor to his race.

Despite his public advice to blacks to abandon voting and officeholding as a solution of their problems, Washington became the leading black political broker in the era of Theodore Roosevelt and Taft. The constituency of black politicians was dissolving in those years because of disfranchisement in the South, while the Northern ghetto populations were still too small to have much political weight. The trend in black patronage positions, therefore, was downward, and Washington could do little to reverse its course. He simply secured places for his friends, particularly black businessmen in the South and well-trained lawyers in the North. He also helped Roosevelt pick white Southerners as judges, revenue collectors, and marshals who gave evidence of conservatism and a paternalistic sympathy for blacks. Washington used his position as a black political boss to try to curb the lily-white Republican movement in the South, to moderate the Republican platforms and presidential utterances on racial matters, and to dampen black protest against the wholesale dismissal of black troops accused of rioting in Brownsville, Texas, in 1906. Although Washington supported Taft in 1908, he was subsequently dismayed by the president's rapid removal of nearly all Southern black officeholders. The

Wilson administration continued this trend and increased segregation in the federal civil service. By the end of his life Boss Washington's political machine was in a state of nearly complete breakdown.

Finally, Washington had an elaborate secret life. In his civil rights activity he presented himself publicly as a social pacifist and accommodationist, while secretly he financed and generaled a series of court suits challenging the grandfather clause, denial of jury service to blacks, Jim Crow cars, and peonage. Working sometimes with the black lawyers of the Afro-American Council, sometimes through his own personal lawyer Wilford H. Smith, and sometimes with sympathetic Southern white lawyers, Washington took every precaution to keep his collaboration a secret. He used his private secretary and a Tuskegee faculty member as go-betweens, and in the Alabama suffrage cases that were carried to the United States Supreme Court he had his secretary and the lawyer correspond using the code names R. C. Black and J. C. May.[6]

It cannot be said that Washington's secret militancy had much effect against the downtrend of race relations. Another secret activity, however, that of espionage against his black enemies, sometimes had devastating effect. When the Boston black radical William Monroe Trotter began openly to denounce Washington and created a disturbance known as the Boston Riot, Washington employed a spy named Melvin J. Chisum to infiltrate Trotter's New England Suffrage League. Chisum acted as a provocateur and informed Washington of secret meetings so that Washington could counter their strategy. Washington also planted a Boston lawyer, Clifford Plummer, in the Trotter organization and arranged with a Yale student to sue Trotter's paper for libel. When W. E. B. Du Bois and some thirty of his friends met at Niagara Falls in 1905 to found the Niagara Movement, Washington paid Plummer to go there and spy on the meeting and to stop the Associated Press from giving it publicity. The following year Washington used a distinguished old black, who hoped Washington would help him regain his political appointment, to infiltrate the Niagara Movement at Harper's Ferry. Washington had many other agents, including Pinkerton detectives and paid and unpaid black informers. Melvin Chisum worked for years as Booker Washington's spy in New York and Washington, infiltrating the Niagara Movement and the NAACP, holding meetings with Washington on park benches to disclose his findings, and obviously enjoying his work. "I am your obedient humble servant, Chisum," he roguishly ended one letter, "your own property, to use as your Eminence desires, absolutely."[7]

In each of these compartmentalized worlds Washington displayed a different personality, wore a different mask, played a different role. At Tuskegee he was a benevolent despot. To Northern whites he appeared a racial statesman; to Southern whites he was a safe, sane black who advised blacks to "stay in their place." To Southern blacks he was a father, to Northern blacks a stepfather; to politicians he was another political boss. In his paradoxical secret life he attacked the racial settlement that he publicly accepted, and he used ruthless methods of espionage and sabotage that contrasted sharply with his public Sunday-school morality.

Perhaps psychoanalysis or role psychology would solve Washington's behavioral riddle, if we could only put him on the couch. If we could remove those layers of secrecy as one peels an onion, perhaps at the center of Booker T. Washington's being would be revealed a person single-mindedly concerned with power, a minotaur, a lion, fox, or Br'er Rabbit, some frightened little man like the Wizard of Oz, or, as in the case of the onion, nothing, a personality disintegrated by the frenzied activity of being all things to all men in a multifaceted society. He "jumped Jim Crow" so often that he lost sight of the original purposes of his motion.

It is possible to explain many of the seeming contradictions in Washington's mature life by examining his biography. A biographical approach may counterbalance a slight distortion introduced by the historical approach. Historians have tended to see Washington's accommodationist behavior as of its time, that is, of the period of his leadership after 1895, and as a deliberate, realistic, pragmatic response to the black man's "time of troubles." While C. Vann Woodward, for example, recognizes that Washington "dealt with the present in terms of the past," he says that "it is indeed hard to see how he could have preached or his people practiced a radically different philosophy in his time and place."[8] The biographical evidence, on the other hand, shows that all the hallmarks of Washington's style of leadership—his conservative petit bourgeois social philosophy, his accommodation to white supremacy and segregation, and his employment of secret weapons against his adversaries—were well developed prior to the 1890's. They were a response to precepts and pressures of the 1870's and 1880's. These decades turn out on close examination to have been not as different from the period after 1890 as some historians have assumed. Perhaps we have too sharply periodized the history of American race relations and have exaggerated the differences between one decade and another. This is not to say that the Progressive era was not characterized by racial violence, disfranchisement, and segregation, but so were the seventies, the age of the Ku Klux Klan and the abandonment of Reconstruction, and the eighties, the era of reversal of civil rights legislation.

Knowledge of Washington's early life is based primarily on his two autobiographies. *Up from Slavery* is more detailed and better written but distorted by its success-story formula. *The Story of My Life and Work*, written a year earlier primarily for the black subscription book market, reveals facets of his career ignored in *Up from Slavery*. These works are supplemented, however, by other contemporary evidence and the reminiscences of a number of close associates of Washington's youth.

Washington was born on a small Virginia farm, the child of a slave cook and a white man of the neighborhood. His birth occurred prior to his mother's marriage to Washington Ferguson, the slave of a neighboring farmer, and prior to the birth of the darker half-sister Amanda. It was a common pattern of slavery that house servants, because of higher status, lighter work load, closeness to the master class, and, sometimes, lighter color often identified themselves in attitude as well as mutual interest with the master and his family. They learned by daily study to interpret and respond to the whims and desires of the white owners. Because he had the softer life and better food of a house servant's child, because he was only five when his master died and only nine when he was freed, because he lived on a small farm instead of a large plantation, Washington never experienced slavery in its harshest forms. He later recalled his horror at seeing a grown man whipped for a minor infraction, but he also recalled "Christmas Days in Old Virginia" with a curious sentimentality, telling how grown slaves hung their stockings on Christmas Eve on the mantel of the master's or mistress' bedroom, and came in next morning shouting "Christmas gift," singing, and bearing the Yule log.[9] One day in 1909, while speaking to the Republican Club at the Waldorf-Astoria, Washington saw in the audience the grandson of his former owner and recalled:

He and I played together as children, fought and wept, laughed and sobbed together. He was the white boy, I was the black boy, on that old plantation.

He liked me then and he likes me yet. I liked him then and I like him now. But until this week I have not met Abe Burroughs since one day away back in 1863 it came to my frightened ears that old "Massa" Burroughs, his grandfather and my owner, had been killed.

There was a skirmish and the Federal troops, I was told, had shot him. I was frightened. I rushed home and told Abe and he and I cried together. Our hearts were broken. That is a long while ago.[10]

Washington probably exaggerated the hardness of his early life for purposes of contrast in conformity with a literary convention of the success-story genre. He recalled in *Up from Slavery* the hard physical work of the salt furnace and coal mine, and he rejected both the work and the exploitative black stepfather who forced him into it, probably within a few months of his arrival in the little West Virginia town of Malden. He moved out of the home occupied by his mother, stepfather, half-brother, and half-sister. He moved into the mansion of General Lewis Ruffner, the leading citizen of the village and perhaps its richest man. "Booker Washington came to me about 1865 as servant," the general's wife Viola later recalled, "and as there was little for him to do, he had much spare time which I proposed he should use by learning to read, which he readily accepted." If Mrs. Ruffner was a godsend to Booker Washington, so was he to her. A Yankee schoolteacher who had married the widowed general after teaching his younger children, Mrs. Ruffner was ostracized by the general's family because of her alien background and sharp tongue, and she threw all the frustrated energies of a New England do-gooder into the training of Booker Washington. She as well as he later recalled his strenuous efforts to meet her exacting demands. "I would help and direct, and he was more than willing to follow direction," she remembered. "There was nothing peculiar in his habits, except that he was always in his place and never known to do anything out of the way, which I think has been his course all thru life. His conduct has always been without fault, and what more can we wish?" And yet there was something more. "He was ever restless, uneasy, as if knowing that contentment would mean inaction. 'Am I getting on?'—that was his principal question."[11] A neighbor similarly recalled: "The reported hard times that he underwent, never really occurred. He lived a thoroughly easy life with General Ruffner."[12]

The general himself was a prototype of those Southerners "of the better class" whom Washington later sought as allies. Of a distinguished Virginia family that owned the Luray Caverns and pioneered in the salt industry of West Virginia, General Ruffner had owned slaves and worked them in his mines and furnaces but believed slavery retarded Southern economic growth and therefore opposed it. He supported the Union and the new state of West Virginia and became a militia general and Republican leader. One day the young houseboy Booker witnessed a riot that dramatized the struggles of race and class with which he would have to live for the rest of his life. A group of whites, largely of the working class, began meeting in the hills at night and called themselves Gideon's Band or the Ku Klux Klan. One day General Ruffner heard the shots of a melee between the Klansmen and the black workers of Malden. The Klansmen were trying to prevent the blacks from testifying about the Klan's activities. Running past the blacks, the general shouted, "Put down that revolver you scoundrel," and was obeyed. When he moved on to reason with the whites, however, a brick one of them had hurled hit him on the back of the head. Relatives dragged the general away unconscious as the battle resumed, and the old man never completely recovered. "It seemed to me as I watched this struggle between members of the two races that there was no hope for our people in this country," Washington later recalled.[13] That there were dangers in transgressing white racial codes was certainly one of the lessons of this incident, but another was that the white paternalist was the black man's only friend, albeit never a perfect one and in this case an ineffectual one.

Not many black boys had an early life as full of generals as Booker T. Washington. He found his beau ideal in General Samuel Chapman Armstrong, the principal of Hampton Institute in Virginia, the Christian soldier, the great white father for whom Washington had long been searching. He began to model his own conduct and thought on Armstrong's. Washington described him as "the most perfect specimen of man, physically, mentally and spiritually" that he had ever seen, and he considered the best part of his education to have been the privilege of being permitted to look upon General Armstrong each day.[14] The general was the child of missionaries in Hawaii, a graduate of the Williams College of Mark Hopkins, and a commander of black troops in the Civil War. One of the war's youngest generals, Armstrong had a quick, nervous, but unhesitating manner, what might appropriately be called a commanding presence; he was the very model of a modern major general. Washington had the opportunity of observing the general closely, for throughout the black youth's three years at Hampton he was janitor in the academic building. Close to the general and the white teachers, picking up all they had to teach, he impressed them as ingratiating, ambitious, and quick to learn.

It was from Hampton and General Armstrong that Washington borrowed what became known in his day as "the Tuskegee idea." Armstrong seems sincerely to have believed that the Polynesians among whom he had grown up and the blacks and Indians at Hampton were lower on the evolutionary scale than the white race, not so much inferior as "backward."[15] They were children who must crawl before they could walk, must be trained before they could be educated. Their moral training was much more important than their intellectual instruction, for it was only after the backward people, as individuals and races, put away childish things, stilled their dark laughter, and learned self-discipline through the imposition of the morning inspection and close-order drill that they would be ready for higher things. Armstrong would not discourage a bright young man from higher education, but he believed that the black race should abstain from politics and civil rights agitation until industrial education should have done its work. Industrial education as Armstrong conceived it was not so much technical as moral, a training in industriousness, abstinence, thrift, in short, the Protestant ethic, the virtues that helped a man get ahead, mankind progress, and the world turn. The bluff General Armstrong was unaware of the cultural and racial arrogance of his faith and program. He was benevolent and earnest, toiling all his life amid the alien corn, a missionary to the benighted blacks. He slept well because his soul was daily cleansed by good works.[16] The contradictions and inner tensions came when one of his black pupils, Booker T. Washington, eager to please and eager to learn all that it took to be a General Armstrong, incorporated not only the method but the rationale and values of this benevolent white racist, and then went forth to preach the gospel of industrial education.

It would be difficult to find in Booker T. Washington's own writings a better statement of his philosophy than the following advice of General Armstrong to Southern black people:

> Be thrifty and industrious. Command the respect of your neighbors by a good record and a good character. Own your own houses. Educate your children. Make the best of your difficulties. Live down prejudice. Cultivate peaceful relations with all. As a voter act as you think and not as you are told. Remember that you have seen marvellous changes in sixteen years. In view of that be patient—thank God and take courage.[17]

General Armstrong's conservative influence on Washington extended far beyond these conventional homilies, however. When the Civil Rights Act of 1875 was passed, for example, the school's magazine, the *Southern Workman*, repeatedly warned blacks "to raise no needless and ill-considered issue under the present law," to use integrated facilities only when none were provided for black people separately.[18] Armstrong openly endorsed the Compromise of 1877 by which Reconstruction was ended, accommodated his school to the new Southern conservative regime, and urged blacks to do the same.[19] Washington along with the other readers of the *Southern Workman* were told not only that the requisites of a gentleman's dress were "cleanliness, quiet colors, and well brushed boots," they were also told that labor unions were conspiracies to defy the laws of economics and get something for nothing.[20] As for federal aid to education in the Blair Bill, Armstrong thought its "fatal error" was that "it is opposed to the doctrine of self-help."[21]

In the graduation exercises of 1875, Washington took the negative in a debate on the annexation of Cuba. It may have been merely accidental that Washington had the conservative role in the debate, but his skill at presenting that side and the warm response from his audience prefigured his later career. His arguments were so terse and vigorous that he carried with him the whole audience, white and black. He argued that Spain had a right to Cuba by discovery and colonization, that the United States should wait until the Cubans were more capable of self-government, that annexation would flood the country with ignorance and crime, that it would increase the power of the Roman Catholic Church, "already so degrading to the great masses of white voters." This sentiment was roundly applauded. "As to helping their ignorance, we have enough of that article already," he said. "Wouldn't it be wise, before we risk a war for Cuba, to redeem ourselves from the meshes of the last war?"[22]

To what extent did Booker T. Washington, Armstrong's aptest pupil, Hampton's most distinguished son, internalize the teachings, values, and example of his master, his teacher? "I require all to keep their clothes neat and clean, and their hair combed every morning, and the boys to keep their boots cleaned," he reported back to Hampton from his first teaching position. "To see that this is done I have a morning inspection, as we did at Hampton." He also began military drill for the boys, marching them up and down the surrounding hills to his shrill "hip! hip! hip!"[23]

"Can we not improve?" Washington asked in a letter to a newspaper in 1877, "I mean the colored people, for I am a colored man myself, or rather a boy." (He was then twenty-one.) He found some things to praise in their first decade of freedom, but the time was coming when bondage could no longer be an excuse for ignorance. Parents should prepare their children by education for the duties of citizenship, but above all blacks should improve their use of leisure time. "I think there are many who, if they would count up the time spend by them in vain and idle street talk, would find it to amount to hours and days enough in which they might have obtained for themselves a valuable and respectable education," he said.[24]

When Washington was invited back to Hampton to give the postgraduate commencement address in 1878, he entitled it "The Force That Wins." He referred to a "tide in the affairs of men" and announced that the key to success was "not in planning but in *doing*."[25] His reward was a teaching position at Hampton, first with the night school students whom he called "The Plucky Class" and then as supervisor of the dormitory for Indian boys, "The Wigwam." The reasoning behind this apparently was that Indians would learn better the white man's values and style of life from a black man who had internalized them. Washington taught them how to make their beds, exhorted them to learn how to farm, and carefully observed the extent of their "enlightenment." For almost a year he wrote a monthly column in the *Southern Workman* on the Indians. In studying the five races of mankind they had to be told that they were the red men, but when reciting the "four conditions of mankind," Washington could hear their subdued whispers, "We savages, we savages."[26]

When Washington established his own school in 1881 in Alabama, he deliberately followed the Hampton model not only in educational philosophy and industrial features but in accommodation to the conditions of Southern life. Samuel R. Spencer, Jr., has pointed out that in his first major national speech, before the National Education Association at Madison, Wisconsin, in 1884, Washington clearly foreshadowed the Atlanta Compromise address in all of its major elements.[27] He was so complimentary of the local white people that a member of the audience, a white woman teacher in a Tuskegee female seminary, wrote a glowing report of it back to her girls. "He represented things as they are at the South, and said some nice things of the Tuskegee citizens," she said.[28] The Civil Rights Act of 1875 had been declared unconstitutional only a year before Washington's speech, but he took the complacent view that good schoolteachers and money to pay them "will be more potent in settling the race question than many civil rights bills." "Brains, property, and character" were the forces that would win, he said. At the bottom of everything "for our race, as for all races, an economic foundation, economic prosperity, economic independence."[29]

That nothing could shake this faith was illustrated in 1885, when a wedding party of Tuskegee teachers of "brains, property, and character" tried to ride a first-class railroad car through Alabama. They were insulted, physically assaulted, and twice forced into the Jim Crow car. Finally they were ejected from the train in a small town where they were arrested and fined. They completed their journey on horseback.[30] Washington wrote a letter of protest to the state's leading newspaper, the Montgomery *Advertiser,* but his first sentences were: "I wish to say a few words from a purely business standpoint. It is not a subject with which to mix social equality or anything bordering on it. To the negro it is a matter of dollars and cents." Washington's complaint was not against separation itself but against the crowded, old, uncarpeted cars, in which drunken or slovenly whites felt free to slouch when ostracized from the white first-class cars. If railroad officials did not want blacks in the first-class cars occupied by whites, said Washington, "let them give us a separate one just as good in every particular and just as exclusive, and there will be no complaint." "If the railroads will not give us first-class accommodations," he added, "let them sell us tickets at reduced rates." He expressed doubt that national legislation or outside attempts would succeed and agreed to wait with "a wise patience" for an equitable adjustment from within the South that would end what he called "these jars in our business relations." He concluded the letter with a remarkable anticipation of the Atlanta Address: "We can be as separate as the fingers, yet one as the hand for maintaining the right."[31]

Acquiescence in segregation was, then, one of the prices Washington believed he had to pay for peace with his white neighbors, in 1885 as in 1895. Another concession was a rather sweeping abandonment of the First Amendment guarantee of free speech. On at least three occasions white opinion in Tuskegee became inflamed by the speeches or writings of those whom the local newspaper called the "dusky Romeos" at the normal school. In 1885 a speech by a Tuskegee graduate was "misunderstood by the whites who heard it."[32] In 1887 Hiram H. Thweatt, a graduate, published in his newspaper, *The Black Belt,* what were alleged to be "incendiary articles against the white race." Booker Washington, "seeing the natural results that would follow from his unwise course, requested Thweatt, so rumor has it, to suspend publication, which he had the good sense to do," said a white reporter. "Washington is a sensible negro," he added, "averse to any intrusion upon our social welfare, and emanations of an agitating character from these senseless babblers, will meet his condemnation."[33] A year later George W. Lovejoy, a young employee and graduate, wrote an indiscreet letter during Washington's absence to a Mississippi black paper saying that the recent effort of a mob to take a black man from the county jail was proof that the white people of Macon County had "caught the spirit of the lynch-law." Readers of the usually drab Tuskegee *News* were startled to read the following headline: "Lying Lovejoy is His Name, Of Ginger Cake Color, The Third Dusky Romeo Turned Out to Roam From the Tuskegee Normal School That Has Ventilated his Spleen and Hate of the White Race. Is it the Purpose of The School to Breed Such Whelps?" The newspaper warned him to leave town as the other two had done. The Tuskegee teachers hastily sent one of their number to say that they "rebuked Lovejoy for his folly and advised him to leave the school." On his return to the school Washington sent a card to the newspaper. "It has always been and is now the policy of the Normal School to remain free from politics and the discussion of race questions that tend to stir up strife between the races, and whenever this policy is violated it is done without the approbation of those in charge of the school." Washington reminded the critics that among three or four hundred students and teachers over a seven-year period there had not been "a half dozen acts performed or utterances made at which any one took offense."[34]

All through the eighties, both locally and regionally, Washington made common cause with the Southern conservative establishment. He exchanged letters with Henry Grady, the principal spokesman of the New South, in which they agreed that "there need be no hostility between the white and the colored people in the South," their interests being "identical."[35] In his solicitation for funds in the North, he carried letters of endorsement from a succession of Alabama governors and superintendents of education, and he seems to have mesmerized the local bankers, businessmen, and planters, for whom Tuskegee Institute was both an economic stimulant and a social tranquilizer. Local white approval constantly soothed him like a balm, and when he said, as he frequently did, that the race problem had been solved in the city of Tuskegee, he generalized from his own experience. He was "one of the best men in the United States," said a visiting legislator. "His influences have all been for the best interest of his own race," said the Montgomery *Advertiser*, "and for peace and good feeling between the whites and blacks."[36] It was not merely that Washington was circumspect, that the mask he turned to Southern whites was a mirror. In many cases Washington not only seemed to agree with those whites who were moderate in their racial views and conservative in their economic views, he actually did agree with them, and they correctly sensed his response.

Washington was a circumspect man, however, full of covert goals and secret devices that would not bear the light of day. Just how far back in his life this habit of secrecy went it is impossible to say, perhaps back to the days of slavery and the saving art of fooling the master, perhaps back to the inevitable deceptions of the house servant. We can be sure, however, that the practice of secrecy was fully developed in Booker T. Washington in the 1880's, when he carried on an elaborate clandestine intrigue against another black school. In 1887, after a student riot between the white Marion Institute cadets and State Colored University students, the president of the latter asked the state to move his school to another city. Montgomery, only forty miles from Tuskegee, was the probable new site, and a move there would threaten an important source of Tuskegee students. Washington tried to prevent this in an astonishing variety of ways. He secretly encouraged a Marion black grocer to try to keep the school in Marion and asked a black doctor friend in Montgomery to pretend to be friendly to the move only to spy on the enemy's councils. He secured the confidential support of a black editor in Montgomery, who subsequently complained to Washington that he was being accused of being "bought off" by Washington. He sent a Tuskegee faculty member to prevent the black Baptist state convention and the state Labor party convention from endorsing the Montgomery site. He paid a Tuskegee white lawyer to lobby against Montgomery with the legislature, governor, and superintendent of education, and to go to Birmingham to persuade both whites and blacks there to invite the school to their town. Washington also secretly paid the state's leading black radical, William J. Stevens of Selma, to seek to secure the school for his town, a safe distance to the west of Montgomery. Stevens was the leader of the "Black and Tan" faction that allied with the white Greenbackers, Independents, and Labor party members rather than with the Black Belt Conservatives. But he was at least as opportunistic as Washington. Stevens promised to "leave no stone unturned" and asked in return that Washington place "as liberal 'ad' as possible" in Stevens' paper, the Selma *Cyclone.* Washington suddenly panicked, however, at the thought that his secret bargain with Stevens might come to light and embarrass his relations with white conservatives. "I have come to the conclusion that we had better have nothing more to do with him in this matter," he wrote privately to Tuskegee's treasurer. "I have just written him a letter asking him to do no more in our interest. Whether the school goes to Montgomery or elsewhere I intend to do nothing that I would be ashamed to have the public know about if necessary and this should be our rule in all actions."[37] The Montgomery school question was actually a tempest in a teapot. Despite all Washington's secret maneuvers the school moved to Montgomery, but it did no appreciable harm to Tuskegee's prosperity or standing. The significance of the episode is in what it reveals about Washington—the insecurity at the threat of even so petty a competitor, his employment of secret aggressive tactics, and the astonishing vigor and complexity of his countermoves.

There were other illustrations of Washington's secret forays and of his separate peace with the conservative white establishment, such as his sub rosa campaign among blacks in the early nineties in behalf of Thomas G. Jones, who was running for governor against the quasi-Populist Reuben F. Kolb.[38] The clearest illustration of Washington's predicament as a black spokesman in the South occurred when, only a few months before the Atlanta Compromise, a wounded black militant, Thomas A. Harris, sought refuge on the Tuskegee campus from a lynch mob.

Tom Harris' problem stemmed from his decision in middle age to practice law in Tuskegee, a town that took pride in its toleration of black farmers, teachers, and businessmen but could not accept black lawyers or editors. Formerly a slave and a Confederate officer's body servant, during and after Reconstruction he was a Republican politician. The local white newspaper described him as "rather a seditious character," "a very ambitious and rather an idle negro man, extremely unpopular with his own race on account of his airs of superiority" and obnoxious to whites because of his "impudent utterances and insolent bearing." Booker T. Washington called him "worthless and very foolish." Yet he appeared before the Alabama bar in 1890 with testimonials to his character and probity from the leading conservative lawyers of Tuskegee, was admitted to the bar, practiced for a time in Birmingham, and then returned to Tuskegee.[39] He had the temerity to entertain an itinerant white preacher in his home. A white mob forced the minister to leave and then sent a note to Harris giving him a deadline for leaving town.

By the time Harris received the note the deadline had already passed. As Harris crossed the street to ask his white neighbor's advice, the lynch mob came down the road with blazing torches. "There they are now, coming to kill me!" Harris shouted, entering John H. Alexander's front yard in an attempt to escape by running through the house and out the back door. Fearful for his daughters seated on the porch, Alexander wrestled with Harris at his front gate until the lynch mob arrived. As Harris frenziedly burst into the yard, one of the mob rushed behind him and in the light of the moon put his pistol within a foot of Harris and fired with intent to kill. The black man squatted in time to avert the shot, which struck Alexander in the throat and lodged in his spinal column. Other shots rang out, one wounding Harris in the leg as he ran down the road toward his own house. His leg bone shattered, Harris lay in the dirt road within a few feet of his gate, screaming for help. Several white physicians in the crowd rushed past the black man to render Alexander all the assistance in their power. Though first thought mortally wounded, he recovered after the lead ball was found and removed.

Since Tom Harris needed medical attention, his son Wiley brought him in the dead of night to Booker T. Washington's home, "where however he was not received," according to the local newspaper, "for Booker T. Washington . . . has ever conducted himself and his school in the most prudent manner, and learning that a mob was in pursuit of Harris he told him that he could not be admitted there."[40]

The report that Washington had turned away Harris pleased local whites but brought much criticism from the black press all over the country. In a debate on the Atlanta Compromise at the Bethel Literary and Historical Society in Washington, an important forum of black expression, the Harris affair was characterized as "hypocritical and showing the natural bent of the man." The house roared its approval when a speaker said: "Mr. Washington, the negro head of a negro institute refused a fellow negro admittance to his negro college, thereby denying the right of medical assistance."[41]

The Reverend Francis J. Grimké, pastor of the Fifteenth Street Presbyterian Church, left the Bethel Literary meeting very disturbed at the conflict the incident created between his friendship for Washington and his commitment to black rights. Writing a letter of inquiry, he received from Washington a detailed explanation:

> After the man was shot his son brought him to my house for help and advice, (and you can easily understand that the people in and about Tuskegee come to me for help and advice in all their troubles). I got out of bed and went out and explained to the man and his son that . . . I could not take the wounded man into the school and endanger the lives of students entrusted by their parents to my care to the fury of some drunken white men. Neither did I for the same reason feel that it was the right thing to take him into my own house. For as much as I love the colored people in that section, I can not feel that I am in duty bound to shelter them in all their personal troubles any more than you would feel called on to do the same thing in Washington.

Washington then told Grimké what he said he had told no one else:

> I helped them to a place of safety and paid the money out of my own pocket
> for the comfort and treatment of the man while he was sick. Today I have no
> warmer friends than the man and his son. They have nothing but the warmest
> feelings of gratitude for me and are continually in one way or another express-
> ing this feeling. I do not care to publish to the world what I do and should not
> mention this except for this false representation. I simply chose to help and
> relieve this man in my own way rather than in the way some man a thousand
> miles away would have had me do it.[42]

Washington was, of course, a genius at self-justification, but his other
correspondence confirms his statements to Grimké. In September 1895,
about ten days after the Atlanta Address, Tom Harris wrote him from
Selma: "Dear friend, I remember all of your kindnesses to me, I will not
take time to mention them, as you know them all." He was getting well. "I
think I will be able one day to walk on my leg as well as ever," he reported.
"It will be a little shorter than the other."[43]

A chastened Tom Harris was eventually allowed to return to Tuskegee,
George Lovejoy became a successful lawyer in Mobile, and Hiram Thweatt
became the head of an industrial school modeled after Tuskegee. In a
physical sense at least, none of these men was victimized by Washington's
conservative approach. On the other hand, it is also clear that in his years
of power Washington was neither a fragmented personality pursuing
contradictory and unclear goals nor an illusion-free pragmatist coolly
adjusting his program to a realistic view of a worsening racial situation. He
confronted a threatening social environment in 1895, but so did he in
1875 and 1885.

If we read Washington's life from front to back, we find that his life was
of a piece. Perhaps the clearest characterization of his program would be
"Uncle Tom in his own cabin," peasant conservatism, originating in the
experience of slavery—the central life experience being emancipation
itself—and practiced in a nation and by a race still overwhelmingly rural
and agricultural. Perhaps because there were few black models in his life
with the charisma of success, Washington from early life became inordinately attached to a succession of fatherly white men, white racists all,
but mild and benevolent in their racism: General Ruffner, General
Armstrong, William H. Baldwin, Jr., Theodore Roosevelt. All his life
Washington followed the precepts that Hampton Institute taught and all

these men subscribed to: a nineteenth-century faith in individual initiative and self-help, an accommodationist strategy toward Southern and American white racism that Armstrong believed to be the lesson taught by Reconstruction, and a faith that men like these could be his effective partners in counteracting Southern proscription and discrimination. Whenever his identity with the black community or his own interest impelled him to actions of which these white counselors and benefactors would not approve, he resorted to secrecy. Some complexities and inner tensions inevitably resulted. Washington's experiences in the 1880's and his responses to them suggest that historians have generally exaggerated the cyclical pattern of race relations in the period after Reconstruction or that Washington's life was more consistent and in a way more principled than we have assumed. If by 1895 he had become a "white man's black man," considering his background it is hard to see how he could have been anything else.

1. "The Atlanta Exposition Address," Sept. 18, 1895, in Booker T. Washington (hereafter BTW), *Up from Slavery* (Bantam ed., New York, 1963), 153-58.

2. See, for example, the red notebook of 1887, Booker T. Washington Papers, Library of Congress, Container 949 (hereafter these papers will be cited as BTW Papers, LC, with container number in parentheses).

3. BTW to Oswald Garrison Villard, Oct. 30, 1908, BTW Papers, LC (42).

4. These included the Dizer, Cockran, and Milholland Funds, the Southern Improvement Company, and Baldwin Farms.

5. See particularly the chapter "Booker T. Washington and the 'Talented Tenth,'" in August Meier, *Negro Thought in America, 1880-1915: Racial Ideologies in the Age of Booker T. Washington* (Ann Arbor, 1963), 207-47.

6. *Ibid.*, 100–18.

7. See "The Secret Life of Booker T. Washington," below.

8. C. Vann Woodward, *Origins of the New South, 1877–1913* (Baton Rouge, 1951), 367.

9. BTW, "Christmas in Old Virginia," *Suburban Life*, V (1907), 336–37.

10. Quoted in New York *Age*, Feb. 18, 1909, BTW Papers, LC, clipping (1052). James Burroughs actually died of "lung disease" in 1861, but several of his sons died in Confederate service.

11. See letters of William Henry Ruffner to his wife written in 1865-66 from the home of his uncle Lewis Ruffner, in Ruffner Family Papers, Presbyterian Historical Foundation, Montreat, N. C.; Viola Ruffner to Gilson Willetts, May 29, 1899, in Willetts, "Slave Boy and Leader of His Race," *The New Voice*, XVI (June 24, 1899), 3. It was actually in 1867 or later, rather than in 1865, that Washington became the Ruffners' houseboy.

12. William A. MacCorkle, *Recollections of Fifty Years* (New York, 1928), 569. A Democratic governor of West Virginia, MacCorkle knew Washington well in his mature years.

13. Charleston *West Virginia Journal*, Dec. 15, 22, 1869, Mar. 30, 1870; BTW, *Up from Slavery*, 54–55. Washington concluded, from the perspective of 1900: "There are few places in the South now where public sentiment would permit such organizations to exist."

14. BTW, *Up from Slavery*, 37–40; BTW, *The Story of My Life and Work* (rev. ed., Naperville, Ill., 1915), 41–42. BTW said of Armstrong: "I shall always remember that the first time I went into his presence he made the impression upon me of being a perfect man: I was made to feel that there was something about him that was superhuman." *Up from Slavery*, 37.

15. Samuel C. Armstrong, "Lessons from the Hawaiian Islands," *Journal of Christian Philosophy*, III (1884), 200–29.

16. On Armstrong's thought and attitudes, see Suzanne Carson [Lowitt], "Samuel Chapman Armstrong: Missionary to the South," Ph.D. dissertation, The Johns Hopkins University, 1952; Meier, *Negro Thought in America, 1880–1915*, 88–90, 95–99; Samuel C. Armstrong, *Armstrong's Ideas on Education for Life* (Hampton, Va., 1940); Edith Armstrong Talbot, *Samuel Chapman Armstrong* (New York, 1904).

17. *Southern Workman*, VI (1877), 10, editorial presumably written by Armstrong.

18. *Ibid.*, IV (1875), 26, 43.

19. Sir George Campbell, *White and Black: The Outcome of a Visit to the United States* (New York, 1879), 277.

20. *Southern Workman*, IV (1875), 26, 43; series of articles by T. T. Bryce, "Labor," *ibid.*, VII (1878), 76-78, "Capital," *ibid.*, 85, "Strikes and Lockouts," *ibid.*, IX (1880), 57. Bryce was a Hampton Institute faculty member who employed hundreds in his private oyster cannery.

21. Quoted in Daniel W. Crofts, "The Blair Bill and the Elections Bill: The Congressional Aftermath to Reconstruction," Ph.D. dissertation, Yale University, 1968, p. 150.

22. Reports of Hampton Institute commencement in New York *Times*, June 15, 1875; Springfield *Daily Republican*, June 26, 1875; *Southern Workman*, IV (1875), 50-51.

23. Letter of "W" in *Southern Workman*, VII (1878), 52; Max B. Thrasher, *Tuskegee: Its Story and Its Work* (Boston, 1900), 19.

24. Letter of "B. T. W." to the editors of Charleston *West Virginia Journal*, reprinted in *Southern Workman*, VI (1877), 62.

25. Nathalie Lord, "Booker Washington's School Days at Hampton," *Southern Workman*, XXXI (1902), 258.

26. BTW, "Incidents of Indian Life at Hampton," *ibid.*, X (1881), 43. This was one in a series of articles of the same title.

27. Samuel R. Spencer, Jr., *Booker T. Washington and the Negro's Place in American Life* (Boston, 1955), 91–94; reprint of speech in *Selected Speeches of Booker T. Washington*, ed. E. Davidson Washington (New York, 1932), 1–11.

28. "M. A. O.," letter in Tuskegee *Macon Mail*, July 23, 1884.

29. *Selected Speeches*, ed. Washington, 3.

30. Samuel E. Courtney, interview, Boston *Journal*, Mar. 29, 1896, BTW Papers, LC, clipping (6).

31. Letter in Montgomery *Advertiser*, Apr. 30, 1885.

32. BTW to J. F. B. Marshall, Dec. 22, 1885, BTW Papers, LC (91).

33. Tuskegee Special, Montgomery *Advertiser*, Aug. 21, 1887.

34. Tuskegee *News*, Aug. 2, 1888; Montgomery *Advertiser*, Aug. 4, 1888; BTW to the editor, and editorial, Tuskegee *News*, Aug. 16, 1888; George W. Lovejoy to BTW from Olustee Creek Post Office, Ala., Aug. 12, 1888, BTW Papers, LC (89).

35. Henry W. Grady to BTW, Jan. 10, 1887, in Montgomery *Advertiser*, Jan. 15, 1887.

36. Montgomery *Advertiser*, Nov. 22, Dec. 13, 1890.

37. Stephen Childs to BTW, Feb. 26, 1887 (85), Cornelius N. Dorsette to BTW, Jan. 11, 1887 (99), J. C. Duke to BTW, Jan. 20, 1887 (85), BTW to Warren Logan, July 15, 1887 (86), all in BTW Papers, LC; Montgomery *Advertiser*, Mar. 24, 1888; Warren Logan to BTW, May 3, 1887 (86), L. H. Watkins to BTW, May 14, 1887 (86), Arthur L. Brooks to BTW, June 14, 1887, and undated letter (85, 86), BTW to Logan, July 17, 1887 (86), Logan to BTW, July 20, 1887 (86), BTW to Logan, July 22, 1887 (86), William J. Stevens to BTW, May 18, 24, 1887 (86), all in BTW Papers, LC; J. K. Jackson to Stevens, May 16, 1887, Booker T. Washington Papers, Tuskegee Institute, Container 1 (hereafter these papers will be cited as BTW Papers, Tuskegee, with container number in parentheses); BTW to Warren Logan, June 15, 1887, BTW Papers, Tuskegee (1).

38. Account of Washington's campaign for Jones, in Jacksonville (Fla.) *Citizen*, Apr. 22, 1897, BTW Papers, LC, clipping (1029).

39. Tuskegee *News*, May 8, 1890, June 13, 1895; BTW to Rev. Francis J. Grimké, Nov. 27, 1895, Booker T. Washington Collection, Moorland Foundation, Howard University, Container 1 (hereafter this collection will be cited as BTW Collection, Howard, with container number in parentheses); Montgomery *Advertiser*, Apr. 30, May 13, 1890.

40. Tuskegee *News*, June 13, 1895; Birmingham *Age-Herald*, June 10, 1895; Montgomery *Advertiser*, June 11, 13, 1895.

41. George W. Lovejoy to BTW, July 17, 1895, BTW Papers, LC (862); Washington *Bee*, Oct. 26, 1895.

42. BTW to F. J. Grimké, Nov. 27, 1895, BTW Collection, Howard (1).

43. Thomas A. Harris to BTW, Sept. 29, 1895, BTW Papers, LC (862). See also Harris to Warren Logan, Dec. 18, 1895, from Okolona, Miss., BTW Papers, Tuskegee (7); Harris to BTW, Oct. 27, 1902, from Anniston, Ala., BTW Papers, LC (229).

Booker T. Washington's
West Virginia Boyhood

Between 1865, when Booker T. Washington was nine years old, and 1872, when he left to attend Hampton Institute at the age of sixteen, he grew up in the Kanawha Valley of West Virginia. Here he learned some of the most significant and compelling lessons of his life. He became one of the earliest of the freedmen to learn to read and write. He learned the equally valuable lesson that freedom could not be conferred by a piece of paper, that the poor and the oppressed were not free. He learned to work as a free youth far harder than he had had to work as a slave child. He learned *how* to work as the houseboy of a frustrated New England former schoolmarm. He learned lessons in class-consciousness that influenced him in later life toward partnership with the white upper classes rather than the masses. And he learned the final lesson that he had to get out of the Valley if he hoped to rise above the poorly paid labor in the extractive industries of the Valley, saltmaking and coal mining.

The slaves on the Burroughs' farm near Hale's Ford, Franklin County, Virginia, learned that they were free in the spring of 1865, but the slave cook Jane, her mulatto children John and Booker, and her black child Amanda, were still milling about the Burroughs' place three months later, searching for aims of their own to replace the purposes given to their lives by the master and mistress. Then from West Virginia came a message to solve their dilemma. Jane's husband, now calling himself Washington Ferguson but soon to lapse again into "Wash" or even "Uncle Wash," sent word that he was working for wages at the salt furnaces of the Kanawha Salines in West Virginia. He sent either a wagon or money to buy one, and about August 1865 Jane and her children set out from Hale's Ford to join him.

The children were ready to skip and dance down Freedom Road. Just as they had never known the harshest aspects of slavery, they had no idea of the tedium and hardships of a mountain journey. Their mother, with **25** palpitations of the heart as her legacy from toil for the Burroughs' comfort, found less joy in freedom and movement and perhaps none at all in the marriage bond, for there were to be no more children. She knew they needed a wagon. They secured a two-horse wagon, perhaps through money sent by Wash Ferguson. On it they loaded clothing, household goods, some coarse-ground corn, and Jane, whose health would not permit her to walk for any long period. Saying goodbye to their aged ex-mistress, who wished them well, the little family started out. The children walked most of the two hundred miles of the journey.

While there is no direct evidence of the route which the family traveled, it seems probable that they traveled to Roanoke and Blacksburg and over the Giles, Fayette and Kanawha Turnpike. This road connected Giles Courthouse, or Pearisburg, with the Kanawha River. Passing through The Narrows, this road went by way of Red Sulphur Springs, Summers County, Beckley, Mount Hope, and Fayetteville to Kanawha Falls, where it joined the James River and Kanawha Turnpike which led along the Kanawha River into Kanawha Salines and Charleston. The Giles, Fayette and Kanawha Turnpike was completed about 1848 and was the usual route of Franklin County slaves hired out to the Kanawha salt furnaces. There is another reason also why that might have been the route. The Union army which moved out of Fayetteville in 1864 went along the turnpike eastward to Beckley and then struck southward to Princeton and Giles Courthouse. In this area many blacks flocked to the Union lines and freedom, and it may have been then that Wash Ferguson, "by running away and following the Federal soldiers," as Booker later recalled it, "found his way into the new state of West Virginia."[1]

The journey took about two weeks. The family camped in the open every night and cooked over fires made of fallen branches of the tremendous virgin hardwood trees that lined the road and almost shut out the sun. One of the most hazardous parts of the journey was crossing the New River gorge, descending from the spectacular towering cliffs on one side, crossing a shallow mountain river, then up again by another winding narrow road to the top of the cliffs on the other side. One evening, coming to an abandoned log cabin on the side of the road at dusk, the little family decided to build a fire inside, cook there, and spread a pallet of rags near its warmth for the night. When the fire blazed up, a tremendous black snake fell from the chimney to the fire and writhed onto the floor, later remembered as fully a yard long, as long as a man. Mother and children hastily grabbed their belongings, abandoned the cabin, and moved on. They were not "tempted by the serpent."

There were many small towns along the way, through which they walked in dusty bare feet. After they passed Gauley, where the Gauley and New Rivers formed the Kanawha, settlements along the narrow valley became almost continuous. They entered Kanawha Salines, recently renamed Malden but frequently still called by the old name, and asked for Wash Ferguson. They soon found him and the cabin he had secured for them. It was not in the largely black part of the Salines known as Tinkersville but in Malden itself. Washington later remembered the experience with the distaste for town life which never left him. The cabins were clustered close together. As there were no sanitary regulations, the filth around the cabins, the rotting garbage and the outhouses, gave off an intolerable stench. Perhaps worst of all to a country child who had been raised in the open was the closeness of contact with other humans, black and white. Some neighbors were black, but crowded next to them were "the poorest and most ignorant and degraded white people." The boy thought of these whites as degenerates and as the enemies of the black people. "Drinking, gambling, quarrels, fights, and shockingly immoral practices were frequent."[2] If freedom meant the conditions of Malden, then the process of disillusionment had already begun. The town seemed an unlikely breeding ground for a black boy's ambition.

During the first half of the nineteenth century the salt industry had thrived in Malden as the principal source of salt for the pork packers of Cincinnati. First known to the buffalo and other game which licked salt at the mouth of Campbell's Creek and then to the Indians who pursued this game, it became known to whites in 1755, when the Shawnees put white captives to work boiling brine dipped from the salt springs into dry salt, and one of the captives escaped. Systematic salt production began in 1794 when Joseph Ruffner, a prosperous Shenandoah Valley farmer, bought a tract and began salt making by the crude process of dipping brine from the springs and boiling it in kettles.

The Kanawha salt industry boomed. Production quickly became more sophisticated, with the boring of wells, piping, vats and furnaces. Wood was an impotant factor for the salt barrels, flatboats, and fuel for the salt furnaces. As the wood supply decreased, the Ruffners were among the first to begin the mining of coal from the nearby hills. The tin and copper piping used in the works attracted skilled tinsmiths from Europe to settle in Tinkersville. Wells were sunk to more than a thousand feet, and as early as 1832 a steam salt furnace came into use. This furnace used the steam produced by evaporation of the brine to heat the "grainer" pan which finished the drying of the salt. The "grainer" pan was emptied once a day onto the salt board, where salt packers such as Washington Ferguson at John P. Hale's Snow Hill Furnace packed it into barrels for shipment.

The Kanawha salt industry declined in the 1850s and was sick nearly unto death when Booker's family arrived in Malden. Its economic basis was undermined by a number of factors, including difficulties of transportation on the rampaging Kanawha River, the shift of the center of meat-packing westward from Cincinnati to Chicago, and the cheaper and better salt of the new Michigan salt furnaces. The Kanawha salt industry tottered on into the post-Civil War period largely because the owners had invested so deeply that they had to continue, when they could, to try to salvage their investment. Put together a decaying aristocracy as represented by the Dickinsons, Ruffners, and Shrewsburys, who had worked slave labor in their furnaces and mines before the war, the social disorganization of a river town, the labor competition and racial hostility of a depressed economy, and you have Malden.[3]

The Civil War had given a brief false revival to the salt industry. The Confederates extracted all they could of this strategic material in short supply, but the Union forces captured the valley in 1861 and a disastrous flood in the same year swept away boats and wharves, melted accumulated salt stocks and further weakened the industry. By the time the railroads reached Malden in 1872, the era of salt was over and available capital went into coal and timber. The nearby town of Charleston became the dominant city of the valley.

How much Booker and his family understood of these economic forces that doomed Malden is uncertain. They may have had some knowledge of the salt works from other slaves, for Franklin County had long been a source of supply of hired-out slaves. In 1839, for example, the Lewis and Shrewsbury salt furnace at Kanawha Salines issued a pass to nine slaves of Asa Holland of Hale's Ford to visit home. Holland lived just down the road from the Burroughs' place, and just across the road was Bowker Preston, who owned seven slaves employed at the Salines at the time of his death in 1851.[4] It may even have been that Wash Ferguson had spent the war there as a salt packer, first as a slave and then as a wageworker.

Quite early one morning, Booker learned one of the reasons his step-father had sent for him to come to Malden. He was routed from bed and he and his brother John went to work helping Wash Ferguson pack the salt. After the salt brine had been boiled to a damp solid state and dried in the "grainer" pan, it was necessary not only to shovel the crystallized salt into the barrel but to pound it until the barrel reached the required weight. The boys' work was to assist their stepfather in the heavy and unskilled labor of packing. Their workday often began as early as four o'clock in the morning and continued until dark, and the stepfather pocketed their pay. Perhaps he was too poor to behave otherwise, and the exploitation of children by their parents was widespread in the nineteenth century in agriculture, textile mills, mining, and all low-wage industries. Nevertheless, the boys deeply resented Wash Ferguson for his greed and shortsightedness. They turned away from him, and he never became a father to them in the sense of a model for their behavior or a person on whom to rely. And in that circumstance was a clue to Booker's later personal success and to some of his later difficulties.

The first thing Booker learned to read was a number. Every salt packer was assigned a number to mark his barrels, and Wash Ferguson's was 18. At the close of every day the foreman would come around and mark that number on all of the barrels that Wash and his boys had packed, and the boy Booker not only learned to recognize that figure but to make it with his finger in the dust or with a stick in the dirt. [5] He knew no other numbers, but this was the beginning of his burning desire to learn to read and write.

Education, the opportunity to learn to read and write, was an immediate and insistent demand of the freedmen everywhere. Literally millions of people felt a hunger to be initiated into the mysteries of the book and the letter. This was not a mere fad. It was a recognition that education was next to land ownership as a symbol of status and an instrument of power. The South had never been a bookish region, but book learning made the difference between the condition of whites and blacks, and the blacks recognized it. All over the South white-haired old men and nursing mothers crowded the children on the benches wherever there were schools. They crowded around any literate black youth to hear him read; they welcomed the Yankee schoolteacher no matter how pedantic. Some wanted to be able to read the Bible before they died; others believed that if they could read and understand the ledger book at the crossroads store they would get a more honest reckoning. Above all, they sought education for their children, for were not the children the seed corn of civilization?

Malden, as a river town in a border state, a place of black mobility, soon felt the quickening of educational enthusiasm. None of the slaves back in

Hale's Ford could read, nor could any of the free blacks of Malden, even Lewis Rice, the Baptist preacher. But one day in Tinkersville Booker saw a large crowd gathered around a young black man to hear him read the newspaper. The man was from Ohio, where the Black Laws before the Civil War had denied public schools to blacks but allowed them to attend private schools if they could afford them. Booker was consumed by envy. He said to himself that if he could ever reach the point of reading as this man was doing, the acme of his ambition would be reached.[6] Every day on the way home from the salt works, he paused with the others to hear the Ohioan read the news aloud.

An "intense longing to learn to read" was among Booker's earliest memories and he induced his mother somehow to secure for him a spelling book. One might assume that Wash Ferguson took money for it grudgingly out of his thin pocketbook, for even the additional labor of his stepsons barely paid the cost of their support. Packing was the least skilled and poorest paid of all the jobs in the salt works. It seems more likely, however, that Jane herself earned the money. Her health had not recovered from the toil and privations of slavery, and instead of domestic service apparently she took in washing.

The alphabet was obviously the place to begin learning to read, and the boy quickly memorized it, but following the alphabet in the Webster blue-back speller were such meaningless combinations as "ab," "ba," "ca," "da." He tried every way he could think of to puzzle out their meaning without a teacher. Knowing no black person who could read and being too shy to ask any white people, he was completely baffled. His mother fully shared his ambition, but she was as totally ignorant of book learning as he.[7]

It was a Sunday school rather than a day school that Booker first saw the inside of. One Sunday morning as he played marbles in the main street of Malden an old black man passed by and spoke harshly to the boys about playing on the Sabbath when they should be in Sunday school. His explanation of the benefit they would derive so impressed Booker that he gave up his game and followed the old man. He began to attend regularly the African Zion Baptist Church in Tinkersville, as did his whole family. Elder Lewis Rice, the pastor, baptized him, and he became a "pillar of the church."[8]

In September 1865, about a month after the arrival of Booker and his family, an eighteen-year-old, light-skinned Ohio youth also appeared in

Malden. He boarded with Elder Rice, and when it was discovered that he could read and write he was hired to conduct a school financed by what little money the poor black people of Malden could pay him. Thus began the educational career of William Davis, Booker's first teacher. Davis had been born at Columbus, Ohio, in 1846, and secured a fundamental education during his stay in Chillicothe from 1861 to 1863. According to one account, his home was a station of the Underground Railroad that helped fugitive slaves toward freedom.[9] Volunteering in the Union army in 1863, he served as assistant cook with the rank of private and a pay of $7 per month. He served in an Ohio cavalry regiment stationed at the national capital and popularly known as the President's Escort, or "Lincoln's Body Guard." Severe pains of the head sent him to the hospital, where he was discovered to have a mastoid infection. The doctors lanced the sore and arranged for his discharge on June 26, 1865, a few months after the end of the war. His infection did not completely heal, and over the years that followed Davis suffered considerable pain, several lancings, and a deafness in one ear of which we may be certain his students took advantage. For several weeks after his discharge, Davis worked on a boat between Gallipolis and Charleston before his appearance in Malden. He was eighteen years old and only five feet, seven inches tall, but the black people were so eager for a teacher that they agreed to try him.[10]

The opening of the Tinkersville school appears to have been entirely a self-help enterprise by the poor black people of the village, without assistance from the local whites, the county or township board of education, or the newly established Freedmen's Bureau in Washington. That the school began is explained partly by the eagerness of the freedmen for book learning and the teaching talent of William Davis, but certainly a crucial factor was the leadership of the Rev. Lewis Rice, the illiterate but wise counselor whose work for education and religion earned him the name of "Father Rice" throughout the Kanawha Valley. It was Rice's own home which became the first schoolhouse of Tinkersville, his very bedroom being the classroom. He was accustomed to the inconvenience, for he had been doing it for his church meetings on Wednesday nights and Sundays. The bed was dismantled and removed to make room for three or four slab benches, hewn by hand and accommodating an average of ten persons each.[11] Though a state law passed on February 25, 1865, required township boards of education to establish separate schools for colored children whenever their number exceeded thirty,[12] the entire support of the Tinkersville school seems to have been borne by the parents. A similar school was established in 1865 at Chapel Hollow, a few miles away, by another Ohioan, the Rev. F. C. James.[13]

When the Tinkersville school opened, Booker suffered a sharp disappointment when Wash Ferguson refused to allow him to attend. The stepfather decided either that he was too poor to allow his son to live at home without working or that children had economic value in the economy of the salt furnaces. And yet, about this time the family felt able to adopt a little orphan boy, James, several years younger than Booker. James was reared as a member of the family. Booker's disappointment at missing school became keener when he looked out from the salt-packing shed and saw other children passing happily to and from the school. He dug deeper into the mysteries of his blue-back speller, and joined the night class that the enterprising Davis organized primarily for adults. Booker was tired by the time he got to school, but his desire to learn was so strong that he believed he learned more at night than more fortunate children did during the day. In his later educational career he would be a strong advocate of the night school.[14]

Finally, after many pleas by the boy and his mother, Ferguson allowed Booker to attend the day school if he would agree to work at the salt furnace from four to nine in the morning and return after school for two more hours of work. Getting to school on time posed quite a problem, however. With quitting time at the furnace nine o'clock and school opening also at nine a mile away in Tinkersville, Booker had no time at all to get there. After several days of tardiness, the boy solved his dilemma by setting forward by half an hour the clock which kept time for the hundred or more employees of the furnace. Being among the first to arrive each morning, he succeeded in this game of deception for some time. This was the earliest recorded instance of the secrecy and deviousness that became part of the pattern of his mature life. Eventually the furnace boss found the time so unreliable that he locked the clock in a glass case.[15]

His attendance at school posed another dilemma also, with regard to his name. According to his own account, it was on his first day at school that he was confronted with the fact that simply "Booker" was an insufficient name. When asked what his last name was, or possibly what was his father's name, he blurted out "Washington" and it was so recorded. Whether this was a deliberate decision to give himself another name than that of his rather unsatisfactory stepfather or simply a confusion about the nature of first and last names by a small boy recently out of slavery is not clear. His stepfather's first name was Washington, of course, usually abbreviated to Wash. In the manuscript census of 1870, the whole family is listed as bearing the name of "Furgerson," but there are so many other errors in the return as to cast doubt on the census taker's accuracy. The head of the family was listed as Watt Furgerson, his wife as Nancy. John was described incorrectly as black and Amanda incorrectly as mulatto. [16] It is not clear when Booker added "Taliaferro," pronounced "Tolliver," as his middle name. He later said that his mother informed him that she had given him that name soon after his birth. [17]

William Davis remained the teacher of the Tinkersville school until 1871, when he left to become principal of the graded school at Charleston. From the records of the Freedmen's Bureau it is possible to reconstruct many of the details of the school. In the summer of 1867 a large crowd of blacks of Tinkersville and surrounding villages congregated to meet with General C. H. Howard and three other high Freedmen's Bureau officials during their tour of inspection of West Virginia educational conditions. Seven black schools were already in operation in the Kanawha Valley, five of them taught by blacks from Ohio. The blacks agreed to "use their best endeavors to build houses and put the schools on a permanent footing," and the Bureau officials promised to send a "first class man" to the region to lead the educational movement and conduct institutes for the black teachers. [18]

The Tinkersville school had only thirty pupils when the Freedmen's Bureau officials visited there, but in the fall of 1867 the number rose to seventy-nine. At that time, the Bureau sent its "first class man," a white New Yorker named Charles W. Sharp, who became principal of the graded school for freedmen in Charleston and supervisor of the smaller schools elsewhere in the valley. He journeyed to Malden to meet with the township board of education. "I presented their own interest in building now, the necessity of some better provision than the present in order to [have] good schools, the state and national policy of educating every class and condition, and met all their objections," Sharp reported confidently to the Bureau. When the board complained that they had already overextended themselves in building white schools, Sharp proposed to get subscriptions from the freedmen. The board eagerly seconded that suggestion. Sharp then visited and talked with the freedmen at Tinkersville, where he got a subscription of $110, and elsewhere. When he made an appointment to meet the board, however, they failed to meet him. He saw them individually, made his proposition again, and finally met them officially and offered $200 from the Bureau toward each of three schoolhouses, as well as the subscriptions. The board offered endless objections, that the houses would cost more than the Bureau agent estimated, that they had no money to build this year, that rented houses would suffice, that log houses were good enough, that they must provide for white children first, that their taxes were too heavy to bear. "At Tinkersville, they thought no house was needed," reported Sharp. "I explained to them the importance of having desks, and other arrangements convenient for a school, but to no purpose." He found that even when he had persuaded individual members, they gave way to the slightest objection. He concluded that "these School Boards are mostly ignorant, coarse-minded men; and while they are disposed to keep the letter of the law, are not willing to be at the slightest inconvenience in this matter." The freedmen of the area, by contrast, he found "wide awake on the subject of schools." Sharp said that the building used for the school at Tinkersville, which with seventy-nine pupils must have been moved out of Father Rice's bedroom, "cannot be made comfortable in winter, and is in no way suited to a school, though it is better than anything the School Boards have yet provided."[19]

In November 1867 the Freedmen's Bureau received its first monthly school report from the Tinkersville School, signed by "Wm Davis Colered." (*Sic.*) He reported that it was a primary school, supported in part by the local school board and in part by the freedmen, in a building owned entirely by the freedmen. He was the only teacher and the enrollment was twenty-nine, seventeen boys and twelve girls, all of them black. He estimated that three were still in the alphabet, sixteen could spell and read easy lessons, and about ten were "advanced readers." Although the township school board provided $40 for the month's expenses, Davis gave a pessimistic estimate of public sentiment. "General apathy prevails," he said, "where there is not decided prejudice and opposition."[20] Charles Sharp agreed with Davis. "Some favor the education of the freedmen in theory," he said, "but do not choose to encounter the violent prejudice of the community, by any positive action."[21]

Davis's success as a teacher is indicated by his report in January 1868 that all but three of his pupils were "advanced readers." By that time the public money required by law to be furnished for four months a year had been expended, and the school continued through the tuition payments of the black patrons. So high was interest in the school that enrollment remained at twenty-nine. In the spring Davis separated his more advanced pupils from the others and called them the secondary school, though he remained the only teacher and presumably taught the secondary pupils simultaneously in the same room as the primary pupils. In the spring of 1868 Sharp reported that the freedmen of Tinkersville had built and owned a good schoolhouse. The white school board of Malden, on the other hand, falsified its enumeration of black children for 1868 in order to reduce the number and hence the public funds due for black schools.[22]

There can be little doubt that at a strategic moment in Booker Washington's growing sense of his own identity and purpose in life, William Davis provided something essential for his development. It would seem from Davis's letters and reports, with their frequent misspellings and fused sentences, that his pedagogical reach sometimes exceeded his grasp.[23] To judge him by these verbal blemishes, the result of his own haphazard education, however, would be a serious mistake. The warm endorsement of Davis by the county superintendent in 1872, after he had left Tinkersville to head the black graded school of Charleston, is closer to an accurate estimate. After visiting Davis's school, the superintendent pronounced him "well qualified in every way" and awarded him a first grade teaching certificate. "He is mild and courteous in his manner, kind to his pupils and conscientious and earnest in the discharge of his duties," the superintendent wrote to a local newspaper. "I found good order, earnest attention, and studied obedience prevailing in his school, and his scholars have profited from his excellent teaching, pious example, and his energy and devotion to the cause of education." Washington was fortunate that his earliest formal education was under a teacher so conscientious and energetic. He looked forward eagerly to the "teacher's day" at his little cabin, when the teacher boarded for a day at the Ferguson home as he did with all of the other patrons in order to make his meager salary cover his expenses.[24]

At some time during his first few years at Malden, Booker Washington took another fateful step in his informal education. He left the family cabin, its smell of rotting garbage and human feces, the drunken street brawls and bawdiness of the town's low life, his inadequate stepfather and the hard and brutalizing labor that Wash Ferguson had put him to. He moved into what was probably the largest and best-appointed house in the town. He became the houseboy of General Lewis Ruffner and his wife Viola, thus following his mother's vocation of house-servant and developing an early closeness to upper-class whites that gave a class orientation to his later racial strategy.

It is not certain exactly when Washington made this change in his life or how completely he separated from his former home. Viola Ruffner recalled three decades later that "Booker Washington came to me about 1865 as servant."[25] This would suggest that the boy came to her quite early, and that his time in the salt works was brief indeed. Governor William A. MacCorkle, who lived in the county and knew both the Ruffners and Washington, similarly recalled: "The reported hard times that he underwent, never really occurred. He lived a thoroughly easy life with General Ruffner."[26] It seems more probable, however, that Washington took up employment in the Ruffner household in 1866 or 1867, worked there sporadically, and lived sometimes with his family and sometimes in the Ruffner house. The census taken in 1870, for example, listed Booker in the family of "Watt Furgerson."[27]

The Ruffners were the leading family of Malden, with the possible exception of the Shrewsburys and Dickinsons, and were the prototypes of those Southerners "of the better class" with whom Booker Washington later sought alliance. Of German-Swiss origin, the Ruffners moved into the Shenandoah Valley in the eighteenth century, discovering and owning the Luray Caverns as well as the farmland around it. They moved into the Kanawha Valley to pioneer in the salt industry, and Lewis Ruffner was the first white child born in Charleston, in 1799. Lewis Ruffner served in the Virginia legislature and engaged in other business in Louisville, Kentucky, but his chief interest throughout a long life was managing the family salt furnaces and ancillary coal mines. Lewis's brother, the Rev. Henry Ruffner, president of Washington College, spoke for western Virginia business interests rather than abolitionist sentiment in his famous "Ruffner Pamphlet" in 1847 which favored gradual abolition of slavery on the ground that the institution retarded southern industrial growth.[28] Lewis Ruffner owned twenty-six slaves in 1860 and also leased others to work in his furnaces, mines, and farm operations.[29] His moderate and paternalistic attitude toward slavery and blacks is indicated by his membership in the American Colonization Society rather than any abolitionist group.[30] Lewis Ruffner opposed Virginia secession, however, aided in the formation of the new state of West Virginia, served in the constitutional convention and the legislature, joined the Republican Party, and became a Union major general of militia. When Booker Washington first knew him in the postwar era, General Ruffner was in his late sixties but seemingly undiminished in vigor, active in Republican politics, busily trying to revive the dying salt industry, opening new coal mines, and farming nearly a thousand acres of land.[31]

At the time of Booker Washington's arrival, General Ruffner lived in a large frame house overlooking the river on the edge of Malden with his second wife and daughter. He had had a large family of children by a first wife, and soon after her death in the 1840s had sent north for a governess for the younger children. Viola Knapp, daughter of a cabinetmaker in Arlington, Vermont, took the position and soon married her employer, to the great unhappiness of his children. She was a sharp contrast to the first wife, who had been "a pretty, gentle, pious lady . . . entirely domestic in her habits." Viola Knapp Ruffner, on the other hand, was described by a member of the family as "a handsome woman of very superior mental capacity & of extensive mental acquirements."[32]

Despite her beauty, something of the Vermonter's granite quality was instilled in Viola Knapp Ruffner by her early life. Her parents were of small means and had seven children. She went to school near her home until she was seventeen, when she began teaching for twenty-six weeks a year for twenty-six dollars and board. Then she asked an acquaintance in Bennington, where there was an academy, if he would board her for three years and trust her to repay him when she could. He cheerfully consented, and after three years in the academy she taught in the same school for two years. The pay as before was a dollar a week, the usual pay of teachers in Vermont, while servant girls got two dollars a week. Seeing she could never pay her debts at that rate, she secured an appointment in Philadelphia but was detained six weeks by snow and ice and reached Philadelphia the same day her place had been filled by another. She had not another dollar, but obtained, almost immediately a position in North Carolina and money to go there, earned $300 a year and repaid her Vermont benefactor. Moving to New Jersey, she headed the English department of a secondary school and then established a school of her own until her health broke down. It was at that point that she received news of Lewis Ruffner's search for a governess, and she accepted the position in order to recover her health for a single season with no thought of remaining. She accepted his unexpected offer of marriage.[33]

From the beginning the shy, introverted Vermont woman was rejected by the older Ruffner children, an outgoing, free-talking brood of country squires. Some of the children refused even to enter the house again, and Lewis's nephew William Henry Ruffner who admired Viola, said of her:

Poor Aunt Viola excites my deepest commiseration. She is a perfectly unique person—the most sensitive person I ever saw—far worse than Sally Wat—& the result is that she has abandoned society & spends her life chiefly in

> brooding over her wounds, griefs & anxieties until she has become the very embodiment of wretchedness. To think of such a woman being married to a Ruffner! I sometimes talk her into a more genial, hopeful mood, but she falls back in a day or two, & for a day or two she scarcely comes out of her chamber.

He wondered that she was sane, or even alive, so out of harmony did she seem with all the world, so nervous and so frequently hysterical. And yet he greatly admired her strength of will, her discriminating literary taste, broad learning, and terse wit. "But after all she craves most *human kindness*," William Henry wrote his wife, "& yet does not know how to encourage it. So it is, that with all her superior mental endowments & all her ardent affection, she has not many friends & knows nothing of domestic happiness."[34]

If Mrs. Ruffner represented to the young mulatto houseboy a godsend to save him from the heavy labor of the furnaces and mines, so must he have been a godsend to her. Married to an old man almost twenty years older, far from her own childhood home, rejected by his children, her own children off to school, Ernest at West Point and Stella at a boarding school in Cincinnati, Booker Washington became the outlet for all the energy, intellectual vigor, and sense of purpose of a frustrated New England schoolmarm.

Viola Ruffner had a reputation in Tinkersville for Yankee strictness, and Booker came at the end of a long succession of houseboys who had tried unsuccessfully for two or three weeks to meet her exacting demands. But he was so anxious to escape from heavier labor that he allowed his mother or stepfather to hire him out to her for five dollars a month, all of which went into his stepfather's pocket. At first he was no exception to her disillusioning experience with houseboys. After a short while, weary of her exacting demands and angry at her badgering tone, he ran away. Going down to the Malden docks, he hired onto a steamboat running to Cincinnati, as a cabin boy. Before the boat had gone many miles, the captain discovered that the boy knew nothing about waiting on table and discharged him. But Booker was so persuasive that the steamboat captain finally agreed to let him go to Cincinnati and back to Malden. As soon as his long voyage ended, he hurried to Mrs. Ruffner, acknowledged his error, and got back his old position. "He left me half a dozen times to try his hand at different occupations," Viola Ruffner later recalled, "but he always came back to me."[35]

There was little on the surface to attract the youth to his job, since all of his earnings went to his parents and his employer seemed impossible to please. At first he trembled whenever he went into Mrs. Ruffner's presence, but soon he came to understand her and even agree with her, and as the years passed he even came to love and honor her as one of the great benefactors of his life. She was the first person to instill in him the puritan ethic of hard work, cleanliness and thrift on which his social philosophy was based. "I soon began to learn that, first of all, she wanted everything kept clean about her," he later recalled, "that she wanted things done promptly and systematically, and that at the bottom of everything she wanted absolute honesty and frankness."[36] Every fence must be kept in repair; no dirt could be swept under a rug. Booker must have noticed the difference in smell, appearance, and feel between the Ruffner way of life on the top of the highest hill in town and the way the common white and black people lived down below. In Malden it was hard to tell black from white among the miners from Monday morning until Saturday night, and low-lying Tinkersville was no cleaner except when occasional floods of the river washed away the debris and sometimes the shacks and even large sections of the village itself built upon the mud flats. In every big rain inhabitants of Tinkersville could be seen half-swimming in mud as they carried their household goods to higher ground.[37]

Washington learned so well the New England message of cleanliness and good order that for the rest of his life he could never see bits of paper strewn in a house or in the street without wanting to pick them up at once. He could never see a yard cluttered with trash without a restless urge to clean it, a paling off a fence without wanting to hammer it back on, a button off or a grease spot on clothes without wanting to attend to it. Years later while on a speaking tour through Vermont, he stopped in front of the little house in Arlington where Viola Knapp was born, took off his hat and bowed his head in silence. "For me it is a shrine," he explained to the person who had driven him there from his speaking engagement in a nearby town.[38]

A remarkable bond of affection and trust grew up between the gentle-spoken black boy and the sharp-tongued white woman. The lonely woman even may have made a confidant of the boy and poured out to him all of her loneliness and bitterness, but it is more probable that the sensitive youth simply silently recognized the signs. At some point, he moved from his nearby home to live in the Ruffner home.[39] Mrs. Ruffner later remembered that, "as there was little for him to do, he had much spare time which I proposed he should use by learning to read, which he readily accepted. I would help and direct, and he was more than willing to follow direction. He was always willing to quit play for study. He never needed correction or the word 'Hurry!' or 'Come!' for he was always ready for his book."[40] Besides her informal schooling, she offered to allow Booker, if he worked faithfully in the morning, to attend William Davis's school again for a few hours every afternoon.[41] Years later Davis loved to tell his black friends what a diligent pupil Booker had been.[42]

The boy did what studying he could during the day, but much of it was done at night, either all by himself or with some other pupil whom he could hire for a few cents a night to teach him what he had missed during the day. "I used to sit up nearly all night burning dear old Mrs. Ruffner's oil," he later recollected. She also encouraged him to acquire a library. He knocked one side out of a dry-goods box, put in shelves, and filled it with every book he could get his hands on. Most of the books came from Mrs. Ruffner. But the most important lessons he learned from her were the informal ones. She had "all the New England ideas about order, cleanliness and truth." And she also offered him a basis for pride and hope. From her he learned "that the difference in social conditions is principally the result of intelligent energy."[43] If a white girl in poverty-stricken Vermont could make her way through "intelligent energy," then so could a black boy in West Virginia.

The youth also learned other things that were perhaps part of the experience of most people in the small towns of America in the nineteenth century, but he surely learned them better and more completely under such a taskmaster as Mrs. Ruffner. She was fond of raising vegetables and grapes, and with characteristic energy she grew more than her own small household could eat, particularly when Ernest and Stella were away at school. Booker not only helped her to cultivate a garden big enough to be called a truck farm, but he was also entrusted with the selling of the vegetables and fruit, as she was too much of a recluse and too much of a lady to hawk her own produce. Filling the boy with the determination to make the farm pay, she sent him off every morning before daylight on a farm wagon to cover the villages and houses between Malden and Charleston, eight miles away. In the narrow Kanawha Valley, settlement was almost continuous along the road into Charleston. The youth went to the homes of the miners and boatmen who were too busy or improvident to raise their own produce, and, as he later recalled, "among the competing neighbors our energy caused consternation and our profits amazement."[44] Booker later wondered if Mrs. Ruffner had completely trusted him at first to be honest with the money he collected, but he responded to the challenge in true Horatio Alger fashion. As the cash he brought home steadily mounted, her confidence in him grew proportionally, until she was willing to trust him with anything she owned. He always brought back every cent and also showed her how much of the produce he had had to bring back unsold.

One day, while Booker was hawking his produce, a grown man of his acquaintance, perhaps presuming on their common darkness of skin, walked up and took from his peach basket the largest of all the peaches, the show peach, whose best side was turned up at the top of the basket. To the man's great surprise, the boy stood up to him. If the peaches had been his he would have given the man one, he said, but under no circumstances could he give away what others had entrusted to his care. Neither the man's bluster nor his plea that the peach would never be missed could shake Booker from his duty. He had begun to internalize the morality that Father Rice preached every Sunday and that Mrs. Ruffner taught him by example. But all along his route he was hounded by the threats and entreaties of larger boys who sought to take from him what he had been assigned to sell. He could not later recall a single instance when he had yielded.[45]

Mrs. Ruffner must have recognized in Booker a very unusual houseboy, and she herself was a rare sort of mistress. Behind his eagerness to please her burned an ambition to escape the toil and poor rewards of the miners and salt packers and to live a life of his own more like that of the Ruffners. He was tractable, but he was also restless. As Mrs. Ruffner later recalled him:

> There was nothing peculiar in his habits, except that he was always in his place and never known to do anything out of the way, which I think has been his course all thru life. His conduct has always been without fault, and what more can you wish? He seemed peculiarly determined to emerge from his obscurity. He was ever restless, uneasy, as if knowing that contentment would mean inaction. "Am I getting on?"—that was his principal question.[46]

While he lived with the Ruffners, Booker Washington witnessed a riot that dramatized the struggles of race and class with which he would have to live for the remainder of his life. Even in that border community there were night riders, white men with masks, who began to meet up the hollows in the night and called themselves Gideon's Band or the Ku Klux Klan. They brought the beast of unreason into the "peaceable kingdom" of Malden. Violence between the Gideons and the blacks began on December 4, 1869, payday Saturday, when a white man and a black man fell out and fought in the dusty street of Malden. When the black man "came out first best," the white man was so humiliated that he swore a hard oath and the black man swore out a peace warrant. The Ku Kluxers, who were cronies of the beaten white man, openly threatened that no black man would be allowed to testify in the assault case before the justice of the peace, a local salt-furnace owner named William D. Shrewsbury. They even went so far as to boast that the black plaintiff, Tom Preston, would not be allowed in town on the day of trial.

The black residents of Tinkersville and Ruffner's Furnace made plans to join with those in the town of Malden to assure Tom Preston a fair trial of his case. Meanwhile, the Ku Klux Klan was making its own plans up George's Creek hollow the night before the trial. What actually transpired at the meeting is unclear, because the Gideons refused to answer questions at a later grand jury investigation on the ground that their oath to the secret order forbade them to "reveal matters talked of in the Order." They refused to say whether there had been any talk of threats or violence "against the niggers at Tinkersville."[47]

The next morning ten blacks armed with revolvers surrounded Tom Preston as he walked from Tinkersville into Malden. Six white men, friends of the defendant John Fewell, ordered the black men to leave town. A fight immediately broke out when John Sneed, a white man, emphasized the point by knocking a black man down with a brick. After a brief round of gunfire, the blacks retreated a short distance to George's Creek bridge. There they met General Ruffner running out of Ruffner's Lane into the main road, with Booker Washington behind him. The General had heard the opening shots of the melee from his house. Finding a growing crowd of blacks at his coal bank, he shouted "put down that revolver you scroundrel," and was obeyed. He moved on, with the blacks behind him, to restore the peace. According to one report, later denied by the General's son, he told the blacks "that they should not leave the place in that manner but to return with him and he would see that they should have a fair trial."

Meeting the white men congregated at Daddow's Foundry, General Ruffner began to expostulate with them and "was struck by a 'brick bat' while thus trying to quiet the minds of the white men." The brick hit the General in the back of the head and removed him from command. He fell to the ground unconscious, and the battle resumed. In a round of revolver fire, a white man was wounded in the arm and another in the thigh. Both sides, however, soon exhausted the loads in their revolvers. They turned to the poor people's ammunition, and went at each other with bricks, rocks, and clubs. Meanwhile, the General's son David and R. A. Coleman dragged the old man, seemingly lifeless, from the battleground. He lay for days in a critical condtion, and never completely recovered from the effects of the blow.[48] The black youth Booker T. Washington took in the whole scene and carried the memory of it through the rest of his life. "It seemed to me as I watched this struggle between members of the two races," he later recalled, "that there was no hope for our people in this country."[49] The danger of a black man transgressing the racial codes of the whites was certainly one of the lessons of this incident. But another lesson was a class one, that the white paternalist was the black man's only friend, albeit never a perfect one and in this case an ineffectual one.

The Klansmen's role in the Malden area continued to be unheroic. None of the blacks were wounded at Daddow's Foundry, and after the wounding of General Ruffner they retreated in good order. That night some two hundred armed night riders entered Tinkersville in search of the blacks involved in the fight but found none of them. A few nights later, they sent a written warning to leave town "or their lives would be taken at first sight." Whether any blacks actually obeyed the order is not clear. What is clear, as a grand jury reported some three months later, is that there existed in the county a secret order, members of which were bound together by solemn oaths. Its object was "to deprive the black race in our midst, of the rights now guaranteed to them by law, and by discrimination against them, in point of labor, and by depriving them of the protection of the laws and other acts of oppression, to render it impossible for this class of citizens to longer live among us in peace and safety." At a Klan meeting they put the matter more succinctly. "To clean out and finish up the niggers at Tinkersville" was, according to a witness, the whole agenda of the meeting.[50] Reputedly under the leadership of a Malden physician, Dr. John Parks, as Grand Cyclops, the Klan was probably more a political instrument of partisan Democrats than a factor in economic competition. They ironically styled themselves the "Board of Education." It is impossible to tell from reading the partisan newspapers of the time how large the Klan was, how much terrorism it practiced, or its relationship to the Democratic Party machinery. It was plain enough, however, as a Republican editor put it, that "their objects are to make things so *hot* among the darkies that they will have to leave the place, and in doing this, every one that is compelled to leave makes a half a vote for the Democratic Party."[51]

The patronage of the Ruffners was of crucial importance in Booker T. Washington's early life. As the twig was bent, so grew the tree. There were many other influences also, however, among the black and white people of Malden. Either before he went to the Ruffners or during one of his several flights from Mrs. Ruffner's employ, he worked in a coal mine about half a mile up Campbell's Creek from Malden, on the east side of the stream.[52] It was a drift mine rather than a shaft mine, as were all of those in West Virginia. That is, it entered the side of the mountain at a "drift mouth" where there was an outcropping coal seam, and tunneled through the sedimentary layer of coal in a more or less horizontal path. Off from the main and subsidiary tunnels of the mine were the many "rooms" or compartments where the miners set explosive charges against the coal face, blasted the coal loose, and shoveled it into the mine carts.

Booker dreaded and detested work in the mines. One reason was that, under Mrs. Ruffner's guidance, he had come to value cleanliness, and coal mining was the dirtiest job in the world. It was so hard to get one's skin clean again after the day's work was over that many miners did not bother until Saturday night. Booker also disliked the darkness everywhere underground, the long trip of more than a mile from the drift mouth to the coal face, the danger of getting lost among the many tunnels and rooms, the occasional dousing of his mine lamp in that day before electricity, and the danger of premature explosions while shooting the coal and of being crushed by falling slate. He had to give up his schooling temporarily, but he took his book into the coal mine and read it during spare minutes by the light of the mine lamp on his cap. Though he sometimes envied those above ground who could stand upright all day and who could seize the educational opportunities denied to the coal miner, Booker's ambition had been kindled by the contact with the Ruffners and lighted his way through the work in the mines that might have been physically and mentally stunting under other circumstances. He sometimes dreamed of what it would be to become a congressman, governor, bishop or even president, or at least a lawyer like Romeo H. Freer, the handsome, friendly young Radical Republican orator of Charleston who, though white, frequently came to Tinkersville to speak of human brotherhood and equality. It was also while he was in the mines that Booker first heard of Hampton Institute in Virginia. He heard two grown miners talking of it, and crept closer to listen. It was his first knowledge of any school for blacks more substantial than the little school in Tinkersville. He learned that poor boys and girls could work for their board if they did not have the money to pay for it.[53]

This interest in Hampton was further whetted by Henry C. Payne, a graduate of Hampton who came to take William Davis's place at the Tinkersville school when the latter moved to Charleston in 1871.[54] Meanwhile, however, the boy helped the adult miners load the coal and led the mules and their train of mine cars in and out of the mine. The mule drivers cracked their whips as they passed through what they called "Ruffner Gate" into the daylight, where in good weather always sat a crippled black ex-miner, "Uncle" Billy De Haven, with his stiff leg and spear-pointed walking stick.[55]

Though Washington returned to live with the Ruffners, Malden was not so large a place that he was cut off from his family. He even kept in touch with his Aunt Sophie from the old Burroughs farm. Jane's sister, who had moved from Franklin County to the little coal town of Handley, ten or fifteen miles up the Kanawha on the south side. She married a man named Agee, worked as a midwife, and had a daughter, Booker's Cousin Sallie Poe.[56] Washington also kept in touch with the black community of Tinkersville through school and through attendance at the Rev. Rice's church. The clergyman, with his usual enterprise, had secured from General Ruffner permission to build a church on a plot of ground of the General's property. He built a single-story frame building with a high roof and sturdy hand-hewn beams. All that was in the church, including the rough but serviceable benches that served as pews for the church and seats for the scholars, was constructed by black carpenters of the congregation. Completed in 1866, it was the first black church building in the Kanawha Valley. The Rev. Rice, who had meanwhile secured a license to preach and an affiliation with the Providence Baptist Association of Ohio, named his church the African Zion Baptist Church.[57]

Politics seems to have been another enthusiasm of the young Booker T. Washington, from which he swung away in his early middle years as he did from organized religion, only to return to both in his years of maturity and power. It is probable that only after his return from Hampton Institute did he become clerk of the African Zion Baptist Church and of the district Baptist association to which it belonged. But even before he went off to school he began to play an active if minor part in local politics.

Looking back later on the Reconstruction period, Washington recalled that even as a youth he had had a feeling that mistakes were being made, that blacks were being used as instruments to help white men into office and to punish the Southern whites, and that in the end it would be the black race that would suffer for this. Besides, the focus on political action distracted black people from the more fundamental need to strengthen themselves by industry and property accumulation. He even came to believe, as a conservative, that it would have been wiser to have made voting a privilege dependent on possession of a certain amount of education or property.[58]

It is evident that the blacks of Kanawha County had a rich and varied political life, even though the elitist character of the local Republican Party meant that the offices and posts of honor were monopolized by the whites. West Virginia was among the earlier states to ratify the Fifteenth Amendment intended to guarantee the black vote, and in May 1870 the blacks of the county celebrated its adoption by enough states to make it the law of the land. It was an all-day affair beginning with a march through the principal streets of Charleston behind a black band imported from Parkersburg, then on to Chalybeate Springs at the foot of the hills in the northeast part of Charleston, a favorite picnic spot. There were speeches in the afternoon by Romeo Freer, the handsome young Radical Republican whose flamboyant oratory later sent him to Congress and a federal judgeship; the local Republican editor George W. Atkinson, later governor; and the current governor, W. E. Stevenson. The orator of the day, however, was the Rev. W. W. DeVan, a black man from Pennsylvania. It was a fact remarkable enough to warrant comment that, contrary to Democratic predictions, "out of the thousand or more colored people in town on that day, not a single one was intoxicated, and not a single one was arrested, for improper conduct, although the police force had been doubled for the occasion."[59]

Whether Washington was among the thousand at the Fifteenth Amendment Celebration, there is no doubt that he was involved at a very early age in local Republican politics. In this he was encouraged, no doubt, by the activities of William Davis and the Rev. Rice, and also by the somewhat paternalistic Republicanism of General Ruffner and of Romeo Freer, under whom he was later to study law. Whatever the reason, the first extant piece of writing by Booker T. Washington was in his capacity as secretary of a local political gathering. Written on July 13, 1872, when he was sixteen years old, it appeared eleven days later in the Republican newspaper in Charleston. At a black meeting at Tinkersville in behalf of the Republican Party, "On motion, H. C. Rice was called to the Chair, and Booker T. Washington was chosen Secretary." Henry B. Rice was also sixteen, the son of the Rev. Lewis Rice. This unusual honor to ones so young may have been necessary, for the Rev. Rice, though a wise and energetic community organizer, was illiterate, as were most of the other adult blacks of the community. A committee drafted three resolutions which the meeting unanimously adopted, that they would support the principles and the candidates of the Republican Party and would "not countenance or support any man who is in any way hostile to the colored people." After speeches by William Davis and other orators of both races, the meeting adjourned and its minutes were signed by Rice and Washington.[60]

It is impossible to know what was in the mind of the sixteen-year-old youth as he drifted off to sleep that July night a century ago. Yet, surely the politician of high purpose, Romeo Freer, crowded in with William Davis the teacher; Lewis Rice, the minister; and General Ruffner, the man of property as images which symbolized the careers open to the ambitious young Washington. To attain distinction in any of these fields, however, he would have to have more education than the village of Malden afforded.

1. Dr. Otis K. Rice, West Virginia Institute of Technology, Montgomery, to the author, Jan. 21, 1969; Booker T. Washington (hereafter BTW), *Up from Slavery* (New York, 1901), Bantam ed., 17; "Sketch of the Birth and Early Childhood of Booker Tallaferio [*sic*] Washington," typescript, President's Office Vault, Hampton Institute.

2. BTW, *Up from Slavery*, Bantam ed., 18.

3. W. S. Laidley, *History of Charleston and Kanawha County, West Virginia and Representative Citizens* (Chicago, 1911), 47-48, 232-34; Writers Program of the Work Projects Administration, *West Virginia: A Guide to the Mountain State* (New York, 1941), 443-46.

4. Pass for slaves, Aug. 24, 1839, Holland Family Papers, Virginia Historical Society, Richmond; William Dickinson, William D. Shrewsbury, and John D. Lewis, appraisal of personal property of the Estate of Bowker Preston, Sept. 25, 1852, Will Book 8, p. 33, Franklin County Courthouse.

5. BTW, *Up from Slavery*, Bantam ed., 18.

6. BTW, *Up from Slavery*, Bantam ed., 19-20; BTW, *The Story of My Life and Work* (Naperville, Ill., 1900), 1915 ed., 23.

7. BTW, *Up from Slavery*, Bantam ed., 19.

8. BTW, *The Story of My Life and Work*, 1915 ed., 25-26.

9. Richard H. Hill, *History of the First Baptist Church* (Charleston, 1934), 5.

10. Service Record of William Davis, Bennett's Company, Union Light Guard, Ohio Cavalry, RG 94, National Archives; Pension Record of William Davis, Folder XC2573366, Veterans Administration, RG 15, National Archives.

11. Thomas E. Posey, *The Negro Citizen of West Virginia* (Institute, W. Va., 1934), 94.

12. Copy of act in Charleston *West Virginia Journal*, May 10, 1865.

13. Carter G. Woodson, *Early Negro Education in West Virginia* (Institute, W. Va., 1921), 28-29.

14. BTW, *Up from Slavery*, Bantam ed., 21.

15. BTW, *Up from Slavery* Bantam ed., 22.

16. Census of 1870, Schedule 1, Inhabitants in Malden Township, Kanawha County, W. Va., enumerated July 21, 1870, p. 30, microfilm roll 1690, National Archives.

17. BTW, *Up from Slavery*, Bantam ed., 23-24.

18. John Kimball, Superintendent of Schools of the District of Columbia, Delaware, Maryland, and West Virginia, to C. H. Howard, Aug. 1, 1867, BRFAL, RG 105, National Archives.

19. Charles W. Sharp to John Kimball, Sept. 20, 1867, Box 9, BRFAL, District of Columbia Superintendent of Education Reports of Sub-District, RG 105, National Archives. According to Carter G. Woodson: "About the only white person who seemed to give any encouragement to the education of Negroes at Malden was General Lewis Ruffner. It seems, however, that his interest was not sufficient to provide those facilities necessary to ease the burden of this pioneer teacher."—*Early Negro Education in West Virginia*, 31.

20. Teacher's Monthly School Report for the Month of November, 1867, District of Columbia Teachers School Reports, BRFAL, RG 105, National Archives.

21. C. W. Sharp, Sub-Assistant Commissioner's Monthly Report from West Virginia, Feb. 1868, BRFAL, RG 105, National Archives.

22. *Ibid.*

23. See, for example, Davis to John Kimball, Nov. 20, 1868, Superintendent of Education of the District of Columbia, Letters Received, BRFAL, RG 105, National Archives.

24. BTW, *Up from Slavery*, Bantam ed., 20.

25. Viola Ruffner to Gilson Willetts, May 29, 1899, in Willetts, "Slave Boy and Leader of His Race," *New Voice*, XVI (June 24, 1899), 3.

26. William A. MacCorkle, *Recollections of Fifty Years* (New York, 1928), 569.

27. For some reason, the Lewis Ruffner family was omitted from the 1870 population census but appeared in that of 1880.

28. Rev. Henry Ruffner, *Address to the People of West Virginia Showing That Slavery Is Injurious to the Public Welfare, and That It May Be Gradually Abolished without Detriment to the Rights and Interests of Slaveholders* (Lexington, Va., 1847), 3, 9, 23-29.

29. Census of 1860, Kanawha County, West Virginia, Free Inhabitants, Reel 1356, p. 256, Slaves, Reel 1392, p. 14, National Archives.

30. He contributed fifty cents to the Society in 1829. See George W. Summers to the Rev. R. R. Gurley, July 30, 1829, Con. 17, American Colonization Society Papers, Library of Congress.

31. Census of 1870, Schedule 3: Production of Agriculture in Malden Township, Kanawha County, West Virginia, in West Virginia State Archives; Charleston *West Virginia Journal*, Sept. 12, 1866, May 17, 1871.

32. MS. genealogy by William H. Ruffner, and Lewis Ruffner to William H. Ruffner, Feb. 4, 1854, Ruffner Family Papers, Presbyterian Historical Foundation, Montreat, N.C.; Dorothy Canfield Fisher, *Memories of Arlington, Vermont* (New York, 1955), 89-90.

33. Her own account of her life, as reported in William H. Ruffner to Harriet Ruffner, Jan. 19, 1866, Ruffner Papers.

34. William H. Ruffner to Harriet Ruffner, Jan. 7, 1866, Ruffner Papers.

35. BTW, *The Story of My Life and Work*, 1915 ed., 27-28; Viola Ruffner to Gilson Willetts, May 29, 1899, in Willetts, "Slave Boy and Leader of His Race," 3.

36. BTW, *Up from Slavery*, Bantam ed., 30.

37. William H. Ruffner to Harriet Ruffner, Dec. 23, 1865, Ruffner Papers; Ernest Rice McKinney to the author, July 5, 1969.

38. Fisher, *Memories of Arlington, Vermont*, 90.

39. BTW to Walter L. Cohen, Feb. 23, 1907, Con. 35, BTW Papers LC.

40. Viola Ruffner to Gilson Willetts, May 29, 1899, in Willetts, "Slave Boy and Leader of His Race," 3.

41. BTW, *The Story of My Life and Work*, 1915 ed., 28; cf. BTW, *Up from Slavery*, Bantam ed., 31.

42. Byrd Prillerman, "Booker T. Washington among his West Virginia Neighbors," *National Magazine*, XVII (Dec. 1902), 353.

43. BTW, quoted in Willetts, "Slave Boy and Leader of His Race," 3.

44. *Ibid.*

45. BTW, *The Story of My Life and Work*, 1915 ed., 28-30.

46. Letter in Willetts, "Slave Boy and Leader of His Race," 3.

47. Transcript of grand jury examination of James F. Donally, in Charleston *West Virginia Journal*, Mar. 30, 1870.

48. Charleston *West Virginia Journal*, Dec. 15, 22, 1869.

49. BTW, *Up from Slavery*, Bantam ed., 54.

50. Report of the grand jury investigation, Mar. 24, 1870, in Charleston *West Virginia Journal*, Mar. 30, 1870.

51. *Ibid.*, Apr. 6, 1870.

52. Charles Carpenter, "Booker T. Washington and West Virginia," *West Virginia Review*, XIV (July 1937), 345.

53. BTW, *Up from Slavery*, Bantam ed., 26-29; BTW, *The Story of My Life and Work*, 1915 ed., 26-27, 31-32.

54. Payne, born in 1847 in Kanawha County, was a member of Hampton's first graduating class in 1871. He later became a teacher in Charleston, an inventor, and owner of city real estate. Helen W. Ludlow, ed., *Twenty-Two Years' Work of Hampton Normal and Agricultural Institute* (Hampton, 1893), 26.

55. William T. McKinney to BTW, Sept. 11, 1911, Con. 429, BTW Papers LC.

56. Sophie Agee to BTW, June 7, 1897 (Con. 124), Sallie Poe to BTW, Oct. 27, 1899 (Con. 163), BTW Papers LC.

57. Hill, *History of the First Baptist Church*, 5-7.

58. BTW, *Up from Slavery*, Bantam ed., 58-59.

59. Charleston *West Virginia Journal*, Apr. 20, May 18, 1870.

60. Charleston *West Virginia Journal*, July 24, 1872.

Booker T. Washington
and the Kanawha Valley 1875-1879

Booker T. Washington returned in 1875 to his boyhood home, the town of Malden in the Kanawha Valley, after three years of training in Hampton Normal and Industrial Institute in Virginia. He was intensely ambitious for his own self-improvement, but the Northern white teachers at Hampton Institute had harped constantly on the duty of graduates to return to their home communities and uplift them. Even before his return home, while he worked through the summer at a Saratoga resort hotel as a waiter, the patrons of the black school in the Tinkersville section of Malden elected him as their teacher. Washington proved a very good teacher, one whose pupils later did him credit. But teaching a public school was no career for an ambitious young man, and a region of obsolete and low-wage industries was a poor place to build a future. The depression of 1873 lingered on, and there was much conflict between capital and labor and between black and white labor. Four years of teaching in the Kanawha Valley, therefore, filled Booker T. Washington with a determination to get out.

When Washington reached Malden, he had his secondary school diploma and a certificate of his qualifications as a teacher. The state required, however, that he be certified by examination. At the Kanawha County Courthouse in Charleston, County Superintendent William M. Fielder and William H. Saxton, then principal of the school at Winifrede colliery up one of the hollows, examined Washington and certified him as fit to teach. Saxton recalled years later "very distinctly the expression of pleasure on Booker Washington's face when he received his first permit to teach."[1]

In his first year of teaching Booker Washington was officially reported as holder of a first grade certificate, the same as his old teacher William Davis, now in Charleston. The county officials may have decided that this certificate cost them too much money, however, for in subsequent years

Washington was reduced to second grade.[2] Teaching a public school in that period was less a career than a means of bare survival, and that only for part of the year. In Washington's first year, Kanawha County paid white men teachers an average of $41.10 per month and white women $36.06, whereas black men teachers received an average of $31.50 and black women $12.50. Two years later the averages were $36.89 for white men, $29.37 for white women, $32.17 for black men, and $13.50 for black women.[3] The black average term of publicly supported school was only 2.75 months, nearly a month shorter than the term of white schools.[4] If Booker Washington received about the average salary, then, he was paid less than $100 for the year. It was customary, however, for patrons to pay privately to keep the school open for a month or two after the public fund was exhausted.

The reduction in Washington's grade of certificate came after a new and stiffer examination required of all teachers in Kanawha County in the fall of 1876. We know something of this because of a letter written to Hampton Institute by one of Booker Washington's former schoolmates, Robert B. Jackson. While teaching in Virginia, Jackson heard from Washington that there was an opening at a school near Malden. When he arrived he found that Washington had gone to Charleston, and, anxious to see his old friend, he went to the Malden landing and got a boat to Charleston. He found Washington at the teachers' examination that he himself would also have to take in order to qualify for a school. He rushed out, bought pencil and paper, and entered the examination. "I have often seen and heard examinations," he reported, "but this was the hardest I ever saw; everything had to be written." Only a few black teachers were there, but many white ones, and all said it was the hardest examination ever given in the county. Many who had held first grade certificates could now secure only third, fourth, or fifth grade this year. Both Washington and Jackson, because of their superior training at Hampton, qualified for second grade. Jackson said his mathematics and history were too low to qualify for first grade. He boarded at Booker Washington's house and taught at a school about two miles from Malden.[5]

Twenty years old now and assuming the role of a man, Booker Washington did not live with his stepfather but moved into bachelor quarters, a small frame house squeezed in between the Kanawha and Michigan Railroad tracks and the towering hillside. It was a two-room structure with a fireplace in each room, and two chimneys, one of stone and the other of brick. Washington and Jackson were a little crowded but comfortable there, and another room was later added in the rear. Each room had a single small window to admit outside light and the fresh air that the teachers at Hampton had proclaimed essential to good health.[6]

What evidence we have of Washington's early teaching suggests that he took to heart what he had been taught and that he was a dedicated teacher who sought not only to teach the young but to uplift the whole community through Hampton's formulae for self-improvement. Tooth-brushing was the heart of his doctrine, along with its concomitants, hair-brushing, clothes-brushing, and scrub-brushing. "In all my teaching I have watched carefully the influence of the tooth-brush," he later wrote, "and I am convinced that there are few single agencies of civilization that are more far-reaching."[7] Washington began his working day at eight in the morning and seldom ended it before ten at night. Though Tinkersville had had a school for a decade, there were many older youths in the town, and adults as well, whose craving for education remained unsatisfied because they had to work all day. So, following William Davis's earlier example, Booker Washington opened a night school. It soon became as large as the one he taught in the daytime and even more demanding. The room was always overcrowded, and the efforts of many older pupils, whose minds had lost their resiliency, were often pathetic. Moreover, as a true son of Hampton, Washington also taught Sunday school. In fact, he taught two of them, at the Reverend Lewis Rice's Zion Baptist Church in Tinkersville and at a church at the Snow Hill salt furnace about two miles away.

Soon the day school attendance rose to between eighty and ninety pupils, and the night school was equally large. Since he had no assistant teacher, Washington was hard pressed to keep all of his pupils interested and advancing in their various subjects and on their different levels. As though this were not enough, however, he also undertook to prepare several of his brightest pupils to enter Hampton Institute. All of them were boys except one, Fannie Norton Smith, the pretty daughter of Celia Smith, whose light-brown color and high cheekbones hinted at the Indian blood said to be part of her complex heritage. Washington fell in love with her and, as soon as he could afford it, married her in 1882.

As an extension of his school activities, Washington organized a reading room, the beginnings of a public library for the black community. He also created a debating society modeled after those at Hampton Institute. Its weekly meeting became a major social event for both young and old in Tinkersville, there being no other public entertainment to compete with it. The Malden debaters frequently challenged similar groups up and down the valley, carrying their claque of supporters with them.

Booker Washington sought by his writings also to further the social ideas he had been taught at Hampton. "Can we not improve?" he asked in a letter to a Charleston newspaper in 1877, "I mean the colored people, for I am a colored man myself, or rather a boy." He was then twenty-one. He found some things to praise in the black people's first decade of freedom, but he warned that "The time is fast coming when bondage can no longer be a plea for our ignorance." The whites who had lifted the slaves out of their bondage now expected them, through self-help and mutual help to achieve on their own. The rise of Abraham Lincoln and Vice President Henry Wilson from humble beginnings was evidence that for anyone "where there is a will there is a way." Washington urged parents to educate their children for the duties of citizenship, but he also remembered how the Hampton teachers had filled every chink in the student's day. "I think there are many," he wrote, "who, if they would count up the time spent by them in vain and idle street talk, would find it to amount to hours and days enough in which they might have obtained for themselves a valuable and respectable education."[8]

In the same year another letter appeared in the *Southern Workman*, a magazine published at Hampton Institute. It was signed simply "W," but it was undoubtedly from the pen of Booker T. Washington. It reveals much about his experiences as a teacher. Thanking his Hampton teachers for sending some textbooks he was using in the classroom, he asked them to send also any newspapers that were not being used at Hampton, and offered to pay the postage costs. "I now have a news table where I keep all the fresh papers and magazines that I can get for the children to read, so that they will know what is going on in the outside world," he reported. "They take great delight in this." He said that his school was much larger in its second year and that he liked teaching more and more each day. He had never really understood algebra until he began teaching it, he confessed. His scholars all seemed anxious to learn, and this gave him pleasure and patience to labor with them. "I require all to keep their clothes neat and clean, and their hair combed every morning, and the boys to keep their boots cleaned," he informed his old teachers. "To see that this is done I have a morning inspection, as we did at Hampton."[9]

Washington continued in his creation of a miniature Hampton Institute by introducing military drill. Having no guns, the schoolboys put sticks on their shoulders, and their teacher put them through their paces in a secluded cove in the hills. One day, as they marched to the shrill "hip! hip! hip!" of their instructor, they met around a turn in the path a half-grown mountain boy walking barefoot toward town. He took one frightened look at the advancing army and ran home to spread the news that the Civil War had broken out again. [10]

Washington seemed to have a catalytic influence on many of his pupils. "When I recall those early school days," one of them later wrote, "I think of how proud we boys were to have one of us, who had been to 'college,' come back and teach us. How our hearts swelled with the feeling that some day we would do likewise, and we went about our tasks with greater energy." And yet, the high earnestness was lightened from time to time with humor. At one of the Friday afternoon speakings by which Washington sought to train his pupils in composition and oratory, one pupil recited a poem:

> Junebug has a glossy wing,
> Lightning bug carries a flame;
> Bedbug has no wing at all,
> But he gits there jis' the same.

On another such occasion, students debated the question, "Which is the most benefit to man, the horse or cow?" Samuel E. Courtney, an almost-white son of a wealthy local white man, later a Boston physician, ended his argument for the horse with the ringing statement, "Give me the horse or give me death!" At this even the earnest Mr. Washington cracked up and joined in the uproarious laughter. At another Friday afternoon speaking, "Si" Randolph entertained the school with a poem of his own authorship. Entitled "No Hafway Doin's," it ran on for forty or fifty lines in the comic misspelling then popularized by Josh Billings and Petroleum V. Nasby, in this vein:

> Belubed feller trablers, in holdin' forth de day,
> I dusent kwote no speshul vurse in what I has ter say.
> But its good old gospul scriptur an' dis am de tex'
> Dat haf way doin's aint no count in dis worl ner de nex.'[11]

The students came to know their teacher intimately from their many hours with him in the schoolroom, and so did most of the black adults and many of the white ones through his many public appearances, in the school closing exercises, church and Sunday school, and the debating society. At the end of every school year the Tinkersville school staged elaborate "Closing Exercises" or Commencement. The whole community took part. Each girl graduate wore a new frock and each boy a new pair of jeans and a roundabout, the tight-fitting jacket worn by boys and many men in the period. These new clothes were usually home-sewn by mothers proud to have children in school. Washington presided over the exercises designed to show his graduates at their best. Single orations and singing made up most of the program, after the Reverend Rice or some passing preacher opened with a prayer. Every parent waited impatiently for his child to "say his piece" and have his sunlit moment, for as soon as school was out most of them would go to sunless work in the mines. In midsummer, however, the school would have its final event, the school picnic, where Mr. Washington always delivered the address of the occasion. [12]

"Father" Rice, who had baptized Booker T. Washington about 1865, continued to preach at the Zion Baptist Church, as he would continue to do for decades to come. As he presided over the monthly meetings of the church as moderator, Booker Washington sat beside him at the front of the gathering as church clerk, reading the minutes of the previous meeting and taking notes on the current one. Though "Father" Rice had learned to read and write a little, he could not nearly match the fluency of his young protegé. As these church meetings furnished the rather unlettered congregation opportunities for rough-hewn eloquence and points of order, questions of parliamentary procedure frequently became a tangled web. Was a proposal debatable or not, was it an amendment or a substitute? "Father" Rice would stroke his sparse whiskers, lean over to Booker Washington for coaching, and make a ruling that would bring the meeting back to order. On one occasion, W. T. McKinney later recalled, the discussion waxed warm indeed. Two disputants, Joe Pete Hughes and Musie Strother, were approaching each other in a belligerent manner, while friends sought to hold them apart. The whole church was on its feet. "Father" Rice quickwittedly struck up the hymn, "Blest be the tie that binds," which he had found on previous occasions to be a reliable crowd-soother. But Booker Washington's stepfather, "Uncle" Wash Ferguson, a deacon, who had been asleep since the beginning of the meeting, was suddenly awakened by the hymn and arose to his feet, shouting, "Put out them lights, put out them lights." This raised quite a laughter, and the threatened melee was forgotten. Frank Randolph, the head deacon, explained Wash Ferguson's confusion. "Be quiet, brothers, be quiet," he said, "brother Wash was 'sleep and when he 'woke he thought he was at one of them dances we used to have in slavery time when the lights would be put out to stop the 'niggers' from fightin'." In good humor again, the meeting proceeded. [13]

Booker Washington was also clerk of the Mount Olivet Baptist Association, which had an annual meeting and picnic every August, "after the watermelons had 'dropped their blossoms' and the spring chickens were well 'feathered'." There, again, he had an opportunity for public speaking. But it was the debating contests that brought Washington's oratorical powers up to full organ tone. He gave his black fellow citizens cause for wonder and pride. Washington's friends, Joe Pete Hughes and Gilbert Lovely, arranged a series of debates with nearby towns, with Booker Washington as their champion. They filled a two-horse wagon with debaters and "rooters" of an early evening, traveled to the town where they were booked, won a debate, and returned in the late evening in triumph. "They would always take 'Booker' along to make their closing arguments," W. T. McKinney later recalled, "and you would always 'clean up' for them."[14]

Booker Washington had no pupils in Malden who ever achieved as much distinction as he, but he did lift a number of youths out of the depressed economy and racial discrimination of the Kanawha Valley. Those who might have had little chance to be anything but underpaid and underemployed coal miners all of their lives were put on the road to professional careers. W. T. McKinney became a lawyer and a minor federal official, as did S. H. Randolph. Samuel E. Courtney graduated from Hampton and Harvard Medical School and became a prominent Boston physician and member of the city school board. Hampton Institute always welcomed "Booker Washington's boys" because of their good preparation, and put them immediately into advanced classes.[15] In addition, Washington arranged to send his brother John and his adopted brother James through Hampton.[16]

Washington's missionary spirit was challenged daily in Malden by the social disorders of a depressed economy. In the late seventies the fog of depression lifted a little, the salt works opened sporadically to fill orders, and the coal mines flourished. But there was a fatal lack of diversity in the valley's economy. It could not employ fully and at all seasons the whole working population, and the widespread use of child labor often threw grown men out of work. Vagrancy and hard drinking at all hours filled out the long stretches of idleness, and they both abetted the labor unrest and the violence for which a lifetime of heavy labor had equipped most of the men.

The witches' brew of all these forces was illustrated by a melodramatic incident near Malden in the winter of 1875–76. On Christmas eve of 1875, on the Campbell's Creek Bridge just outside the town, two white men, Rufus Estep and John Dawson, both about twenty years old, brutally murdered another white man, Thomas Lee. They were duly arrested and imprisoned in Charleston jail, but the word went through all the mines and furnaces of Malden and Cabin Creek that Lee's family and friends would not allow his murderers to escape through loopholes of the law. The talk was so open that by the time a lynch mob was on the march to Charleston, few people in the county did not know of their coming. The sheriff tricked the mob in its first effort by sending persons to argue with it while he used the delay to transport the accused men out of the county.[17]

Three weeks later, a mob again entered Charleston, after Estep and Dawson had been indicted and the eloquent young Republican lawyer Romeo Freer and his law partner had been assigned by the court to defend them. Freer asked for a change of venue, claiming that a fair trial was impossible in Kanawha County, and word spread among the Malden "regulators" that their vengeance might be thwarted. While the white lynch mob was gathering, another incident in the black community turned it also toward the white American pattern of vigilantism. A "drunken Irish tailor," Thomas Hines, cut the throat of a quiet, industrious black man, J. William Dooley, a Charleston shoemaker, who died within the hour. The Irishman was said to be having a love affair with the black man's wife. A black mob of fifty joined the white mob of 450 in front of the county jail. They took a vote to lynch Hines as well as Estep and Dawson, and an interracial mob broke in the jail door and seized its victims.

The mob began to segregate itself again during the long walk to Campbell's Creek Bridge, scene of the murder of Lee. The blacks moved to a nearby honey-locust tree to hang their victim, but hardly had the whites strung their pair on the bridge preparatory to hanging than they began to cool toward the idea of black men doing any hanging. "Even in their great excitement it was seen that the hanging of a white man by negroes must be productive of the most awful consequences," said a newspaper account. The blacks offered to let the whites do the hanging, but a white leader insisted that the whites had their work to do and the blacks theirs. This display of logic impressed both mobs, and the black men promptly hanged Hines upon the tree. Estep and Dawson, with ropes around their necks, at this point made the ultimate appeal to white superiority. They objected to being hanged in the presence of blacks. The white mob obligingly withdrew from the scene and hanged them elsewhere.[18]

Some respectable citizens sought to blame the lynchings on the poor administration of justice. One supporter of "law and order," alleging that only one man in twenty-five years had been hanged for murder in the county, though there had been an average of two murders per year, demanded speedier trials and harsher punishments as the remedy.[19] But lynching was only the most dramatic of the symptoms of social disorganization. Saturday night in Malden, after payday at the Campbell's Creek mines, was always enlivened by several street fights. Mad dogs ranged the streets with alarming frequency, and the only hope of cure of hydrophobia was the use of a madstone.[20] A week seldom passed without a violent death or maiming accident in the coal mines, a drowning in creek or river, or a scalding among the boilers and vats of the salt works.[21]

One challenge to the way of life Washington had been taught at Hampton was the almost continual labor friction of the Kanawha Valley. In 1876 and in 1877, an unparalleled year of labor violence all over the United States, the Kanawha mines contributed their share. At the Cannelton Coal Company, a few miles upriver from Malden, a strike broke out when the company lowered payment from eight cents per bushel to seven and a half cents. The company compromised on a reduction of one-fourth cent, but discharged the leaders of the trouble. Thereupon all hands refused to work at any rate. The company announced that they "did not propose to allow their employees to dictate to them who should do their work" and locked the workers out of the mine until they should be ready to accept "a new deal all around."[22] The Campbell's Creek Coal Company, where Booker and John Washington had worked as children, also had a strike in 1876. The miners demanded two and a half cents more than they had been receiving per bushel, but soon settled on the management's terms.[23] The Cannelton miners, on the other hand, carried their resistance into 1877 and threatened violence when Pennsylvania strikebreakers were brought in. A visit of the Governor and compromises by the company, however, soon quieted the trouble.[24]

Washington had been taught at Hampton that the efforts of labor unions were immoral folly, and this viewpoint continued to find expression in Hampton's magazine, *The Southern Workman*, that came to Booker Washington every month. Thomas T. Bryce, owner of a large oyster company and lecturer at Hampton, wrote: "All 'strikes,' or rather all forcible strikes, arise from a misconception of the right of property that is vested in every man, as regards his own labor." If a man wanted to work eighteen hours a day or at low pay, that was no labor union's business. Strikes, according to his logic, were successful only when capital could afford to pay more wages than it had been paying. "Strikes generally cost more than they come to, even if they are apparently successful," he counseled. The only one who benefited in these Pyrrhic victories was the "agitator," a man Bryce described as an incompetent workman, "generally as lacking in skill at his craft and in habits of industry, as he superabounds in loquacity and effrontery." Clearly any self-respecting graduate of Hampton should stay clear of the agitator and particularly the radical. Bryce said radicalism was a "mental illness" founded in knavery and flourishing best "with ignorance and filth as surroundings." He warned the freedmen ominously: "If the dreams of those who would destroy all capital could be realized, the sun would rise on the world's people, naked, homeless, foodless, and with nothing saved, not even seed to plant."[25]

In a public statement he made on the labor question in 1910, Washington asserted that he had "for a number of years" been a member of the Knights of Labor. There is no reason to doubt this factual statement, but it must have been in the late seventies, when the school term was too short and the pay too small to entirely support him, that he entered the mines again and joined the union, for the Knights of Labor did not enter West Virginia until after 1875. Whether he was a union man or not, Washington's outlook probably was close to that of Bryce and the employers, as it was in later life.[26] In speaking of his youth in his autobiography, he said that a strike "usually occurred whenever the men got two or three months ahead in their savings. During the strike, of course, they spent all that they had saved, and would often return to work in debt at the same wages, or would move to another mine at considerable expense." In either case, the miners were worse off at the end of a strike, Washington believed, the victims of "the professional labour agitators."

Washington later remembered his years as a teacher in Malden as "one of the happiest periods" of his life because of the opportunity "to help the people of my home town to a higher life."[27] But public school training provided little better living than coal mining, and Booker Washington was ambitious. His pupils noticed his strangeness, his differentness from others in the town. "You always appeared to be looking for something in the distant future," one of them recalled. "There was always a future look in your eyes."[28] He searched about for a career that would give scope to his talents. Before he decided finally on his lifelong career as an educator, he tried two other professions that also grew out of his skill as an orator, the law and the ministry.

Hampton Institute warned her sons not to make politics a career, but Washington found in the location of West Virginia's state capital at Charleston an issue consistent with Hampton's teachings and made to order for him. It was an issue on which the overwhelming majority of the local citizens of both races agreed, hence one that united rather than divided men. There was in the issue, at least in the Kanawha Valley, no partisanship or social friction. Charleston white men anxious to locate the capital permanently in their city, and hoping to secure the maximum black voter turnout, asked Washington to be their stump speaker to black audiences all through the surrounding counties of southern West Virginia. Some had heard him on the debating circuit. The Republican Romeo Freer and the Democrat John E. Kenna were co-chairmen of Charleston's campaign, and they persuaded Washington to spend the summer of 1877 on a speaking tour.

West Virginia's capital had floated about within its weirdly artificial boundaries ever since the state detached itself from Virginia during the Civil War. Wheeling, in the northern panhandle, was the first capital city. In 1869, however, as soon as the state legislature managed to free itself from the clutches of the Baltimore and Ohio Railroad, it made Charleston the capital as the new Chesapeake and Ohio Railroad approached that city under the control of Collis P. Huntington, a leading railroad baron and one of the nation's leading lobbyists. Amid much lobbying the legislature in 1873 turned its back on the free capitol building, the free hotel, and the railroad accommodations offered by Charleston, and returned the state capital to Wheeling. This decision produced fresh dissatisfaction particularly in the southern part of the state, and in February 1877 an act passed the legislature to submit the choice of a capital city to the voters of the state. At an election on August 7, 1877, West Virginians had to choose between three cities or would-be cities, Charleston, Clarksburg, and Martinsburg. "Regardless of color," the largest vote would win the prize. Here was an issue in which Kanawha Valley residents, black or white, Ku Klux or Radical, could go to the polls together and vie for the home town. It was an issue made to order for the young Booker T. Washington, lion and lamb.

Charleston's bid for the state capital of West Virginia was in no small part a real estate venture of the founding fathers. The railroads also had a share in the speculation. Collis P. Huntington, builder of the C. & O., lent $24,000 to the Charleston entrepreneurs who offered the state a capitol building free of cost.[29] And the great national railroad strike of 1877 brought federal troops to Martinsburg, one of the contending cities, where striking workers had seized the depot and stopped all trains. Martinsburg was a symbol viewed differently according to the perspective. "From the number of strikers in Martinsburg and the boldness they display," said a newspaper friendly to Charleston, "one may easily see that were the capital of the State situated at that town or Clarksburg it might be put under the power of the mob, in case that body thought proper to amuse themselves by subjecting the legislature to the lord of misrule."[30]

Booker T. Washington began his speaking for the capital on June 27, 1877, at a rally in Charleston of "the colored citizens of Kanawha." He shared the platform with the principal of the black graded school in Charleston, William Davis, who had been his first teacher. The meeting passed a resolution designed to muster the black vote, declaring "the right to a fair portion of the public institutions" for their part of the state.[31] While white speakers traveled in a body to a succession of white audiences in their part of the state, Booker Washington made a circuit of the black communities, speaking at Hinton, Lewisburg, White Sulphur Springs, and elsewhere. At Hinton he spoke to black citizens from the steps of the courthouse. "He aroused the people to a sense of their duty," according to a reporter at Hinton, and left behind him a committee pledged to work and vote for Charleston.[32] At Lewisburg, again at the courthouse, he addressed "quite a large audience" of both races, despite inclement weather. "Mr. Washington made a very good speech indeed," it was reported, "giving the arguments in favor of Charleston in good style, and expressing his idea in a clear manner and with appropriate words, interspersing his speech with apt anecdotes, illustrating his arguments. We would urge upon our colored friends to turn out and hear this champion of Charleston when the occasion presents itself, and by all means on the 7th of August, vote for Charleston."[33]

When Greenbrier cast 1,902 votes for Charleston, 4 for Clarksburg, and 0 for Martinsburg,[34] the proportion of the votes was due more to local self-interest than to Washington's eloquence, but surely his "apt anecdotes" deserved some credit for the size of the voter turnout. He even wandered into such little black communities as Anthony's Creek, where "Booker Martin . . . was listened to with marked attention." He told them not only why they should vote for Charleston. "He also gave them much sound and sensible advice in regard to their general course in voting, calling their attention to the identity of interest between the races, &c., &c."[35]

Washington's speeches in behalf of Charleston, he later recalled, "rather fired the slumbering ambition . . . to become a lawyer," and he "began in earnest to study law, in fact read Blackstone and several elementary law books preparatory to the profession of the law." Most of this reading was done, he said, "under the kind direction of" Romeo Freer.[36] Whether he actually read law in the white Radical Republican's office or merely borrowed books to take home is not clear. According to William A. MacCorkle, "Washington did not study law in his office as was currently reported. Freer loaned him books and examined him on the law, which he had studied during the week at his home."[37] On the other hand, MacCorkle was a Democrat and racial moderate, and perhaps he could not countenance a white man helping a black man to pore over law books. Washington kept up a lifelong friendship with Freer, who became a judge and a congressman.[38] His commitment to the law, however, was only provisional. As he later said, "notwithstanding my ambition to become a lawyer, I always had an unexplainable feeling that I was to do something else, and that I never would have the opportunity to practice law." Somehow, there was a nagging feeling that to confine himself to legal work "would be going contrary to my teaching at Hampton, and would limit me to a much smaller sphere of educating my people after the manner in which I had been taught at Hampton."[39]

Curiously, Washington did not so much as allude to his study of law in *Up from Slavery*, the better known of his two autobiographies. He freely discussed, however, the temptation to enter into a political career. Perhaps fortunately for his own future, he decided not to cast his lot with the black lawyers and politicians whose sun was setting. He reached the decision in the wake of Reconstruction, when the federal government, the white Northerners, and even the ardent civil rights leaders were deserting the black politicians to the mercies of a resurgent white South. When black voting was sharply reduced, black politicians were consigned to limbo. Washington thought that Reconstruction, with its political emphasis, was "on a false foundation." Political agitation, he thought, drew black men away from the fundamental task of organizing their lives by developing work skills and securing property. So he stayed out of political life because of "the feeling that I would be helping in a more substantial way by assisting in the laying of the foundation of the race through a generous education of the hand, head, and heart."[40]

Another career that Washington dallied with in his formative years was the ministry, and his interest in it came about naturally through his early religious experiences. In the Tinkersville section of Malden, the little Zion Baptist Church was about the only institution that the black people owned and controlled. Washington participated fully in it, but even this early he may have developed the skeptical attitude toward the black clergy that he expressed as a mature man. In his autobiography he spoke of some black ministers as "not only ignorant but in many cases immoral men" who sought to escape heavy toil in the hot sun by a "call." This call usually came, he said, within a few days after the man had learned to read, while he was sitting in church. Suddenly, the called one without warning would fall on the floor "as if struck by a bullet" and lie there speechless and motionless for hours. The word would spread through the community that this individual had received a call. If he resisted or pretended to resist, he would fall into the trance a second or third time, and in the end he always yielded. "While I wanted an education badly," said Washington, "I confess that in my youth I had a fear that when I learned to read and write well I would receive one of these 'calls'; but, for some reason, my call never came."[41] If Washington had more fully confessed, however, he would have admitted that, if he was not called in such a cataleptic way, he was at least tempted.

Whenever he thought of churches and preachers, Washington must have remembered an incident during the services at Zion Baptist Church during his mother's lifetime, before 1874. Aunt Jane Ferguson, as she was called, was sitting one Communion Sunday, as she always did, in the "amen" corner with the other "old mothers in Israel," Aunt Violet Taylor and Aunt Mary Rice. One Doctor Baty, the first black man to come that way wearing the title of "Doctor," appeared to preach at the morning service. After warming to his subject, he proceeded to emit those peculiar sounds that always set the brethren and sisters to rocking and moaning and giving vent to their feelings in various ways. Doctor Baty himself became so carried away by the spirit that he grabbed the heavy Bible up from the pulpit and threw it into space, proclaiming, "Here, God, take the Bible!" It struck Jane Ferguson on the arm. For a time it appeared the arm was broken but fortunately it was only bruised. This outburst of spiritual extravagance on the preacher's part was soon overlooked, for he was obviously "in the spirit" and not responsible for his actions.[42]

After some thrashing about in efforts to avoid the Jacob's Ladder of the ministry, in the fall of 1878, at the age of twenty-four Booker T. Washington left the Kanawha Valley to enroll in Wayland Seminary in Washington, a school for the training of black Baptist ministers. The year he spent there is the most obscure year of his life. He hardly mentioned it in his autobiography, and the school's records were destroyed by fire. It is not even clear whether he failed to meet Wayland's standards or whether the school and a ministerial career failed to satisfy Washington's interests. This year of experiment with the ministry coincided also with Washington's first sustained experience with urban living and with higher education. He later became reconciled with the church and the clergy, but he retained a lifelong aversion to cities and a mistrust of higher education. Washington found even a Baptist seminary in the big city too urbane for his taste. He thought the students learned too little of self-reliance, character-building, and civic duty, in contrast to those at Hampton. "In a word, they did not appear to me to be beginning at the bottom, on a real, solid foundation, to the extent that they were at Hampton. They knew more about Latin and Greek when they left school, but they seemed to know less about life and its conditions as they would meet it at their homes." Whereas Hampton students went out to lives of service to their communities, Washington thought that despite their calling many Wayland students would end as drifting Pullman porters and hotel waiters.[43]

Returning home to Malden rather at loose ends, somewhat chastened by his venture in higher education and city life, Washington could not resume teaching his school, for his brother John had graduated from Hampton and taken over the school when Booker Washington left for Wayland.[44] Perhaps it was in this period rather than earlier that Washington began the study of law. It was, ironically enough, at this period of frustrated ambition and indecision that Washington received a letter in the late winter of 1879 from General Armstrong of Hampton. Armstrong asked his promising graduate to deliver the annual Post Graduate Essay at the next Commencement in May. "The idea is to bring out the facts of actual experience," the General wrote, "to show what clear heads & common sense colored graduates of the school have attained, and to win the respect of all by a generous noble manly spirit."[45]

At Armstrong's suggestion, Washington went to Hampton three weeks before his speech, and he and his old teacher Nathalie Lord hammered out and polished his speech, "The Force That Wins." She was as thrilled as he by the challenge, and kept the original copy of Washington's address among her choicest possessions. When the great day arrived and the slim young black man stood before his audience, he said in his winning, natural voice that his humble experience as a teacher had shown him "that there is a force with which we can labor and succeed and there is a force with which we can labor and fail. It requires not education merely, but also wisdom and common sense, a heart bent on the right and a trust in God." He discovered "a tide in the affairs of men" and declared that the key to success was "not in planning but in *doing*." These sentiments pleased everyone, so strong was a commencement audience's appetite for platitudes. Booker Washington in that time and place personified "the force that wins."[46] A few weeks later, back at Malden still casting about for a fresh start, Washington received a letter from Armstrong offering him a position at Hampton as a "graduate." Hampton had something of a double standard. The flower of New England that Armstrong attracted to teach at Hampton were called "teachers," whereas the black graduates of the school whom he hired also were called "graduates" and even, for decades, ate in a separate dining room.

It was not only the speech but the good performance of his Malden pupils he had sent that caused Washington to be called back to Hampton. John Washington, James Washington, Fannie Smith, Henry Rice, W. T. McKinney, Sam Courtney, and Si Randolph all brought credit to their teacher. And Booker T. Washington had found his vocation as an educator like Samuel C. Armstrong, a calling that combined the talents of the teacher with those of the politician and the preacher.

Though Booker T. Washington made his career elsewhere, he had an abiding fondness for the friends and the scenes of his youth, and every year he returned one or more times to West Virginia, to see his sister Amanda and to pass the time of day with his old friends, black and white. He spoke several times to overflow audiences at the Charleston Opera House, and spent many days resting at a fishing camp on the banks of the Gauley River, which one of his friends facetiously named Tuskegee-on-the-Gauley.

1. Charleston *Mail*, Nov. 1915, clipping, Con. 530, Booker T. Washington Papers, Manuscripts Division, Library of Congress (cited hereafter as BTW Papers).

2. *Biennial Report of the State Superintendent of Free Schools of the State of West Virginia for the Years 1875 and 1876* (Wheeling, 1877), 39; *ibid.*, *1877 and 1878* (Wheeling, 1878), 80.

3. *Ibid.*, *1875 and 1876*, 2; *ibid.*, *1877 and 1878*, 2.

4. *Ibid.*, *1877 and 1878*, 11.

5. R. J. to Dear Teacher, Oct. 24, 1876, in *Southern Workman*, V (Dec. 1876), 94.

6. Charles Carpenter, "Booker T. Washington and West Virginia," *West Virginia Review*, XIV (July 1937), 345-47.

7. Booker T. Washington (hereafter cited as BTW), *Up from Slavery* (New York, 1901, Bantam ed.), 52.

8. "B. T. W." in Charleston *West Virginia Journal*, reprinted in *Southern Workman*, VI (Aug. 1877), 62.

9. Letter of "W," Mar. 26, 1877, in *Southern Workman*, VII (July 1878), 52. There may have been a typographical error in the date of the letter; 1877 maybe should have been 1878.

10. Interview with a former student in 1899, in Max B. Thrasher, *Tuskegee: Its Story and Its Work* (Boston, 1900), 19.

11. William T. McKinney to BTW, Sept. 11, 1911, Con. 249, BTW Papers. BTW's reply, Sept. 21, 1911, confirmed McKinney's accuracy. BTW said: "The scenes, figures and incidents described by you are all so vivid, that for a few moments I felt myself carried back once more to my boyhood days."

12. *Ibid.*

13. *Ibid.*

14. *Ibid.*

15. *Ibid.*; BTW, *Up from Slavery*, 67; Helen W. Ludlow, ed., *Twenty-Two Years' Work of Hampton Institute* (Hampton, Va., 1893), 129-30.

16. See "Scholarships, 1876-7," 22, 24, record book in Treasurer's Office Vault, Hampton Institute.

17. Charleston *West Virginia Courier*, Jan. 5, 1876.

18. *Ibid.*, Feb. 2, 1876; eyewitness account in George W. Atkinson, *History of Kanawha County* (Charleston, 1876), 335-36.

19. Letter of "Citizen" to the editor, Charleston *West Virginia Courier*, Feb. 9, 1876.

20. *Ibid.*, Aug. 1, 1877.

21. *Ibid.*, Jan. 26, July 19, Aug. 30, 1876, July 25, 1877.

22. *Ibid.*, Aug. 16, 23, 1877.

23. *Ibid.*, Oct. 18, 1876.

24. *Ibid.*, Aug. 15, 1877.

25. Articles in *Southern Workman*, VII (Oct. 1878), 76-78, VII (Nov. 1878), 85, IX (May 1880), 57.

26. BTW telegram to St. Louis *Post-Dispatch*, Nov. 18, 1910. August Meier and Elliott Rudwick, "Attitudes of Negro Leaders toward the American Labor Movement from the Civil War to World War I," in Julius Jacobson, ed., *The Negro and the American Labor Movement* (New York, 1968), 39, 402, assume that BTW worked as a miner only before 1872, and therefore conclude that he could not have been a member of the Knights of Labor, who did not organize in the West Virginia coal fields until after 1872. It is probable, however, that BTW worked in the mines when school was not in session, as his brothers, John and James, did.

27. BTW, *Up from Slavery*, 48, 52.

28. McKinney to BTW, Sept. 11, 1911, Con. 429, BTW Papers.

29. Charleston *West Virginia Courier*, Aug. 4, 1877.

30. Lewisburg *Greenbrier Independent*, Aug. 4, 1877. The history of the capital question is discussed in Charles W. Ambler and Festus P. Summers, *West Virginia: The Mountain State* (2nd ed., Englewood Cliffs, N. J., 1958), 276; Elizabeth Cometti and Festus P. Summers, eds., *The Thirty-Fifth State: A Documentary History of West Virginia* (Morgantown, W. Va., 1966), 476-77; Works Progress Administration Writers Program, *West Virginia: A Guide to the Mountain State* (New York, 1941), 182-84.

31. Charleston *West Virginia Courier*, July 4, 1877.

32. *Ibid.*, July 18, 25, 1877.

33. Lewisburg *Greenbrier Independent*, July 21, 1877.

34. *Ibid.*, Aug. 18, 1877.

35. *Ibid.*, Aug. 4, 1877.

36. BTW, *The Story of My Life and Work* (Naperville, Ill., 1900, rev. ed., 1915), 46. A biographical sketch of Romeo Hoyt Freer is in George W. Atkinson, ed., *Bench and Bar of West Virginia* (Charleston, 1919), 216-17.

37. William A. MacCorkle, *Recollections of Fifty Years* (New York, 1928), 569-70.

38. See W. B. Carroll to BTW, Mar. 21, 1900, Con. 168, BTW Papers.

39. BTW, *The Story of My Life and Work*, 46-47.

40. BTW, *Up from Slavery*, 58-60.

41. *Ibid.*, 57-58.

42. McKinney to BTW, Sept. 11, 1911, Con. 249, BTW Papers.

43. BTW, *Up from Slavery*, 61-62.

44. Tuskegee *News*, Nov. 18, 1915.

45. Samuel C. Armstrong to BTW, Feb. 10, 1879, Armstrong Letterbooks, President's Office Vault, Hampton Institute.

46. Account of the speech in Nathalie Lord, "Booker Washington's School Days at Hampton," *Southern Workman*, XXXI (May 1902), 258.

Booker T. Washington
and the White Man's Burden

Those who have thought of Booker T. Washington as a provincial southern American black, intellectually as well as geographically isolated from the rest of the world, will be surprised to find that he was substantially involved in African affairs.[1] This involvement, however, did not require any fundamental readjustment of Washington's outlook. The position of blacks in American society at the turn of the twentieth century was, after all, roughly analogous to that of blacks in the African colonies. Both groups were politically disfranchised, socially subordinated, and economically exploited. Black Americans were engaged largely in raw material production in the South, that "underdeveloped" part of the American land empire that closely resembled a colony. The Darwinist mode of social thought supported both European colonialism and proscriptive American racial practices. Washington's cooperation with white colonial authorities and promoters in Africa, likewise, was consistent with his public acceptance of most of the southern white racial practices and his partnership with American white elite groups of both North and South. He urged black peoples overseas as well as those in America to seek their individual and group interests within the existing political and racial order. Though Washington, abroad as at home, occasionally endorsed surreptitious attacks on the prevailing race system, his African experience illuminates his essential conservatism. He is seen, as in a tailor's mirror, from new angles but in the usual posture. Though he occasionally associated with more militant blacks at home and overseas, he so thoroughly subscribed to the "White Man's Burden" of leadership and authority that, in seeming forgetfulness that he was black, he actually took up the burden himself.

Early in his career as a black leader Washington even endorsed the white stereotype of the naked African savage, as a story he told on the lecture platform in 1897 illustrates. "A friend of mine," said Washington, "who went to Liberia to study conditions once came upon a negro shut up with-in a hovel reading Cicero's orations. That was all right. The negro has as much right to read Cicero's orations in Africa as a white man does in America. But the trouble with the colored man was that he had on no pants. I want a tailor shop first so that the negro can sit down and read Cicero's orations like a gentleman with his pants on."[2] A growing knowledge of African history and the new ideas of anthropology, sociology, and archaeology modified the image.[3] "I am deeply interested in any discoveries that your expedition on the Upper Nile has brought to light," Washington wrote to James H. Breasted. "I have long wished to know something more about the early history of the dark people of Africa. During the past two or three years, I have been taking advantage of such leisures as I had to dig into the history of the African people."[4] There is other evidence of this reading program, and by 1909 Washington was emphasizing the size of the continent and the multiplicity and variety of its peoples. "It is impossible," he said, "to tell the story of Africa in a few sentences."[5] But Washington was a man of action, and what sophistication his conception of Africa acquired was largely through the role he played there. Washington and other Tuskegeans were actively involved in Togo, Sudan, South Africa, Congo Free State, and Liberia. These activities and his many contacts with African teachers, missionaries, and nationalist intellectuals shaped a view of Africa resembling that of the more enlightened European colonialists.

On the first day of the twentieth century Tuskegee's first venture into Africa began. A Hamburg freighter put ashore in the German colony of Togo three Tuskegee graduates and a faculty member, along with their teaching equipment—plows, wagons, a steam cotton gin, and a cotton press. Their dual task was to train Africans in cotton culture and to experiment with interbreeding of local and imported cotton to develop a hardy, commercially successful variety. This was one of many projects of the *Kolonial-Wirtschaftliches Komitee* (KWK), a private German organization anxious to accelerate the economic exploitation of the German colonies. While the *Komitee's* lobbyists sought to divert their government from absorption in *Weltpolitik* to more systematic administration of its present possessions, the *Komitee's* experts were busily focusing modern technology on the colonial opportunities. They sought Tuskegee advice on cotton growing not only in Togo but in Morocco and East Africa.[6]

Through the influence of the German ambassador and the American Secretary of Agriculture, a team of KWK experts visited Tuskegee to secure expert and practical cotton farmers. "Some members of the company have certain misgivings whether your negro-planters might find some difficulties in starting and developing their work in Togo," Baron Herman of the *Komitee* wrote to Washington, "in finding the necessary authority towards the native population and in having at the same time the necessary respect towards the German government official[s] who of course would try to help them as best they could in their work."[7] What he was really asking, though Washington may not have understood this, was whether the Tuskegeans would accept the highly authoritarian German colonial administration. According to one authority the Germans in this period "treated the people as conquered subjects of the German empire who had few or no legal rights."[8] Washington reassured the Baron: "I do not think in any case that there will be much if any difficulty in the men who go from here treating the German officials with proper respect. They are all kindly disposed, respectful gentlemen. I believe at the same time they will secure the respect and confidence of the natives."[9] It was decided that James Nathan Calloway, a Fisk University graduate with knowledge of German who had managed one of the Tuskegee farms, should accompany the young Tuskegee graduates for the first year.

One can picture the first party of Tuskegeans standing on the shore of the Gulf of Guinea beside their pile of equipment, forty miles from their destination in the bush, without a beast of burden within a hundred miles. The Africans who met them refused to draw the wagons over the rough roads, but offered to bear the wagons on their heads. This proved impracticable, and the Americans loaded only the most important articles on the heads of a hundred bearers and made the four-day journey on foot. While the mechanic of the party built a grass-covered mud hut and made plans for housing the gin and cotton press, the two farmers attacked the twenty-foot tree trunks and the fifteen-foot elephant grass. Calloway meanwhile went off in search of draft animals and laborers. Wild cattle and horses were secured from the Sudan, but the tsetse killed them before they could be broken to yoke and harness. Clouds of locusts, armies of ants, the "bug-a-bug," and the jigger—presumably an Africa-sized chigger—plagued the Tuskegee pioneers. For lack of draft animals, they harnessed four Africans to each plow and thirty-six Africans to the sweeps that turned the ginning machinery. Despite obstacles and challenges, in the first year they grew, processed, and shipped to Germany a small cotton crop of twenty-five bales. The Missahöhe experiment station was successfully launched.[10]

Nine Tuskegeans worked for various periods in Togo between 1901 and 1909. Their many letters back to the school would make an interesting case study of early black American contact with Africa. They worked hard, with a single exception. Four of them died in Togo, and five others returned after a few years.[11] The weakest of the first party died of fever, and two members of the second party died in 1902 before they could get ashore in a small boat through the heavy surf. This incident inspired an alumnus to write "Tuskegee's First Martyrs," only part of which is quoted here:

> So into life boats and canoes,
> They climbed like Jonah of old;
> But never would they have done it,
> If their fortunes had been told.
>
> Soon after they had left the ship,
> An hour's time or shorter;
> The boat was upset and they all
> Were hurled into the water.
>
> Way down beneath the briny waves,
> Two martyrs Simpson and Drake;
> Who gave up school and native land,
> For their race and country's sake.
>
> Their images no sculptor carved,
> Nor biography detailed;
> But in every Tuskegee heart,
> Their monument stands unveiled.[12]

For almost a year after this disaster, Tuskegee students refused to take the places of the martyrs, despite vigorous recruitment by George Washington Carver and Emmett J. Scott of the Tuskegee faculty.[13] Eventually only John W. Robinson, of the class of 1897, one of the original party, was left in Togo.

An exemplar of the Tuskegee virtues of industry and humility, Robinson was determined to "make good" in Africa. "I am doing nothing that most people would consider great or noble, or either very honorable— 'Growing Cotton' because it is commonly thought that any fool with a mule could do that," he wrote home. "Yet it has become the main object of my life to do most successfully that so-called simple thing 'Grow Cotton.' . . . How well I am succeeding my work must tell, not my words." He carefully reported his achievements, however. In 1903 some 122 bales were sent to

Germany, and Robinson made two hundred dollars that year as a 5 per cent commission on his share of the cotton produced. The *Komitee* increased his salary 25 per cent.[14] After Robinson became the only Tuskegean left in Togo, he continued to seek advice from Carver, the school's distinguished agriculturist, on such matters as cross-pollination and insect pests. Marrying a Tuskegee graduate, Robinson took her to Africa for several years. "I feel that my future is sealed up in these cotton stalks," he wrote Carver, "then why should I run away from it?"[15] In 1905 Robinson began a cotton school for African farmers, with one hundred pupils, increased the next year to two hundred.[16] His school was enlarged eventually into a general agricultural school, and he was assigned to a new experiment station and cotton school farther inland in 1908. As Robinson's health began to break, he resolved to serve for only two more years. "The pioneering part seem[s] to fall always to me," he wrote wistfully.[17] A few months later he was drowned while crossing a swift river in a canoe. "It is due to his important services . . . that the Togo cotton has attained the high reputation it has," wrote the KWK in reporting the death.[18] Because Robinson's body was not recovered, the German officials would not issue the death certificate. His widow waited for years to collect his back pay and finally employed a Berlin lawyer to sue his insurance company.[19]

The KWK program is hard to assess with fragmentary evidence. It reported in 1908 that cotton production in the German colonies had risen from nothing to more than three thousand bales of marketable product, that from Togo excelling American "middling" grade. To gin the Togo cotton, ten power stations were set up in the colony, and German industrialists began the manufacture of gins and presses to supply the colonial market.[20] A historian of Togo reports, on the other hand, that the cotton experiments were less successful practically than technically. When the Togo cotton stations shipped five different varieties to Germany in 1904, all of them marketable but of different staple length, German importers caused an uproar. They demanded that the *Komitee* concentrate on a single variety.[21] Evidently the cotton program prospered until the end of German control of Togo, however, for cotton production at seven Togo stations rose steadily from 129,797 kilograms in the cotton year 1904-1905 to 530,763 kilograms in 1910-1911.[22] Washington, for his part, gave German colonial policy toward the African population a sweeping endorsement on the occasion of a visit to Berlin in 1910. "I have followed with great care the policies and the plans according to which the German officials have dealt with the natives of Africa," he said. "Their work succeeds by these means in a wholesome and constructive manner. They do not seek to repress the Africans, but rather to help them that they may be more useful to themselves and to the German people. Their manner of handling Negroes in Africa might be taken as a pattern for other nations."[23] In actual fact, German administration had been so arbitrary and disruptive of tribal organization and traditional ways that the Africans had refused to cooperate. The German parliament investigated and insisted on some reforms in 1907, but even after that the tenor of Togo administration remained less than "wholesome and constructive."[24] As he frequently did in America, Washington construed white men's actions more favorably than they deserved.

Tuskegee graduates helped to introduce cotton culture also into other parts of Africa. Some of them were employed by British promoters in Nigeria and others apparently in the Belgian Congo.[25] More importantly, the man who opened up the fabulous cotton region of the Anglo-Egyptian Sudan chose three Tuskegee Seniors to assist him in his pioneer experimental farming in that area. Leigh Hunt, an American capitalist, acquired with British associates a large tract at Zeidab on the banks of the Nile. He brought a Tuskegee carpenter, agriculturist, and blacksmith there to organize a plantation and prepare the way for a larger colony of American blacks. Hunt told Washington that hardheaded business motives rather than philanthropy guided his actions, and there is every reason to believe him. "What race of men is best adapted to assist in this pioneer work,—to serve as model farmers, to train the natives and teach them how to make the best use of these lands?" Hunt asked. "I should like to try the American Negro as I believe him best fitted to work with advantage to himself and to the Sudanese."[26]

Washington's parting advice to the young men bound for the Sudan was amusingly similar to what one would expect from a Victorian parent, a warning against "going native." After reminding the boys that they had the school's reputation in their keeping, he concluded: "One point I wish to impress upon you is this, a great many persons going to a warm climate, go to ruin from a moral standpoint. I hope you will keep this in mind and remember that if you yield to the temptation and lower yourselves in your moral character, you will do yourself, the school and the race the greatest injustice; but I feel sure you are going to stand up and be men."[27]

The Tuskegeans took hold of their work in the Sudan with such a will that Hunt wrote enthusiastically to Washington: "To tell you the truth I am delighted with these boys and therefore very hopeful that my experiment in blazing the way to this land of promise is going to prove beneficial to at least some of your race."[28] Hunt arranged for two other Tuskegee graduates to join the staff of the experimental plantation, but in about two years one of them died and the others returned home with "African fever."[29] Hunt soon withdrew from the syndicate, which went on to develop the Gezira irrigation and cotton-growing enterprise a few miles north of Zeidab. Tuskegeans apparently were not further involved.[30]

Colonial officials in Southern Africa meanwhile sought Washington's advice on race policy. Lord Grey of the British South Africa Company, which controlled Rhodesia, suggested in a conversation with the editor William T. Stead that Washington might be employed to tour Rhodesia and report on the best methods "to raise, educate, and civilize the black man." Grey told Stead that his company would be willing to pay Washington's expenses for a period of six to nine months. After Stead enthusiastically relayed the offer through his American colleague Albert Shaw, Washington's consideration of it was given wide newspaper publicity. He consulted with President Roosevelt and other prominent Americans and finally declined on the ground that his primary responsibility was to his institution and black Americans, but he agreed to reconsider at a future time.[31]

Washington was consulted also when "Milner's Kindergarten" was launching the new Union of South Africa. E. B. Sargant, appointed South African Commissioner of Education by Lord Milner, was instructed to devise a plan of education for the Orange Free State and Transvaal. His request for advice on the proper education for black Africans was forwarded to Washington by a mutual friend.[32] Washington's answers to Sargant's questions are particularly revealing because of Washington's stated assumption that there was "no very great difference between the native problem there and the Negro problem in America." For blacks in South Africa he proposed the same accommodation, economic and cultural subordination, and incentives to individual self-help that characterized his racial philosophy in the United States. "Since the blacks are to live under the English Government," Washington wrote, "they should be taught to love and revere that government better than any other institution. To teach them this, they should receive their education and training for citizenship from or through the government. It is not always true that the Missions teach respect for the rulers in power."[33] Washington thus supported those conservative South Africans who considered missionaries, particularly black American ones, as subversives.[34] Washington also urged that the Africans be taught English in order to give them a common language and to absorb them more fully into Western culture. All should receive industrial as well as common school training, he felt, so as to "fit them to go out into this rich country and be skilled laborers in agriculture, mining and the trades." He urged that the educated class of African men be accorded civil equality with Europeans, a position that was consistent with his support of educational qualifications for suffrage in the United States. "The tribal system of government should gradually be replaced by an allegiance directly to the government of the land," wrote Washington. His principal answer to the complex racial problems, however, was a black version of the nineteenth-century "Gospel of Wealth." "Experience shows," he said, "that the black, as other men, work better and more profitably when induced to this labor by reward and it is voluntarily performed. If proper inducements are offered these people they will labor more and more as their wants are increased by education." There is no evidence that Washington's recommendation of industrial education was seriously heeded by the South African government. Africans were rigidly excluded from skilled trades, and many white South Africans considered industrial education of the Africans a threat to the social order.

Washington became involved in a more congenial African role as defender of mistreated black people in King Leopold's Congo Free State. Early in the twentieth century a world-wide scandal began with the exposure of forced labor and police brutality in this supposedly model colony. Washington readily assented to the request of Thomas S. Barbour, American organizer of the Congo Reform Association, that he use his influence with high American officials in behalf of Congo reform. He called personally on his friend President Roosevelt and on members of the Senate Foreign Relations Committee to urge American diplomatic pressure on the Belgian government and monarch.[35] Washington carried with him to the White House a protest committee of the National Baptist Convention, the largest of all black organizations, which he had helped to arouse to a state of concern.[36] He became a vice-president of the Congo Reform Association, persuaded influential white friends to take an interest,[37] and discussed the Congo scandal in his public lectures. In 1904 an article on "Cruelty in the Congo Country" appeared in the *Outlook* under Washington's name, but he sent the royalty check to Robert E. Park, the young, white secretary of the Congo Reform Association, who had written all or most of it.[38] Park thus began a career as his principal ghost writer that lasted until Washington's death. The article described in detail the nature of the European exploitation and urged "careful investigation and swift action" to end the abuses. Washington and Park warned that "The oppression of the colored race in one part of the world means, sooner or later, the oppression of the same race elsewhere."

Washington's success in bringing black pressure to bear on American policy makers is indicated by the reaction of his opponents. "Dr. Washington is no small enemy to overcome," Colonel Henry I. Kowalsky wrote to the King of the Belgians.[39] A New York lawyer, Kowalsky was the highest paid of Leopold's several American lobbyists. In letters and an interview with Washington, Kowalsky sought to dissuade the black leader from his course by convincing him that his sympathies were misplaced. Kowalsky assured Washington of his own lack of racial bias, flattered him, slandered the missionaries, and excused the cutting off of hands as merely "an old tribal custom." "I recall with great pleasure my visit with you the other evening," Kowalsky wrote in March 1905, "not because I did all the talking, but because I found you deeply impressed with the subject and your honest and manly attitude towards me." Kowalsky put in writing an offer of a free trip to the Congo. "You can select your own route," he wrote to Washington, "in every way be your own master, free from suggestion or dictation,—the fullest and widest latitude of your own choice alone shall map your footsteps, and every dollar of expense I will place in the bank for you to defray your wants. All I want is 48 hours' notice of the fact that you will go."[40] Washington apparently did not seriously consider the offer, which is interesting chiefly for what it reveals of Leopold's lobby. Washington was more tempted, however, by an invitation to speak at a Congress on Economic Expansion in Belgium under the more respectable auspices of the Belgian ambassador to the United States and an American professor.[41] Park urged him to go, and his reasoning indicates the sort of influence Park had on Washington's view of colonialism:

> I say by all means "go." I believe it will give you an opportunity to say something, at once for your school and our own colonial system, more fundamental than has yet been uttered. The difference between our colonial system and others consists in the fact that we are preparing the peoples we govern for citizenship, either in the United States or as independent states; other countries are interested only in the *economic development* (a vague term, which may be interpreted in many ways) of their possessions. . . .

Park warned Washington, however, that "the King of Belgium hopes to win you over to his theory of dealing with the Blackman. It is part of his cynical view of things in general that everyone can be purchased with money or flattery."[42] Possibly for this reason, Washington found an excuse not to go.[43]

Washington continued to lecture on Congo reform and spoke with Mark Twain at a series of meetings in major American cities. When Park wrote Washington in mid-1906 that "there seems to be a feeling here that you have not as much interest in the work of the association as [you] formerly did," Washington agreed to sign another article written by Park.[44] Then in December 1906 Hearst's New York *American*, at the height of its sensational crusade for Congo reform, published the purloined letters of Kowalsky to King Leopold, one of which stated that "I then reached out and got to Dr. Booker T. Washington. . . . "[45] Kowalsky did not explain what "getting to" meant, but there is no other known evidence to support a view that Washington aided Kowalsky or faltered in his support of Congo reform. It is uncertain how much Washington or American opinion influenced the moderate reform in the Congo after the King surrendered his colony to the Belgian government.

It was in Liberia that Washington played his greatest African role. While his actions in this case were immediately useful, they served to support a semicolonial relationship of Liberia to the United States. During the final months of the Roosevelt administration and early in the Taft administration, when the little black republic seemed on the verge of both internal collapse and absorption by its European colonial neighbors, it was Washington who rang the fire bell, and kept ringing it. He used the leverage of the black American vote to engage in international as well as interracial diplomacy. This resulted in American's first serious commitment in Africa, an area far from the range of America's national interests. Washington's unofficial diplomacy in this crisis of black self-government illustrates the strong points of his personal style. He showed patience and mastery of detail in the untying of Gordian knots, diplomatic skill and agility developed in a lifetime of interracial negotiation, and ability to play several roles simultaneously in dealing with various groups. On the other hand, the weaknesses of Washington's approach and outlook are suggested by the nature of the American commitment in Liberia that emerged from his negotiations. Liberia became an American protectorate similar to that which had recently been imposed on the Dominican Republic. It involved an international bankers' loan and the control of customs and border police by American officials.

Liberia's plight was indeed serious, intricate, and seemingly endless.

Established early in the nineteenth century by the efforts of white Americans who hoped to return manumitted slaves to the Dark Continent, Liberia at the turn of the twentieth century was still only an Americo-Liberian coastal fringe with an undeveloped and rebellious tribal hinterland. Liberia had never received enough immigration or capital to become an outpost of Western civilization, but it lacked the cohesion or isolation requisite to a hermit kingdom. And so it limped downhill, saved from absorption by powerful neighbors less through its own efforts than through the unstable European power equilibrium on the eve of the First World War.

When the able West Indian Arthur S. Barclay became President of Liberia, his efforts at reform only made bad matters worse. He brought in as adviser Sir Harry H. Johnston, the famous explorer, intellectual, and colonial administrator. Johnston promptly negotiated the £100,000 loan of 1907 with Emile Erlanger and Company of London to help the nation pay its creditors. In return, Johnston's Liberian Development Company was granted a sweeping concession to exploit Liberian rubber and other resources, and the British Colonial Office was given control over the Liberian Frontier Force. These changes precipitated a Liberian political crisis. The Erlanger loan proved inadequate to pay off all the creditors; it was also such a burden on the customs revenues, which were administered by a British official, that the Liberian government could not pay its employees and had to procure government supplies and services on credit at ruinous rates. Moreover, the French government, alarmed by Barclay's pro-British policies, occupied a section of the Liberian hinterland precipitately and then reached out for more. A factor adding to the confusion was a divergence of policies among the British officials. While the British Foreign Office supported Liberian independence and integrity, the Colonial Office, as in the case of South Africa before the Boer War, pursued an imperialistic policy. The British consul at Monrovia took advice from the governor of Sierra Leone, for whom he had formerly worked under the Colonial Office. The head of the Liberian Frontier Force was a former British colonial administrator who employed many Sierra Leone troops, clothed them in British uniforms with OHMS on their caps. At a strategic moment in Liberia's internal crisis he led a mutiny of his unpaid frontier troops that threatened the capital. Possibly he acted on orders from the British consul, and a British ship aptly named the *Mutiny* arrived offshore with a company of British troops from Sierra Leone. President Barclay managed to put down the mutiny by winning over most of the Liberian troops and deposed its commander, but Liberia's weakness was manifest.[46]

At the request of several Liberians and black Americans resident there, Washington meanwhile had told President Roosevelt in the name of black voters that Liberia needed substantial American assistance.[47] When three Liberian commissioners arrived in the summer of 1908 to appeal formally to the United States government, Washington served as their host. He arranged for their accommodation at white hotels, special consideration aboard trains, and treatment by government officials with "just as much courtesy as the customs of the United States will allow." He accompanied the commissioners to meetings at the State Department, with President Roosevelt and presidential nominee Taft, and later took them to Tuskegee for a three-day conference.[48] Meanwhile, Second Assistant Secretary of State Alvey A. Adee was "grubbing among papers inch deep in dust" to find the record of Liberian-American relations. Though he himself favored "some form of quasi-protectorate," Adee failed to find precedent or treaty sanction for this and concluded that Great Britain claimed "as much right to feel interested in the welfare of Liberia as the United States does."[49] Secretary of State Elihu Root, therefore, listened in a fatherly way to the Liberians, but did not commit himself until an American commission should be sent to Liberia.[50] Roosevelt expressed to Emmett Scott his desire to settle the Liberian question "on the broad ground of the square deal to the Liberian Republic." Two days after the Liberians had visited him, however, Roosevelt said in reference to Haiti's and Liberia's predicament: "It is a question of race."[51] It is evident that a somewhat ludicrous racialism also governed the thinking of Adee in the State Department. "It must always be borne in mind that the climate of Liberia is against any effective Americanisation," he wrote in a memorandum. "Only full-blood Africans seem to stand it. The half-bloods have to go through two or three attacks of the fever before they can be acclimated." He continued:

> I think, with the experience we have gained in the Philippines, we could administer and self-develop Liberia in practical ways, with the aid of trained African mestizos from Puerto Rico and perhaps some Philippinos, and sending some full-blooded southern Africans. . . . To do that, however, we would have to assume an administrative protectorate, in short a colonial control in all but the name. The practical administration might be under the Secretary of Agriculture.[52]

Washington was regarded by Secretary Root as an indispensable member of the Liberian commission because the Liberians "would listen to him when perhaps they would not to any one else, for a large part of the problem to be worked out is with these people themselves."[53] Root thought Liberian problems should be solved primarily through self-help, with a minimum of technical assistance from such Americans as Washington. When William Howard Taft became President, however, he insisted on Washington's presence in the United States during during the early months of his term as his adviser on black and southern affairs.[54] Washington therefore made arrangements for Scott, his private secretary, to be a commissioner in his place. Washington also submitted to the State Department the list of white men experienced in colonial administration and development from which the other two commissioners were selected.[55] After much negotiation and the resignation of several more experienced men, Roland P. Falkner, chairman, formerly superintendent of education in Puerto Rico, and George Sale, superintendent of Baptist mission schools in Puerto Rico and Cuba, were appointed.[56]

"LIBERIANS INSULTED BY U.S. SENDING COLORED CLERK AND UNKNOWN WHITES" was the headline of the Boston *Guardian*. This organ of Washington's black opponents charged inaccurately that it was on Washington's advice that the commission had a white majority.[57] On the other hand, New York *Times* reporters tried to stir up a race issue in the selection of Scott. Finding that Scott was to travel on the cruiser *Birmingham*, whose officers were preponderantly southern, the reporters interviewed officers who said that they would ask for a transfer and eat below rather than sit at table with a black man.[58] The commissioners were moved to another cruiser, the *Chester*, whose captain Scott found to be kind and considerate. "The officers *in the main* have also been agreeable," Scott later reported. "We have had our meals in the Cabin Mess the Captain's sumptuous quarters & he alone has been a fellow diner."[59] During part of the time in Liberian waters Scott also traveled on the *Birmingham* without racial incident.[60]

The commissioners returned from Liberia suspicious of the designs of the British, French, and German. Their report recommended an all-American banker's loan to refund the entire debt of Liberia and free it of dependence upon any colonial power. It also urged that the United States arrange for a firm delimitation of the Liberian boundary, take over the Liberian customs service, and furnish United States Army officers to lead and retrain the Liberian Frontier Force.[61] Washington and Scott threw the weight of the so-called Tuskegee "Machine" behind these recommendations, for they believed that "subterranean forces are at work to prevent anything being done for Liberia." They influenced both the black and white press against southern and isolationist opposition to a Liberian protectorate.[62] Washington persuaded the Secretary of the Navy to dispatch a warship to aid the Americo-Liberians in suppressing a tribal revolt and to send at least one warship a year thereafter. He warned President Daniel Howard of Liberia, however, that "the whole future of Liberia hinges upon its ability to get hold of the native population," that a redress of the very real grievances of tribal Liberians was a prerequisite to both civil concord and settlement of chronic border disturbances.[63]

Through Henry Cabot Lodge and Elihu Root of the Senate Foreign Relations Committee, Washington influenced the Senate's approval of the Liberian convention.[64] The administration was forced to compromise, however, in order to overcome Senate reluctance to involve the nation in a bilateral commitment in Liberia and to satisfy the colonial powers' continued interest in the black republic. By the arrangement that the Senate finally approved, four American banking firms shared the American part of a $1,500,000 international loan in 1912 in which British, French, and German banks were also equally involved. To secure the loan, the United States appointed the general receiver of customs, while the three assistant receivers were appointed by the other powers whose bankers were parties to the loan.[65] Black American army officers took over direction of the Liberian Frontier Force.[66]

Washington continued to influence Liberian finance, economic development, and education. While the State Department was negotiating the political settlement, Washington wrote to the banker-philanthropist Isaac N. Seligman. He asked him to "find parties in New York who would like to take up the Liberian debt, something in the way that was done in the case of San Domingo."[67] Seligman showed interest, but it was Paul M. Warburg, a Tuskegee trustee and partner of Kuhn, Loeb and Company, who led the American banking consortium involved in the Liberian loan. Through Warburg's family firm in Germany was already interested in the loan, there is evidence that Washington also influenced his decision.[68] In a letter to Secretary Philander C. Knox, Warburg took a philanthropic view of the loan, saying that "our associates and we hardly look upon this small transaction as a matter of business, but we rather consider it from the point of view, of attempting to assist that Republic in its struggle to free itself from the oppressive influences, which are well known to you."[69]

Washington realized that American fiscal aid was only a rescue measure for Liberia; it would do little good if economic conditions continued as before. He sought, therefore, to encourage American capital investment in Liberia. The most notable of such schemes was that of John Stevens Durham, a black Philadelphian, to plant sugar in Liberia on a large scale. Warburg's refusal to supply the capital brought the plan to an end.[70] Washington also urged Liberians to accumulate their own capital by heroic measures of self-denial and enterprise. There were many things that Washington, with an outlook forged in the mid-nineteenth century, did not understand. His lifetime in the colonial economy of the American South, however, gave him a ready understanding of many of the problems of an undeveloped country such as Liberia. He may also have sensed that Liberia's experience was a harbinger of the hopes and trials of independent Africa. He advised a Liberian editor:

> A nation must export more than it imports or financial disaster follows. This means but one thing, that the Liberian people should try to get their living out of the natural resources of their country instead of depending to any extent upon the resources of foreign countries. Every time a Liberian eats a tin of canned goods imported from any other country, it means poverty for the Liberians; it means that the Liberians are paying somebody else to manufacture the tin cans, and paying the freight upon the cans, and all this of course means money taken out of Liberia. . . . All this means another thing, and that is, that a large proportion of the brightest men and women should receive scientific, technical and industrial education in order to enable them to understand and master these natural resources.[71]

The First World War interrupted all plans and was disastrous to Liberia's economy precisely because it stopped all trade with industrial countries. A postwar American loan was insufficient, and a better day for Liberia awaited the arrival of large-scale rubber investment in the 1930's and the end of forced labor by tribal Liberians.

Washington became the best-known black man in the world when his autobiography became a world-wide best seller. It was translated into Zulu as well as the chief European languages, and some of the Africans who corresponded with him may have done so simply because he was a celebrity. Many Africans, however, responded hopefully to his message of self-help and industrial education. Students went to Tuskegee from all over Africa, though not in large numbers because scholarships and travel funds were lacking. Olivia E. P. Stokes, whose ancestors had been involved in the founding of Liberia, began in 1908 a Tuskegee scholarship fund for both Americo-Liberians and the sons of Liberian tribal chiefs. She and Washington began a correspondence that resulted, years after the death of both, in the creation of the Booker T. Washington Industrial Institute in Liberia under the auspices of the Phelps-Stokes Fund.[72] In every part of Africa other industrial schools were started in imitation of Tuskegee by whites and blacks, by missionaries and governments.[73]

Washington's most prominent African disciple was the Zulu educator the Reverend John L. Dube, who was educated in the United States. After a visit to Tuskegee, Dube returned home to found the Zulu Christian Industrial School at Ohlange, near Phoenix, Natal. Though his school was on a tract of land given by one of the Zulu chiefs, it was supported almost entirely by American philanthropists. Dube had to overcome the suspicions of white South Africans who considered black American missionaries subversive. He earned the title of "the Booker T. Washington of South Africa" by sponsoring a type of education calculated to mollify the local whites and by his example of middle-class conservatism and dignity. He succeeded in gaining the support not only of white leaders but the militant African nationalists as well. After his election as president of the South African National Congress by the more militant Africans, Dube wrote to his American sponsors: "I believe in being moderate as you will see in my letter of acceptance, and I regard it as a duty to my people to keep in check, the red-hot republicanism that characterize[s] some of our leaders, and is calculated to injure rather than help our cause."[74] A number of Dube's graduates later attended Tuskegee.

Another South African political moderate and educational leader, Davidson D. T. Jabavu, was more directly influenced by the Tuskegee educator. This graduate of the University of London spent three months at Tuskegee in 1913 under instructions from the South African Minister of Native Affairs to report on the adaptability of Tuskegee methods to South Africa. Jabavu and is father led in setting up the South African Native College at Fort Hare three years later.[75]

A curious anomaly of the Washington Papers is his friendly correspondence with most of the leaders of African nationalism. There is no evidence, however, that he encouraged or even clearly understood their nationalistic and Pan-African views.[76] He initiated none of this correspondence, and about the only thing he seems to have had in common with the nationalists, beyond skin color, was an acquiescence in segregation, which they may have construed as similar to their desire for national separatism.

In 1895 Washington made a celebrated address known as the Atlanta Compromise which won such enthusiastic support from whites of both sections that it established his position as a black leader. In this speech he acquiesced in segregation while at the same time pleading for economic opportunities for blacks in agriculture and the trades. Soon thereafter he received a letter from Edward W. Blyden, the intellectual father of Black Nationalism, endorsing his position. Born in the West Indies of Togo slave parents, Blyden returned to Liberia for his education and then served the American Colonization Society and the governments of Liberia and Sierra Leone. Deeming Christianity a white man's religion, Blyden was converted to Islam. In other ways also he anticipated the Black Muslims of a later era: he glorified *negritude* and believed in a distinctive and somewhat mystical "African personality."[77] He wrote Washington that his 1895 speech was "an inspiration" and would go down to posterity alongside George Washington's Farewell Address. In some ways, he told Washington, his work was greater than that of the Father of his Country for whom he was named. "He freed one race from foreign domination, having another chained and manacled. But your words and your work will tend to free two races from prejudice and false views of life and of their mutual relations which hamper the growth of one and entirely cripple the other." The maxim in Washington's speech that Blyden particularly praised was that which said: "In all things that are purely social we can be as separate as the fingers, yet one as the hand in all things essential to mutual progress." The separatist concept which was Tuskegee conservatism in the American context became radical nationalism in the African context. The simile of the separate fingers of the hand, wrote Blyden, "is a common one among the aborigines of Africa." He also endorsed as "common sense" Washington's assertion that the opportunity to earn a dollar in a factory was more important than the opportunity to spend the dollar in an opera house. Blyden wrote:

> I recognize as healthful and encouraging elements in the condition of the Negro in the South his desire for material and intellectual improvement, his thirst for physical comfort, his craving for justice, which your work tends to stimulate. I do not understand his hunger for social equality with the dominant race, because equality depends upon so many things. It is a matter of taste which it is not in our power to regulate.[78]

When Washington had dinner with President Roosevelt at the White House in 1901 and thus revealed that he was not at heart a segregationist, Blyden reversed his position to one of criticism of Washington.[79]

Another central figure in the history of the African nationalist idea, the

Washington as a Hampton Institute student, 1873

(Above) Washington, circa 1880; (below) Washington in the principal's office at Tuskegee Institute, 1902

(Above) Washington and his secretary, Emmett J. Scott, circa 1902; (below left) Washington hunting in West Virginia, 1902, courtesy of *National Magazine*; (below right) Washington's first wife, Fanny Norton Smith Washington, who died in 1884, courtesy of Booker T. Washington National Monument.

(Above left) Washington's second wife, Olivia A. Davidson Washington, who died in 1889, courtesy of Booker T. Washington National Monument; (above right) Washington's third wife, Margaret James Murray Washington; (below) lithograph of White House dinner with Theodore Roosevelt by C.H. Thomas and P.H. Lacey, 1903, courtesy of Smithsonian Institution.

Faculty and guests at Tuskegee Institute's twenty-fifth anniversary celebration in 1906. Seated l to r: Robert C. Ogden, Margaret M. Washington, Washington, and Andrew Carnegie

(Above) l to r: Robert C. Ogden, William H. Taft, Washington, and Andrew Carnegie, 1906; (below) Washington and his sons, Booker T. Washington, Jr., (center), and E. Davidson Washington

Washington speaking in Louisiana in 1915, during one of his last tours, photograph by A. P. Bedou

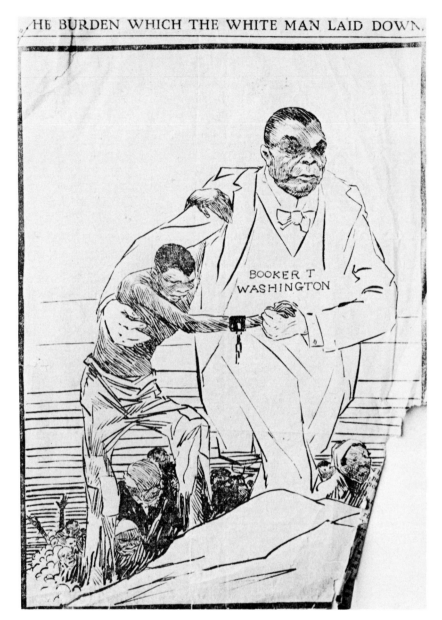

Unidentified cartoon published in 1915 after Washington's death, courtesy of Booker T. Washington Papers

white missionary Joseph Booth, wrote to Washington in behalf of several causes. Perhaps best known for his slogan, "Africa for the Africans," Booth inspired and fostered John Chilembwe's insurrection in Nyasaland in 1915, which was "Ethiopian" or national rather than tribal.[80] Booth first corresponded with Washingon in the interest of a scheme to colonize American blacks in East Africa.[81] Later he asked Washington to persuade Andrew Carnegie to promote racial peace in South Africa by giving a hundred thousand dollars a year toward black American colonization there. Park, Washington's chief advisor on Africa, dismissed Booth as a "little dinky missionary" whose peace fund "would be used in fighting the English government in South Africa to whose policy he is opposed and by whom he is regarded as an enemy of public peace."[82] Washington's reply to Booth, drafted by Park, concluded that "the introduction of another alien element into South Africa would only increase the present irritation and make conditions worse."[83]

The chief Gold Coast nationalist of the early twentieth century, J. E. Casely Hayford, wrote to Washington in 1904: "I have recently had the pleasure of reading your autobiography, and it occurred to me that if leading thinkers and workers of the African race had the opportunity of exchanging thoughts across the Atlantic, the present century would be likely to see the solution of the race problem." To further the dialogue to such an end, Hayford sent Washington copies of his own books.[84] Washington's rather perfunctory reply enclosed some Tuskegee printed matter and invited him to visit the institution. Washington's friendship seems to have been closer with his brother, the Reverend Mark C. Hayford, who visited Tuskegee in 1912. Mark Hayford wrote from London:

> I am here endeavoring to raise funds for the purpose of opening on the Gold Coast what I trust may in time be a sort of "Tuskegee," if only in miniature form, for the development, among other things, of industrial & technical education in that part of West Africa, where at present we have nothing at all adequate to meet the needs of the place—in fact nothing which gives any systematic industrial & technical training such as has proved so useful & helpful to the race in America, where under your able leadership so much has been accomplished which is destined to influence the future of the Negro more than any of us can conceive at present.[85]

Mark Hayford arranged to give financial aid to at least one Gold Coast student at Tuskegee in 1912.[86] Casely Hayford in the same year sent Washington copies of his pamphlets attacking British colonial policies.[87]

Some lesser figures of African nationalism also had contact with Washington. Pixley Ka Isaka Seme, a Zulu who later was a founder of the African National Congress, visited Tuskegee in 1906 while a student at Columbia University. He described himself as "carried away with" the Tuskegee plant, and added: "We need your spirit in South Africa." Seme gained admission to Tuskegee of a cousin interested in learning the printing trade.[88] Seme himself, after graduating from Columbia, studied at Jesus College, Oxford, where he organized a club of African students. He wrote Washington to ask for an endorsement of the club, whose purpose was not agitation but "the interchange of general ideas." He assured Washington that "violence in word or deed has no place in our programme." Yet, in the long run the club might have great influence. He noted "that here are to be found the future leaders of African nations temporarily thrown together and yet coming from widely different sections of that great and unhappy continent and that these men will, in due season, return each to a community that eagerly awaits him and perhaps influence its public opinion."[89] Washington's reply indicated good will, but counseled moderation and even conservatism:

> I am sure that English statesmen, the men whose counsels will finally prevail, believe as you and I do, that in the long run Africa can prosper only on condition that, not only the riches of the soil and the mines but the latent powers of the native people are developed in a rational manner. What that implies is a practical problem that can only be solved by study and experiment. You can and should help in the solution of that problem and there are ways that you can be helpful, as no one else can, both to your own people and to the government. More and more I am learning that you face in South Africa, in a somewhat different and more difficult form, the same task we have in this country.[90]

When the two men met in London in 1910 Washington apparently rejected Seme's appeal to take a more active interest in African national causes. "I shall always regret that our meeting in London had to be marred by incidents of a personal character," Seme wrote. "Africa is certainly awakening mighty and hopeful. I know that it will be a great cause of inspiration and encouragement to us if you could enlist your interest to our course." Washington replied simply that he was "sorry that our meeting in London was not more satisfactory than it was."[91]

Washington refused to endorse a similar club at Liverpool University, the Ethiopian Progressive Association,[92] but he encouraged the efforts of Moussa Mangoumbel, a Senegalese living in France, to promote world-wide black brotherhood.[93] He also took an interest in similar Pan-African efforts of West Indian and African expatriates in London, most notably those of Duse Mohammed, editor of the *African Times and Orient Review*.[94] Two important South African black nationalists, A. Kirkland Soga[95] and F.Z.S. Peregrino,[96] sought to introduce the Tuskegee educational system into South Africa and to send students to Tuskegee.

A suitable culmination of Washington's long interest in Africa was the International Conference on the Negro held at Tuskegee in 1912. The conference involved the same ambiguity of relationship to the blacks and whites that was evident in his other African activities and in his role in American society. Washington had attended none of the earlier international race conferences, at Atlanta in 1895 and in London in 1900 and 1911, to all of which he was invited,[97] perhaps because his chief American antagonists were prominent in them. As early as 1905 Park asked Washington: "Would you be willing to write an article recommending that the Powers in Africa, the missionaries and educators, come together in an international conference to devise means for the systematic and harmonious extension of Industrial training in Africa[?]" Park had already gathered much information on the subject, and in 1906 an article by Washington, or perhaps Park, in the *Independent* urged such a conference. Washington hoped that it would lead to the formation of a permanent society that would be "a sort of guardian of the native peoples of Africa, a friendly power, an influence with the public and in the councils where so often, without their presence or knowledge, the destinies of the African peoples and of their territories are discussed and decided." The society should include "explorers, missionaries and all those who are engaged, directly or indirectly, in constructive work in Africa."[98]

Washington's formal call for the 1912 conference ignored the important but controversial issues of race and nationalism and stressed "a more systematic development of constructive educational work on the part of missionaries and governments."[99] Invitations were sent to the leading missionary societies and to thousands of individual missionaries. The State Department at Washington's request publicized the conference among European governments that had colonial possessions in Africa or the West Indies.[100] In view of the type of publicity, the distance from Africa, and the restrictions on travel of subject peoples, it is not surprising that most of the delegates were white. West Indians were present "in three colors," and twenty-five missionaries of twelve denominations and eighteen countries or colonies were represented, but very few black Africans.[101]

Several influential West Africans, however, gave their blessing to the conference from a distance. Blyden, who died before the meeting, had sent a letter commending its purposes. Washington read it to the delegates, as well as one from Casely Hayford. "There is an African Nationality," Hayford asserted, "and when the Aborigines of the Gold Coast and other parts of West Africa have joined forces with our brethren in America arriving at a national aim, purpose, and inspiration, then indeed, will it be possible for our brethren over the sea to bring home metaphorically to their nation and people a great spoil." Hayford went on to commend Washington's methods. "We feel here," he wrote, "that the great work that is being done at Tuskegee Institute has a mighty uplifting force for the race."[102]

One of the principal speakers at the conference was Mark C. Hayford of the Gold Coast. He was scheduled to speak on industrial education in Africa, but, according to one report:

> He had prepared a long historical paper, giving an account of the antiquity and past grandeur of some of the tribes who had reached the West Coast in the region where he lives. His paper was so learned and so long that Mr. Hayford did not succeed in completing it, but he told some very interesting facts in his cross examination by Dr. Washington, after he had finally given up the attempt to read his paper.[103]

The delegates might have done well to have listened more respectfully to Hayford. The "tribes" referred to were probably the medieval kingdom of Ghana. Another speaker who was given a less respectful hearing than he deserved was Bishop Henry M. Turner of Atlanta, the "back to Africa" leader of his day. The general tone of discussion is suggested by the report that "There was no politics and very little theory in any of the three days' sessions."[104]

On the last day the missionaries met to discuss the possibilities of greater cooperation among their denominations in the mission field. White South Africans were said to be suspicious of the purposes of black American missionaries. The representatives of the black Baptists, African Methodist Episcopal Church, African Methodist Episcopal Zion Church, and Colored Methodist Episcopal Church "were unanimous in saying that their only purpose in going to Africa was to help their brethren there and that in no case did they wish any of the people not to be loyal to the Governments under which they were living." They unanimously urged

Washington to go to South Africa and explain to the whites that their purpose was "to uplift their brethen and not to incite sedition."[105] Plans for a second conference three years later were disrupted by the First World War and Washington's death.[106]

A mere review of Washington's activities and expressed attitudes still leaves his role somewhat enigmatic. He never went to Africa, though he found time for three trips to Europe. He considered his principal mission in life to be the spreading of the educationl system and social philosophy symbolized by Tuskegee Institute. It was consistent with this commitment to encourage black American enterprise and ethnocentric philanthropy in Africa. On the other hand, Washington rejected the proposals of emigrationists, visionaries, and missionaries as inconsistent with the Tuskegee ideal.

Just as Washington had built a career in the United States by telling blacks what influential whites wanted them to hear, so in Africa he supported the principle if not all the practices of colonialism. There as here, Washington's role and outlook were complex, but they supported the concept of the white man's burden. This burden was not entirely hypocritical, of course. Washington acquiesced in the leadership of white men, but he was prompt to remind them when they neglected the responsibilities of power. In Togo and South Africa he supported the colonial structure, if not the *status quo*. In the Congo he reminded the white rulers of their obligations. To Liberia Washington offered the form of black nationalism and self-government, while the substance of political and economic power went to American officials and international bankers, though he showed more sensitivity than the usual white man toward the problems of the Liberian tribal aborigines. Washingtón's extensive if fruitless correspondence with African nationalists is also hard to explain. It is important to remember that the nationalist leaders initiated the correspondence and that Washington yielded to them no important concessions. He remained a social pacifist for whom industrial education was a universal panacea. Its method and ethos seemed to him as applicable to African problems as to those of black Americans.

1. The Booker T. Washington Papers, Manuscript Division, Library of Congress, hereinafter cited as BTW Papers, are an important neglected source on early American black contacts with Africa. George Shepperson, "Notes on Negro American Influences on the Emergence of African Nationalism," *Journal of African History*, I (No. 2, 1960),

310-11, recognizes BTW's significance, but his brief investigation of this huge collection missed most of the pertinent manuscripts there. Two other recent surveys of the same theme ignored the BTW Papers: Harold R. Isaacs, "The American Negro and Africa: Some Notes," *Phylon*, XX (Fall 1959), 223-24; Robert Collins and Peter Duignan, *Americans in Africa: A Preliminary Guide to American Missionary Archives and Library Manuscript Collections on Africa* (Stanford, Calif., 1963).

2. Entry for Oct. 20, 1897, in *Indianapolis in the "Gay Nineties": High School Diaries of Claude G. Bowers*, ed. Holman Hamilton and Gayle Thornbrough (Indianapolis, 1964), 99.

3. Robert Ezra Park to BTW, June 2, 1908 (42), Franz Boas to BTW, Nov. 30, 1904 (550), James H. Breasted to BTW, Apr. 29, 1909 (387), Mar. 8, 1910 (903), BTW to Breasted, May 6, 1909 (387), BTW Papers [container number in parenthese].

4. *Ibid.*

5. BTW to Mrs. C. Foremint Pober, Oct. 23, 1909 (397), BTW telegram to Brentano's booksellers, May 17, 1905 (298), BTW Papers.

6. Mary E. Townsend, *The Rise and Fall of Germany's Colonial Empire* (New York, 1930), 256-59. On Tuskegee's assistance to the *Komitee* in Morocco and East Africa, see BTW to George Washington Carver, Sept. 11, 1910 (604), Dr. Mathiesen, KWK, to Washington, Feb. 20, 1912 (919), BTW Papers.

7. Baron Herman, Berlin, to BTW, Nov. [should be Sept.] 3, 1900 (177), *ibid.*

8. J. D. Fage, *An Introduction to the History of West Africa* (3rd ed., Cambridge, Eng., 1962), 180.

9. BTW to Baron Herman, Sept. 20, 1900 (282a), BTW Papers.

10. Unidentified Tuskegean in Togo to BTW, Jan. 13, 1901 (218), Calloway to BTW, Feb. 3, Apr. 13, 1901 (213), Shepherd L. Harris to BTW, May 15, 1901 (199), Nov. 3, 1901 (213), John W. Robinson to BTW, May 26, 1901 (215), speech of Robinson at Tuskegee twenty-fifth anniversary celebration, press release, Mar. 31, 1906 (571), *ibid.*; James N. Calloway, "Tuskegee Cotton-Planters in Africa," *Outlook*, LXX (Mar. 29, 1902), 772-76; interview of Calloway, Indianapolis *Freeman*, Mar. 15, 1902, clipping in American Colonization Society Papers, Manuscript Division, Library of Congress. For several references to this collection I am indebted to Edwin S. Redkey, Yale University.

11. Reprint from *Tropenflanzer*, official organ of the KWK, Berlin, sometime in 1910 (255), BTW Papers.

12. In W. E. Dancer, *Treasured Thoughts: Tuskegee Days and Ways* (n.p., 1909).

13. Warren Logan to BTW, June 13, July 22, 1902 (233), Scott to BTW, June 24, 1902 (241), KWK to BTW, July 15, Oct. 21, 1902 (232), Scott to Carver, Jan. 13, 1903 (241), BTW to Alexander McKenzie, Apr. 25, 1903 (22), BTW Papers.

14. Robinson to BTW, Jan. 25, 1904 (294), *ibid.*

15. Robinson to Carver, July 2, 1904 (871), *ibid.*

16. Robinson to Robert C. Bedford, Sept. 12, 1906 (358), *ibid.*

17. Robinson to BTW, Oct. 21, 1908 (380), Robinson to Bedford, Jan. 24, 1909 (897), *ibid.*

18. KWK to BTW, Sept. 14, 1909 (53), *ibid.*

19. BTW to KWK, Oct. 14, 1909, Sept. 26, 1910 (53), KWK to BTW, Dec. 2, 1909, Sept. 9, 1910 (53), BTW to Mrs. Danella F. Robinson, Oct. 27, 1910 (53), Apr. 6, 1912 (62), Mrs. Robinson to BTW, Sept. 27, 1910 (53), Oct. 16, 1911 (53), Mar. 25, 1912 (62), BTW to Karl Supf, Jan. 10, 1911 (440), *ibid.*

20. KWK to BTW, Aug. 25, 1908, enclosing Karl Supf, "German Colonial Cotton (Reports of 1900-1908)" (375), *ibid.*

21. Robert Cornevin, *Histoire du Togo* (Paris, 1962), 186; O. F. Metzger, *Unsere Alte Kolonie Togo* (Neudamm, 1941), 241-53.

22. Cornevin, *Histoire du Togo*, 187.

23. Reprint from *Tropenflanzer*, sometime in 1910 (255), BTW Papers.

24. Fage, *History of West Africa*, 180; Harry R. Rudin, *Germans in the Cameroons 1884-1914: A Case Study in Modern Imperialism* (New Haven, Conn., 1938), 212-13.

25. William E. Curtis, in Washington, D. C., *Evening Star*, Mar. 24, 1905, clipping (299), Henry F. Downing to BTW, Sept. 2, 1902 (225), J. Wesslay Hoffman to Isaac Singer, Mar. 1, 1908 (381), BTW Papers.

26. Hunt to George Roberts, Nov. 29, 1903 (871), Hunt to BTW, Dec. 6, 1903, Sept. 24, 1904 (29), *ibid.* BTW was introduced to Hunt by a mutual friend, James S. Clarkson, who had an intense personal interest in the experiment with black technicians in Africa. (See Clarkson to Hunt, June 19, Oct. 19, Nov. 28, 1903, Hunt to Clarkson, Oct. 7, 30, 1903, Hunt to Earl of Cromer, undated copy, James S. Clarkson Papers, Manuscript Division, Library of Congress.)

27. BTW to Cain Triplett, Poindexter Smith, and John P. Powell, Dec. 12, 1904 (294), BTW Papers.

28. Hunt to BTW, Feb. 3 [1905] (29), *ibid.*

29. BTW to Clarkson, Apr. 9, 1905 (299), BTW to the five Tuskegeans at Zeidab, May 23, 1905 (308), July 28, 1906 (322), J. B. Twitty to BTW, Apr. 17, 1907, C. C. Finlator, report of death of Smith, Aug. 27, 1907 (340), BTW to Powell, Sept. 2, 1907 (357), *ibid.*

30. Hunt's career in the Sudan is briefly traced in Arthur Gaitskell, *Gezira: A Story of Development in the Sudan* (London, 1959), 51-52, 75; J. S. R. Duncan, *The Sudan: A Record of Achievement* (London, 1952), 122-24.

31. Stead to Shaw, Feb. 11, 1903, Shaw to BTW, Mar. 7, 21, 1903, Stead to BTW, June 3, 1903, (277), BTW to the Reverend A. E. LeRoy of Natal, Apr. 29, 1908 (818), BTW Papers; see also Clarkson to Hunt, June 19, 1903, Clarkson Papers.

32. Mrs. Grace Lathrop Luling (Mrs. Theodore Luling) to BTW, Jan. 17, 1905, Sargant to Mrs. Luling, Nov. 30, 1904 (307), BTW Papers.

33. BTW to Mrs. Luling, Jan. 23, 1905 (303), *ibid.*; see also Mrs. Luling to BTW, Feb. 12, 1909 (895), Sargant to BTW, June 12, 1909, BTW to Sargant, June 30, 1909 (398), *ibid.*

34. See George Shepperson, "Ethiopianism and African Nationalism," *Phylon*, XIV (Winter 1953), 9-18, and "The Politics of African Church Separatist Movements in British Central Africa, 1892-1916," *Africa* XXIV (Jan. 1954), 233-45; Thomas Hodgkin, *Nationalism in Colonial Africa* (New York, 1957), 93-114; Ambassador Whitelaw Reid to Earl of Selborne, High Commissioner for South Africa, introducing AME Bishop William B. Derrick, Oct. 30, 1907, Whitelaw Reid Papers, Manuscript Division, Library of Congress.

35. Barbour to BTW, May 17, 1904 (284), June 22, 1904 (2), July 1, 1904 (284), BTW to Barbour, July 11, 1904 (284), Robert E. Park to BTW, July 18, 1904 (30), July 23, 1904 (870), BTW to Park, July 19, 1904 (30), BTW Papers.

36. George E. Stevens to BTW, Nov. 14, 1905, BTW to Stevens, Nov. 18, 1905 (881), L. G. Jordan to BTW, Nov. 16, 1905, BTW to Jordan, Nov. 28, 1905 (877), *ibid.*

37. BTW to Barbour, undated (reply dated Oct. 26, 1904) (284), Robert C. Ogden to BTW, Nov. 10, 1904 (23), BTW to H. P. McCormick, Nov. 25, 1905 (878), *ibid.*

38. BTW, "Cruelty in the Congo Country," *Outlook*, LXXVIII (Oct. 8, 1904), 375-77; Park to BTW, July 23, Sept. 10, 1904 (870), BTW to Park, Oct. 11, 1904 (293), BTW Papers.

39. Undated letter in New York *American*, Dec. 11, 1906.

40. Kowalsky to BTW, Mar. 1, 10, 1905 (303), BTW Papers.

41. Louis Frank, Brussels, to BTW, Mar. 8, 1905, BTW to Frank, Mar. 8 [*sic*], 1905 (301), Professor James H. Gore to BTW, May 1, 1905, Robert H. Terrell to BTW, May 17, 1905 (308), Baron L. Moncheur, Belgian ambassador to the US, to BTW, May 23, 1905 (804), *ibid*. Gore apparently was one of Leopold's lobbyists. (New York *American*, Dec. 12, 1906.)

42. Park to BTW, undated, about May 1905 (30), BTW Papers.

43. BTW to Baron Moncheur, May 30, 1905 (804), *ibid*.

44. Park to BTW, June 29, 1906, BTW to Park, July 5, 1906 (33), *ibid*.

45. Kowalsky to King Leopold, undated, in New York *American*, Dec. 11, 1906. On activities of Kowalsky and other lobbyists, see Paul McStallworth, "The United States and the Congo Question, 1884-1914," doctoral dissertation, Ohio State University, 1954, 255, 276-86; Ruth M. Slade, *English-Speaking Missions in the Congo Independent State, 1878-1908* (Brussels, 1959), 305-15; Joseph O. Baylen, "Senator John Tyler Morgan, E. D. Morel, and the Congo Reform Association," *Alabama Review*, XV (Apr. 1962), 130-31. The name Congo Reform Associations is used throughout this essay to avoid confusion, though it went by other titles at first.

46. The preceding three paragraphs are based on many manuscript items in the BTW Papers and in the National Archives. The most useful secondary accounts of the topic are Raymond W. Bixler, *The Foreign Policy of the United States in Liberia* (New York, 1957), which is based on archival sources, but fails to note BTW's influence; Raymond L. Buell, *The Native Problem in Africa* (2 vols., New York, 1928), esp. II, 786-802; Léonce A. N. H. Jore, *La République de Libéria* (Paris, 1911), 110-14; Nnamdi Azikiwe, *Liberia in World Politics* (London, 1934), 111-19; Sir Harry H. Johnston, *Liberia* (New York, 1906).

47. Ernest Lyon, US minister to Liberia, to BTW, July 15, 1907, BTW to Roosevelt, Sept. 19, 1907, BTW to Lyon, Sept. 28, 1907 (7), Emmett J. Scott, telegram, to BTW, Sept. 27, 1907 (133), BTW Papers; State Department cable to Reid, US ambassador to Great Britain, Sept. 12, 1907, Reid Papers.

48. BTW to Roosevelt, Mar. 21, 1908 (7), BTW to Lyon, Apr. 8, May 12, 23, 25, 26, June 3, 15, 1908, C. R. Branch to BTW, Apr. 27, 1908 (368), BTW to P. O. Gray, the Reverend S. G. Ferguson, Jr., and editor of the *African League* [J. H. Green], June 15, 1908 (371), BTW Papers. The commissioners were so grateful for BTW's aid that both he and his secretary, Scott, were awarded knighthood in the Order of African Redemption. BTW was also offered the post of Liberian chargé d'affaires in the United States, which he declined. (BTW to Secretary Elihu Root, June 15, 1908, Root to BTW, June 19, 1908, State Department 12083/30, National Archives [hereafter cited as NA]; Lyon to BTW, June 23, 1908 [375], BTW Papers.)

49. Adee, memo to Secretary of State, Mar. 24, 1908, State Department 12083/71, NA.

50. Root, memo of interview with the Liberian commissioners, June 1, 1908, State Department 12083/14, *ibid*.; G. W. Gibson, James J. Dossen, and Charles B. Dunbar to the Secretary of State, June 11, 1908, in *Papers Relating to the Foreign Relations of the*

United States, 1910 [hereafter cited as FR] (Washington, D. C., 1915), 696; BTW to Roosevelt (sent on to Root), June 16, 1908, Elihu Root Papers, Manuscript Division, Library of Congress.

51. Scott to BTW, undated [late Sept. 1908] (1), BTW Papers; Roosevelt to Ray Stannard Baker, June 3, 1908, and to Johnston, July 11, 1908, in *The Letters of Theodore Roosevelt*, ed. Elting E. Morison *et al.* (8 vols., Cambridge, Mass., 1951-54), VI, 1048, 1125-26. Gentler public attitudes of both Roosevelt and Root are indicated in Roosevelt's message to Congress (Jan. 19, 1909), quoting extensively from a report from Root, reprinted in FR, 1910, 699-701. See also Philip C. Jessup, *Elihu Root* (2 vols., New York, 1938), II, 61.

52. Adee, memo, to Assistant Secretary Robert Bacon, Nov. 10, 1908, State Department 12083/50, NA.

53. Root to Seth Low, Jan. 19, 1909, State Department 12083/60, *ibid.*; BTW to Low, Feb. 16, 1909 (45), BTW Papers.

54. BTW to Robert C. Ogden, Mar. 4, 1909 (895), *ibid.*; Adee to Assistant Secretary Huntington Wilson, Mar. 11, 1909, Fred W. Carpenter, secretary of President Taft, to Secretary Philander C. Knox, Mar. 6, 1909, State Department 12083/110-11, NA.

55. Of the voluminous correspondence on this topic in the BTW Papers, see particularly BTW to Root, Dec. 14, 1908, Root to BTW Dec. 16, 1908 (895) BTW to Ralph W. Tyler, Dec. 23, 1908, Tyler to BTW, Dec. 25, 1908 (8), BTW to Root, Dec. 28, 1908 (6), BTW to General Leonard Wood, Dec. 29, 1908 (385), Wood to BTW, Jan. 2, 15, 1909 (895), undated lists of suggested names for commissioners (895).

56. When the State Department prematurely announced appointment of BTW and two others without their consent, all of them declined. (BTW to Robert C. Ogden, Mar. 4, 1909 [895], *ibid.*; New York *Evening Post*, Mar. 2, 1909, clipping [1052], *ibid.*) BTW blocked efforts of his black opponents to put J. Douglas Wetmore on the commission. (See letters between BTW and Charles W. Anderson in Apr. 1909 [43], *ibid.*; Taft to William Loeb, Apr. 7, 1909, Letterbook Ser. 8 [Presidential], II, 320, William Howard Taft Papers, Manuscript Division, Library of Congress.)

57. June 19, 1909 (1090), clipping BTW Papers.

58. New York *Times*, Apr. 17, 23, 1909, New York *Tribune*, Apr. 18, 1909, clippings (1089), Boston *Guardian*, May 1, 1909, clipping (1092), Scott to BTW, Apr. 17, May 3, 1909 (587), Leander T. Chamberlain to BTW, Apr. 18, 1909 (389), Fred R. Moore to editor of New York *Times*, Apr. 19, 1909, copy (396), *ibid.*; memo for Assistant Secretary Wilson, Apr. 21, 1909, Frank Abial Flower to Wilson, Apr. 18, 1909, State Department 12083/188 and 193, NA.

59. Scott to BTW, May 3, 1909 (587), BTW Papers.

60. Interview of Scott in New York *Age*, July 8, 1909, clipping (1089), *ibid.*

61. Suggestions submitted to the American commission by the government of Liberia, 1909 (394), *ibid.*; another copy of same in State Department 12083/290, NA; Report of the Commission of the United States of America to the Republic of Liberia (typescript), State Department 12083/288-89, *ibid.*; Emmett J. Scott, "The American Commissioners in Liberia," typescript (394), BTW Papers.

62. BTW statement sent to Associated Press, Feb. 14, 1909 (896), copy of newspaper interview of BTW, undated, about Nov. 1909, Scott to Carpenter, Feb. 8, 1910, BTW to Carpenter, Mar. 28, 1910 (50), Scott to George A. Finch, Apr. 14, 1910 (905), Scott to

Hamilton Holt, Apr. 18, 1910 (907), Scott to BTW, Apr. 21, 1910 (596), Scott to Ernest Lyon, Apr. 21, 1910 (908), Scott to Bishop Isaiah B. Scott, Sept. 26, 1910 (408), Scott to Burelle's Clipping Bureau, Feb. 3, 1911 (418), *ibid.*

63. BTW to James J. Dossen, Mar. 19, 1910 (905), BTW to Howard, Feb. 6, 1912 (918), *ibid.*

64. BTW wrote to Scott, April 10, 1910 ([596], *ibid.*), after an interview with Secretary Knox and President Taft: "Both are deeply interested and mean to stand by Liberia as far as they can, but of course their hands are tied by the Senate committee." Scott replied on April 13, 1910 ([596], *ibid.*), expressing gratification but adding: "From what I have seen in the newspapers, however, I am not very optimistic as to the outcome. Of course as you clearly appreciate, Liberia's plight is likely to be worse now than before, for the reason that the United States has pretended an interest which it may not prove." For evidence of their redoubled efforts with the Senate, see BTW to Dossen, Mar. 16, 17, 1910 (905), Scott to Lyon, Apr. 9, 1910 (908), BTW to Lodge, Apr. 10, 1910, Lodge to BTW, April 12, 1910 (411), BTW to Dossen, Apr. 10, 19, 1910 (404), BTW to Lyon, Apr. 21, 1910 (411), *ibid.;* George A. Finch, "The Liberian Program and the Senate," memo filed Apr. 17, 1913, State Department 882.51/200, NA.

65. Roland P. Falkner to Secretary of State, Mar. 8, 1912, enclosing signed agreement between the Liberian government and banking firms of the United States, Great Britain, France, and Germany, State Department 882.51/306, *ibid.*

66. BTW to Charles D. Hilles, secretary of President Taft, July 29, 1911, Hilles to Secretary Knox, July 31, 1911, Knox to Reed Paige Clark, Aug. 9, 1911, State Department 882.51/242 and 245, *ibid.;* Clark to BTW, Nov. 10, 1911 (441), Charles D. Young to BTW, Nov. 24, 1911 (446), Feb. 5, 1912 (922), Clark to BTW, Dec. 4, 1911 (419), Mar. 8, 1912 (916), BTW to Clark, Feb. 28, 1912 (916), BTW Papers.

67. BTW to Seligman, Sept. 5, 1909 (394), Oct. 21, 1909 (898), Seligman to BTW, Sept. 10, 1909 (393), Sept. 20, 1909 (898), *ibid.*

68. BTW to Scott, Sept. 23, 1909 (587), Scott to Warburg, Sept. 25, 1909 (898), *ibid.*

69. Warburg to Knox, Nov. 17, 24, 1909, State Department 18222/16-17, NA.

70. Durham had been US minister to Haiti and Santo Domingo and manager of an American sugar plantation in Cuba. (See scores of letters on the Liberian sugar planting project between these men and also with Roland P. Falkner, Hollis B. Frissell, and R. Mackay Mackay [alias R. Mackay Cadell] [5, 44, 58, 63, 65, 404, 405, 408, 411, 421, 441, 450, 453, 891, 908], BTW Papers.) Though BTW encouraged this and several other black American enterprises elsewhere in Africa, he avoided any capital investment there and emphatically refused the use of his name by promoters of the Liberian-American Produce Company. (See particularly BTW to D. E. Howard, Secretary of the Treasury of Liberia, May 9, 1910 [905], *ibid.*)

71. BTW to J. L. Morris, editor of Monrovia *Liberian Register,* Jan. 6, 1911 (428), *ibid.*

72. Olivia E. Phelps Stokes to BTW, Aug. 24, 1908, Aug. 19, Nov. 16, 1909 (47), Caroline Phelps Stokes to BTW, Oct. 14, 1908 (47), W. E. Stokes to BTW, Oct. 23, 1908 (381), and much other correspondence with the Stokes family after 1908, *ibid.*

73. Space limitations prevent fuller development of the influence on Africans of BTW's industrial education ideas and social philosophy. The BTW Papers indicate that the schools listed below were substantially influenced by Tuskegee: Zulu Christian Industrial School, Ohlange, Natal; South African Native College, Fort Hare, Cape of Good Hope;

Lovedale Industrial Institute, Lovedale, Cape of Good Hope; Pretoria Polytechnic Institute in Transvaal; American Baptist industrial mission at Mt. Silinda, Southern Rhodesia; Church of Scotland missions at Blantyre, Domasi, and elsewhere in Nyasaland; Lumbwa Industrial Mission in Kenya; Mittel und Gehelfen School of Kidugalo, German East Africa; African Training Institute, Colwyn Bay, North Wales; S. B. Thomas Agricultural Academy, Freetown, Sierra Leone; and industrial institutes founded or contemplated at Cape Coast, Gold Coast, and at Lagos and Ibadan in Nigeria. (See esp. Emmett J. Scott, "Tuskegee in Africa and Africa at Tuskegee," undated typescript [335], *ibid.*) BTW's influence on the African educator J. E. K. Aggrey seems to have been indirect, though he had some correspondence with Franz Boas about him. (See Edwin W. Smith, *Aggrey of Africa: A Study in Black and White* [New York, 1929], 140-41.)

74. Francis M. Sutton to BTW, June 25, 1903 (261), Louis Stoiber to BTW, Mar. 22, 1906 (261), Mar. 30, 1906 (321), BTW to Dube, Aug. 10, 1907 (346), Dube to BTW, Sept. 21, Oct. 25, Nov. 30, Dec. 3, 1907 (346), Sutton to Mrs. Horton, June 17, 1911, copy (439), Dube to members of the American Committee of the Zulu Christian Industrial School, Jan. 27, 1911, copy to BTW from Stoiber (921), BTW Papers.

75. Catherine Impey, Somerset, Eng., to BTW, June 11, 1913, (479), BTW to Impey, July 16, 1913 (479), Sept. 29, 1913 (927). Jabavu to BTW, Sept. 4, 1913 (927), Jabavu to Scott, Sept. 5, 29, 1913 (927), Minister of Native Affairs, Pretoria, cable to BTW, Sept. 2, 1913, and BTW's reply by cable, Sept. 5, 1913 (927), BTW to John H. Harris, Sept. 9, 1913 (926), *ibid.* On Jabavu's subsequent career, see Mary Benson, *The African Patriots: The Story of the African National Congress of South Africa* (London, 1963), 33, 79, 81-86; Edward Roux, *Time Longer than Rope: A History of the Black Man's Struggle for Freedom in South Africa* (2nd ed., Madison, Wis., 1964), 77, 286, 291, 293.

76. Shepperson, "Negro American Influences," 310-11, and George Padmore, *Pan-Africanism or Communism? The Coming Struggle for Africa* (New York, n. d. [1956?]), 108-12, correctly describe BTW as unsympathetic to militancy, and Shepperson recognizes BTW's ambiguity. BTW was an inactive director of the Philafrican Liberators' League in 1896. (Heli Chatelain to BTW, Oct. 5, Nov. 6, 1896 [115], BTW Papers.) The complexity of Pan-Africanism is shown by the essays in *Pan-Africanism Reconsidered*, ed. American Society for African Culture (Berkeley, Calif., 1962). The dilemma of black Americans, torn between the desire to become fully integrated into the land of their birth and part of their ancestry and the appeal of *negritude* and the African "blood tie," is discussed in Harold R. Isaacs, *The New World of Negro Americans* (New York, 1963), but more perceptively in St. Clair Drake, "Hide My Face? On Pan-Africanism and Negritude," in *Soon One Morning: New Writing by American Negroes 1940-1962*, ed. Herbert Hill (New York, 1963), 78-105.

77. Padmore, *Pan-Africanism or Communism?* 54-55; Colin Legum, *Pan-Africanism: A Short Political Guide* (London, 1962), 20-22; obituary of Blyden in *African World*, Feb. 10, 1912, clipping (1060), BTW Papers; Hollis R. Lynch, "The Native Pastorate Controversy and Cultural Ethno-centrism in Sierra Leone 1871-1874," *Journal of African History*, V (No. 3, 1964), 395-413.

78. Blyden to BTW, Sept. 24, 1895 (112), Oct. 3, 1895 (862), BTW Papers.

79. For this information I am indebted to H. L. Wilson, University College of Wales, Aberystwyth, at work on a life of Blyden; see also Blyden to J. Ormond Wilson, Aug. 11, 1897 (Vol. XXVII, Pt. 1), June 9, 1900 (Vol. XXVIII, Pt. 2), Blyden to the Reverend A. F.

Beard, Oct. 20, 1899 (unbound letters received, 1894-99), in American Colonization Society Papers; Shepperson, "Negro American Influences," 299-301, 309-10.

80. Booth's career in Africa is described in detail in George Shepperson and Thomas Price, *Independent African: John Chilembwe and the Origins, Setting, and Significance of the Nyasaland Native Rising of 1915* (Edinburgh, 1958), 19-123.

81. Booth to BTW, Jan. 19, 1902 (222), Apr. 2, May 12, July 22, 1902 (192), May 14, 1903 (249), leaflet by Booth, Dec. 13, 1901 (1), BTW Papers.

82. Scott to Park, Nov. 6, 1913, Park to Scott, Nov. 8, 1913 (66), *ibid.*

83. BTW [actually Park, written on Park's typewriter] to Booth, undated draft about Nov. 1913 (66), *ibid.*

84. See J. E. Casely Hayford to BTW, June 8, 1904, BTW to Hayford, July 6, 1904 (289), *ibid.* BTW's reply may not have reached Hayford, for it was addressed to "Ainn" instead of Axim, Gold Coast. The best source on Hayford is David Kimble, *A Political History of Ghana: The Rise of Gold Coast Nationalism, 1850-1928* (Oxford, Eng., 1963), 541 *et passim.*

85. Mark C. Hayford to BTW, Jan. 31, 1912 (918), BTW to whom it may concern, recommending Hayford, Apr. 19, 1912 (455), BTW Papers.

86. Mark C. Hayford to J. H. Palmer, registrar of Tuskegee, Sept. 14, 1912, BTW to Hayford, Dec. 22, 1912 (456), *ibid.*

87. J. E. Casely Hayford to BTW, Apr. 17, 1912 (456), Aug. 7, 1912 (455), *ibid.*

88. Seme to BTW, Jan. 29, 1907, BTW to Seme, Feb. 19, 1907 (359), *ibid.*

89. Seme to BTW, Apr. 15, 1908 (381), *ibid.*

90. BTW to Seme, Apr. 29, 1908 (381), *ibid.*

91. Seme to BTW, Jan. 13, 1911, BTW to Seme, Feb. 22, 1911 (439), *ibid.* On Seme's career as a nationalist leader, see Benson, *African Patriots*, 25-32; Roux, *Time Longer than Rope*, 108-13.

92. Kwesi Ewusi and I. A. Johnson to BTW, Feb. 14, 1906, BTW to Ewusi and Johnson, Mar. 9, 1906 (324), BTW Papers.

93. Mangoumbel to BTW, Oct. 6, Nov. 12, 1906 (327), Dec. 6, 1906, Feb. 24, June 16, 1907 (353), *ibid.*

94. Mohammed to BTW, Apr. 4, 1912 (465), May 1, 1912 (61), Scott to Park, May 13, 1912 (61), BTW to Mohammed, Apr. 18, 1912 (465), *ibid.*

95. Soga, editor of *Izwi Labantu*, East London, Cape Colony, to BTW, Dec. 9, 1903 (294), *ibid.*

96. Peregrino, managing editor, *South African Spectator*, Mafeking and Cape Town, to BTW, Jan. 25, 1911 (436), June 12, Sept. 4, 1912, BTW to Peregrino, July 13, 1912 (462), *ibid.*; see also typescript of Peregrino's paper, "The Black Man in South Africa," sent to the International Congress on the Negro at Tuskegee in 1912 (917), *ibid.* Peregrino had once lived in Buffalo, New York. (Indianapolis *Freeman*, May 14, 1898.)

97. H. L. Williams, Pan-African Conference Committee, to BTW, Jan. 6, June 29, 1900 (187), Soga to BTW, Dec. 9, 1903 (294), W. E. B. Du Bois to Scott, Feb. 6, 1911 (421), BTW to Anderson, Jan. 23, 1911 (52), Park to Scott, Dec. 14, 1910 (54), BTW Papers.

98. BTW, "Industrial Education in Africa," *Independent*, LX (Mar. 15, 1906), 616-19.

99. BTW printed call for International Conference on the Negro, Apr. 17-19, 1912 (917), BTW Papers.

100. BTW to Knox, Feb. 19, 1911 (427), BTW to Park, Aug. 3, 1911 (54), *ibid.*

101. Press releases, printed program, and lists of arrivals (917), *ibid.*

102. Quoted in BTW's address of welcome, Apr. 16, 1912 (917), *ibid.*

103. Report on first day of conference, Apr. 17, 1912 (917), *ibid.*

104. Unsigned, undated typescript, "Some Results of the International Conference on the Negro" (917), *ibid.* A white South African who attended the conference was struck by the atmosphere of optimism that the Tuskegee hosts imparted to the conference and noted that one great question was never alluded to: the discrimination against blacks in the United States. (See Maurice S. Evans, *Black and White in the Southern States: A Study of the Race Problem in the United States from a South African Point of View* [London, 1915], 135, 205.)

105. Reports of the committee of missionaries (917), BTW Papers.

106. Press release on the conference (917), *ibid.*

Booker T. Washington and the National Negro Business League

Since the death of the great black conservative leader Booker T. Washington in 1915, there has been such a tremendous reorientation of black social thought that we have tended to read black history backward. That is, we have tended to find, in the past, spokesmen for our present ideas—our own conventional wisdom—contesting with spokesmen for the now repudiated conventional wisdom of the past. Historians looking back a half-century have discovered there the accommodationist Washington and his allies, mostly whites, locked in mortal combat with W. E. B. DuBois and his militant "Talented Tenth." A total war between the powers of light and darkness, with DuBois on the side of light. This simplistic view is now being re-examined by a number of scholars, who find consensus as well as conflict in the black social thought of the turn of the century. As August Meier has pointed out, in his excellent book, *Negro Thought in America, 1880-1915*, Washington and DuBois, born twelve years apart, were products of the same age and, to a considerable extent, shared underlying assumptions. Both were products of a nineteenth-century education; and at the turn of the century both looked backward in different ways to nineteenth-century ideals. This essay may, it is hoped, contribute in a minor way to the dispassionate examination of black thought in the Progressive Era by exploring one idea that DuBois and Washington shared: the idea of black business enterprise as a means of advancement for the race. Let me say in advance that it is not my intention to disparage DuBois, whose ideas changed radically after 1900. He was ever learning, searching for the truth, even when the trail led to China. Further, I have not attempted a systematic study of the actual condition of black business, which has been fully treated by other scholars.

The idea of the National Negro Business League was born in the brain of **98** W. E. B. DuBois, but it was Washington who took the idea and made of it an institution, an important part of the so-called "Tuskegee Machine." In 1899, a year before Washington took up the idea, DuBois sponsored an Atlanta University conference on "The Negro in Business," and was a member of the committee which drafted the conference proposal for "the organization in every town and hamlet where the colored people dwell, of Negro Business Men's Leagues, and the gradual federation from these of state and national organizations." The Atlanta professor expressed not only the organizational idea of the Business League but also its general social outlook. Reiterating the black nationalist cry of "Negro money for Negro merchants," he deplored the shortage of black businessmen and business institutions, which gave the race "a one-sided development" and put it "out of sympathy with the industrial and mercantile spirit of the age." It is clear that DuBois himself was very much in sympathy with the *Zeitgeist* of a commercial age. At the 1899 meeting of the Afro-American Council he was made director of a bureau on black business, with the duty of organizing business leagues. As a social scientist, rather than an action leader, he began by gathering statistical information and drafting organizational plans.

When Booker T. Washington called the organizational meeting of the National Negro Business League in the summer of 1900, he was accused by DuBois and his friends in Boston, Chicago, and elsewhere of stealing the idea and of dividing the black ranks by creating a new organization outside the Afro-American Council, "a new organization of which he will be president, moderator and dictator," as the Chicago *Conservator* put it. At the 1899 meeting of the Afro-American Council, which Washington refused to attend, the *Conservator* said, "he had ample opportunity to suggest plans along business lines and Prof. DuBois, the most scholarly and one of the most conservative members of the Council, who is chairman of the Business Bureau would have been glad to receive Mr. Washington's co-operation." Washington gave no public attention to these criticisms, nor ever acknowledged any debt to DuBois for the idea of the Business League, though he occasionally quoted from DuBois's 1899 report. Washington insisted that the idea had come from his tours all over the country, where he had found many successful black businessmen living isolated and unsung, and that he had organized the Business League in order to give publicity to their achievements and to help them help themselves. Nevertheless, Washington's secretary, Emmett J. Scott, wrote to the editor of the *Conservator* that Washington was "not especially concerned as to the matter of leadership," that he did not seek to "throw obstacles in the path of any organization working in the interest of his people," and that he was creating a separate business organization because "its attention will not be divided as between sociological and other such questions. . . ." And Washington himself made a point of attending the next Afro-American Council meeting, to confront his critics. By 1903, the Afro-American Council had been destroyed by the intensity of its internal dissensions, and the Washingtonian H. T. Kealing was able to say that "the Sage of Tuskegee had a long and true vision. He also knew the value of singlemindedness and the danger of hydraheadedness, so he went ahead. The event now justifies his prescience, for the Afro-American Council is dead and the Business League is at the period of its greatest activity. Success is the best witness wisdom can have."

The 300 businessmen and other Washington supporters who gathered at Boston in 1900 "to take stock" faced a crisis in race relations, and Washington moved forcefully, and even brutally, to control their response to this crisis. Just before and during the meeting, the papers were full of news of race riots in New Orleans, New York, and Akron. These events, Emmett Scott later said, "painted a sombre picture of racial friction and planted in the hearts of many the seeds of dark despair." And yet, in the two days and nights of the conference, "there was not one single reference to the riots or to the conditions that gave rise to them," Washington later reported with pride. "These were business men, come to Boston for a definite purpose with which politics had no connection, and they attended strictly to business." Washington and "the powers that governed the Business League," to maintain this unanimity, prevented a delegation of New Bedford, Massachusetts, businessmen from rendering their report, for fear that it would "deal with topics which were forbidden at that gathering." One New Bedford delegate was still angry two years later, when he wrote to Emmett Scott:

> They knew we [the New Bedford delegation] were all members of the Union League . . . and they knew we were accustomed to speak out. But their fears and suspicions were unjustified, not a word in our report but dealt with business pure and simple. We did not agree with Mr. Washington's fiat (with the New Orleans horror and the Georgia outrages still burning in our memories) but we respected the wishes of the callers of the meeting and laid supreme questions of manhood by, for the sordid materialism of business, although our hearts throbbed in unison with that lofty, manly sentiment of Emerson's
> > "For what avail the plough or sail,
> > "Or land, or life, if FREEDOM fail."

Possibly to allay criticism, Washington brought William Lloyd Garrison, son of the abolitionist, to speak. "The particular word I wish to leave with you is this: Aim to be your own employers," said Garrison. "If the title deeds to the land of the South were in the hands of the colored people, there would be no Negro problem, but, instead, a very large white one."

The National Negro Business League grew rapidly, the 300 delegates of 1900 swelling to some 3,000 when the national convention returned to Boston in 1915, the year of Washington's death. By 1915, there were about 600 local leagues, of which approximately 300 had been organized and chartered by the national league. Membership was estimated at anywhere from 5,000 to 40,000, in thirty-six states and West Africa. The organization remained under the tight control of the Tuskegeean. Though not himself a business man, Washington remained the president throughout his life, and his successor at Tuskegee, Robert R. Moton, also became head of the Business League. The corresponding secretary of the Business League, until 1922, was Washington's private secretary, Emmett J. Scott. A succession of national organizers—Fred R. Moore, Ralph W. Tyler, Charles R. Moore, and Albon W. Holsey—spent their time largely in Northern cities, stimulating or reviving local business leagues, thus keeping the headquarters in the small Alabama town in touch with the leading centers of black enterprise.

Financial records of the Business League are incomplete, but they make clear that the businessmen's organization was not affluent enough to finance itself. Life memberships, at $25 each, reached about a hundred by 1915; but the League was about $500 in debt to Tuskegee Institute; and in 1916 it got out of debt at a cost of $1,500, thanks to a gift from Julius Rosenwald. The private correspondence of the national organizers indicates that many of the local leagues were largely on paper, reviving each year to send delegates to the national meeting, or torn by schisms and leadership struggles. Nevertheless, the Business League was strong enough during Washington's lifetime to be the organizational center of black conservatism. The businessmen held the center of the stage at the annual meetings, but the League absorbed the Washingtonian lawyers, doctors, educators, and other professional people after the collapse of the Afro-American Council. Affiliated with it were a black press association, bar association, and similar organizations of bankers, insurance men, undertakers, and retail merchants. In every community the local business league gave conservatives a rallying point against the militants organized in suffrage leagues, the Niagara Movement, and the NAACP. The Richmond Business League gave Washington a forum there during the Virginia disfranchisement convention in 1901; the "Boston Riot" of 1903 occurred at a meeting sponsored by the Boston businessmen.

The National Negro Business League was significant not only as a help to Washington in the black leadership struggle, but also as a promoter of black enterprise and as an expression of Washington's social outlook. The League unabashedly presented the case for a segregated black economy and the exaltation of black businessmen to a high place parallel to that of white businessmen. The annual meetings never systematically analyzed the status, problems, and opportunities of black business. Instead, the meetings were given over almost entirely to highly personal accounts by businessmen of their "ups and downs," ending with Horatio Alger formulas for business success. Since plain men of business were seldom natural orators, however, the "life of the meeting" was Washington himself, who conducted the "quizzing" of the speakers. By propounding leading questions at the close of a paper or talk, Washington and other "quizzers" from the floor extracted information and homilies that would otherwise not have come to the surface. As one delegate facetiously put it, "'The Wizard' thus compels a man to make a good speech whether he knows how or not." All these colloquies were taken down by a stenographer and published in the annual reports, allegedly as objective evidence of black business progress.

At the local level, the League members stimulated small retail businesses, through "buy black" campaigns, to persuade people to "pass by the Dago store, the German establishment, the Irish institution, and give their trade and spend their money with their own struggling people. . . ." Scott organized a black business service to advise and aid small businesses, but it seems to have died through lack of support. Although there was much talk of black millionaires and black trusts, the League never seriously grappled with the real problems of black business: lack of capital, because poorly paid blacks had small savings, and because white bankers refused to lend to or invest in black enterprises; lack of a business tradition among blacks recently out of slavery, so that few blacks had the chance to grow up in a business, and most successful black businessmen educated their children, not for business, but for professions; the virtual impossibility of a successful black economy, because of the narrowness of a market confined to blacks of low average income; and, finally, the perilous condition of all small business in an age of mass production, giant corporations, and chain stores.

It seems a legitimate question why Washington was so involved in a business organization, since he was an educator. Part of the answer is that he was more a businessman than he seemed to be. His role as principal of Tuskegee was somewhat entrepreneurial, in that he used the capital of philanthropy and the cheap labor of students to build a one-room school into a multimillon-dollar educational enterprise; and in the early years Tuskegee sold everything from bricks to buggies in the local market. Even before Andrew Carnegie's large personal gift to him in 1903, Washington's personal property in land, residences, and business buildings gave him a rental income of nearly $100 a month. He also owned stock in a Birmingham coal company, $500 of stock in a Massachusetts shoe company, $600 of stock in the Tuskegee Cotton Oil Company, a secret investment in at least two black newspapers and a magazine, and, probably, stock in black cotton mills and oil mills in which he took an active interest. At Tuskegee Institute were a savings bank, to encourage thrift on the campus, and the Southern Improvement Company, with philanthropic capital to encourage black land ownership by selling on long terms at low interest. Washington was actually a bigger businessman than any but a handful of the members of the Business League.

Washington's interest in the Business League also stemmed from his evolutionary approach to the race problem. The Progressive Era was, paradoxically, an era of retrogression for black Americans, when political proscription was accompanied by racial violence all over the nation, and followed by segregation and discrimination more extreme than ever before. The scholarship of C. Vann Woodward, Rayford Logan, and others attributes these developments to economic depression and political turmoil in the South, Darwinistic racialism and imperialism, and a strangely *laissez-faire* attitude of the federal government during the age of reform. To Washington, however, as to most of his contemporaries, the worsening position of black Americans seemed to result from the reaction of whites against pushing blacks into positions for which they were unready. Washington expressed this view in 1909 in these words:

> He [the black man] came out of slavery with the idea that somehow or other the Government, which freed him, was going to support and protect him, and that the great hope of his race was in politics and in the ballot. In the last decade the Negro has settled down to the task of building his own fortune and of gaining through thrift, through industry, and through business success that which he has been denied in other directions.

The gospel of thrift, industry, and property ownership had been instilled in Washington during his student years at Hampton Institute, where its founder, General Samuel C. Armstrong, gained a lifelong dominance over Washington's thought. Armstrong, the son of New England missionaries in Hawaii, believed that blacks, like that other "backward," or childlike, race, the Polynesians, were lazy and shiftless, and that all of them needed to be sent to school to learn the Calvinistic virtues of industry and thrift before they would be ready for higher civilization. This viewpoint, which underlay Washington's industrial curriculum at Tuskegee, was reinforced by his contacts with successful Northern businessmen during his fund-raising campaigns. The advice of John Wanamaker and Andrew Carnegie—and of Theodore Roosevelt too—was that blacks needed to get out of politics and get into business. There were "acres of diamonds" all around blacks, particularly in the South, just awaiting an enterprising hand to gather them.

"Man may discriminate," said Washington, "but the economic laws of trade and commerce cannot discriminate." A man of action, rather than an intellectual, Washington accepted the conventional economic ideas of his time, the nineteenth-century climate of classical economics. He thought that economic life and all men's economic actions were controlled by natural laws, which men defied at their peril. These perfect laws had no place for anything so irrational as race prejudice. "When an individual produces what the world wants," Washington believed, "the world does not stop long to inquire what is the color of the skin of the producer." This article of faith ignored the fact that, in reality, the world was very conscious of skin color. To this black Polonius, it followed, as the night the day, that whenever blacks demonstrated the virtues of good businessmen by getting property, nice houses with several bedrooms, bank accounts, and property taxes, the Southern whites who surrounded them would give them the ballot, the Pullman berth, and other unspecified perquisites of full citizenship without a qualm. Northern whites would likewise recognize proven ability and give blacks whatever place they had earned in their society.

In Washington's opinion, business success would gain white recognition of blacks more surely than any other achievement; for the world measured men and races by "certain visible signs of civilization and strength," outward signs of an inward grace. Washington said:

As one goes through our Western states and sees the Scandinavians in Minnesota, for example, owning and operating nearly one-third of the farms in the state; and then as he goes through one of the cities of Minnesota and sees block after block of brick stores owned by these Scandinavians; as he sees factories and street railways owned and operated by these same people, and as he notes that as a rule, these people live in neat, well-kept cottages where there are refinement and culture, on nice streets, that have been paid for, he can't help but have confidence in and respect for such people, no matter how he has been educated to feel regarding them.

Through a thousand speeches extolling the business career for blacks and promoting the Business League, Washington seemed to say that blacks should turn away from the avenues of political action and civil rights agitation which, for the time being anyhow, were already blocked, and travel up the economic road to affluence and consequent economic strength. In this opportunism, he avoided complete acquiescence and accommodation by asserting that the economic approach would re-establish political and civil rights on a firmer basis, and thus provide a new emancipation. Washington illustrated this point with many dubious examples. He recounted the story of "Old Jim Hill," whose name was changed to "Mr. James Hill" after he had acquired property and a bank account. The celebrated Indianola, Mississippi, postmistress, whose post office the local whites forced President Theodore Roosevelt to close, was better off in the banking business with her husband, and even lent money to local whites. Washington alleged that, "almost without exception, whether in the North or in the South, wherever I have seen a Negro who was succeeding in business, who was a taxpayer, a man who possessed intelligence and high moral character, that man was treated with respect by the people of both races."

There was some ambiguity in Washington's attitude toward the separate-economy concept. He always opposed colonization schemes, either within or outside the United States; he insisted that there was "no color line in eggs," and that natural resources knew nothing of skin color; and he constantly harped on the effect that black success would have on white attitudes. Nevertheless, he urged black businessmen to come South precisely because the chief market for black business was among their own people, more of whom were in the South than anywhere else in America. The effect of segregation, he said, "has frequently been to create for the Negro a special business opportunity." Although he tried to keep Madame C. J. Walker, a wealthy manufacturer of hair straightener, off the Business League program, even though she was a life member and a donor to many black causes, including Tuskegee, and although he kept saloonkeepers out of the League on moral grounds, even though they were a leading class of black businessmen, Washington recognized that the chief black business opportunities lay in performing services that whites would not perform and in marketing products designed for blacks. And he showed particular fondness for such all-black, segregated towns as Boley, Oklahoma, and Mound Bayou, Mississippi, which the Business League declared "the finest possible concrete argument that the negro is ready for citizenship." In these self-segregated towns blacks could enter naturally and easily into any occupations for which their talents qualified them, Washington believed. Hoping that Mound Bayou could become a model of black enterprise, with a diversified economy parallel to that in the white world, he persuaded Julius Rosenwald to invest $25,000 in a $100,000 oil-mill enterprise at Mound Bayou, which soon failed, and he introduced Charles Banks of the Bank of Mound Bayou to a number of New York bankers in an effort to save that business concern. Washington ignored the fact that these segregated businesses and segregated towns gave black economic leaders a vested interest in segregation.

Washington's public optimism about black opportunities was not always borne out by his private correspondence. In 1904, for example, black businessmen who exemplified the qualities Washington extolled were molested in West Point, Mississippi. Isaiah T. Montgomery wrote him that:

> Thomas Harvey runs a neat little Grocery, he kept a Buggy and frequently rode to his place of business, he was warned to sell his Buggy and walk. Mr. Chandler keeps a Grocery, he was ordered to leave, but was finally allowed to remain on good behavior. Mr. Meacham ran a business and had a Pool Table in connection therewith, he was ordered to close up and don overalls for manual labor. Mr. Cook conducted a hack business between the Depots and about town, using two Vehicles, he was notified that he would be allowed to run only one and was ordered to sell the other.

A printer named Buchanan, also of West Point, had a piano in his home and allowed his daughter, who was his cashier and bookkeeper, to ride the family buggy to and from work, until "a mass meeting of whites decided that the mode of living practiced by the Buchanan family had a bad effect on the cooks and washerwomen, who aspired to do likewise, and became less disposed to work for the whites." A mob forced Buchanan's family to flee, during his absence, and refused to allow him back in town even to pack. So much for the economic panacea for black ills.

Although the Business League's heyday was a period of tremendous economic, social, and ideological readjustment for blacks, the League and its exaltation of the business ideal met surprisingly little resistance before the First World War. One reason was that such white champions of black militancy as Oswald Garrison Villard and John E. Milholland also supported the Business League. By the 1920s, white and black leaders of the NAACP supported identification of blacks with labor; but in Washington's day the alienation of black leaders from the lily-white unions was almost complete. What muted opposition there was to business leadership came from a minority of blacks of the professional class. To understand their response, it may be helpful to employ the concept of the status revolution which Richard Hofstadter has used to interpret the Progressive Movement in the same period.

The industrial revolution of the nineteenth century, said Hofstadter, threw self-made industrial millionaires to the top of American society. The old elite of the Northeast—preachers, teachers, lawyers, and merchants—had no choice but ruin or subservience. In the Progressive Movement, members of this elite saw a chance to lead a popular movement which would restore them to their former status.

Application of this concept of the status revolution to the black professionals and their leadership of black militancy might prove fruitful, but in this essay only its relation to the thought of Washington and DuBois can be explored.

In an interesting article for *The Outlook*, in 1909, Washington noted that the political leaders of Black Reconstruction were "what may be called the aristocracy of the race," many of whom had been free, or practically free, before the Civil War. A number of them had been favored house servants or sons of their masters and were given special educational opportunities. After the war, while these leaders found scope for their talents in politics, in the professions, and in services catering to the white upper class, they and their descendants were also singled out by Northern philanthropy for higher education and professional training. For, in the nineteenth century, before the industrial *nouveaux riches* had assumed much social responsibility, the center of philanthropy was still in New England and among the old elite. The very Northern elements which were losing power attempted, through philanthropy, to create a black elite in their own image. While this older elite suffered loss of status through the withdrawal of suffrage and political offices and the loss of white patronage for their services there grew up what Washington referred to as "a middle class among the colored people," slaves before the war, but now becoming landowners, artisans, and businessmen. Washington identified himself with these self-made black men of enterprise; DuBois was never of them.

Although DuBois said in 1898 that "The day the Negro race courts and marries the savings-bank will be the day of its salvation," by 1903 he deplored many changes in black society. He wrote:

> The old leaders of Negro opinion . . . are being replaced by new; neither the black preacher nor the black teacher leads as he did two decades ago. Into their places are pushing . . . the businessmen, all those with property and money. And with this change, so curiously parallel to that of the Other-world, goes too the same inevitable change in ideals. The South laments to-day the slow, steady disappearance of a certain type of Negro,—the faithful, courteous slave of other days, with his incorruptible honesty and dignified humility. He is passing away just as surely as the old type of Southern gentleman is passing, and from not dissimilar causes,—the sudden transformation of a fair far-off ideal of Freedom into the hard reality of bread-winning and the consequent deification of Bread.
>
> What if to the Mammonism of America be added the rising Mammonism of the re-born South, and the Mammonism of this South be reinforced by the budding Mammonism of its half-awakened black millions?

If DuBois was a "radical" by 1903, he was clearly one who looked back nostalgically to an earlier society more to his liking. The early volumes of the *Crisis* under his editorship, however, indicate that he had not rejected capitalism. Its columns of racial news were full of friendly notices of black enterprises. Increasingly critical of capitalism, DuBois was always more of a race-conscious black nationalist than was Washington. By the 1930s, the depression conditions, his discouragement about the results of his lifetime struggle for integration, and his latent racial chauvinism caused DuBois, for a brief period, to advocate a separate black co-operative economy and separate schools. He justified these proposals, just as Washington had done two decades earlier, as tactics in the struggle for black integration into American society, but he later changed his mind. As we would hesitate to apply the term "accommodationist" to DuBois for this aberration, so, perhaps, we should be slow also to apply the term to Washington for his promotion of black segregated business.

We have seen that, in their economic thought, Washington and DuBois, at the turn of the century, were not far apart, and that Washington thought that, by promoting black business, he was putting his race's evolution in harmony with the economic revolution of his day. Washington's own life had shown that it was possible to be both black and a successful, self-made American of the late nineteenth century. Along this line of reasoning, if not of action, he drew not only a handful of black businessmen and would-be businessmen, but most of DuBois's "Talented Tenth" of professional men whose interests were linked with his. This fisher of men caught many a lawyer, doctor, and teacher in his net, and their private correspondence is sprinkled with friendly references to the Business League. A *minority* of professional men—the group which Washington's friends called "the kickers" or "the soreheads"—were opposed, not to promotion of black business, but to its corollary: Washington's seeming lack of interest in black political and civil rights, and his optimistic conviction— redolent of Samuel Armstrong and Adam Smith—that every black American's pursuit of his self-interest would, in the long run, result in the race's interest. Even Washington's opponents, though called "radicals," were not anticapitalistic. Instead, they looked backward to an era when the black professional class was dominant in the black community, hopeful of future integration into American society, and favored by Northern philanthropy.

The Secret Life
of Booker T. Washington

The historian inquiring into the black people's experience in America must sooner or later confront the presence in the black past of men who do not fit the conventional mold of heroic history. Nevertheless, a study of their lives may be instructive. One such man was Booker T. Washington, the conservative black leader of the early twentieth century. What strikes a later generation about Washington is not so much his accommodation to segregation and other aspects of white supremacy, which has long been recognized, but his complexity, his richness of strategic resource, his wizardry. He used the white money and favor won by his bland accommodationism to build a personal political machine, sometimes by ruthless methods. While he smiled and nodded in his public life, like the man in the moon he had his dark side, a secret life in which he could cast off the restraints of conventional morality and conservatism and be himself. Surreptitiously, Washington supplied money and leadership for an assault on racially discriminatory laws in the courts. With more success, he employed spies, secret agents, and provocateurs to countermaneuver against his black-militant enemies.

Washington's public image, which in time became a deception, was fixed in the minds of his generation by two highly publicized events, a speech and a book. In 1895 he suddenly moved out of the ranks of obscure young black men through his Atlanta Compromise address, which eloquently presented the conventional formula for interracial cooperation to which most whites and many blacks of the day subscribed. Holding out his hand in a dramatic gesture, Washington promised that blacks would accept segregation "as separate as the fingers," if whites would provide them with opportunity for economic progress and unite with them, "one as the hand in all things essential to mutual progress."[1] Washington's speech was delivered when a tide of white aggression was engulfing the black communities and when white Americans were either joyfully or sadly proclaiming the final failure of the political approach of Reconstruction. Washington offered both races a negotiated peace. This peace was never actually consummated, but Washington's proposal of it enhanced his influence as a black spokesman who had the ear of whites. In 1901 he added his personal example to strengthen the formula. In his autobiography, *Up from Slavery*, Washington carefully edited his past to present himself as the black version of the American success-hero, the slave boy who "by luck and pluck" made good. Like the white heroes of the Horatio Alger novels, Washington lived a virtuous life, manfully overcame odds, and saved his pennies, and though he did not in the end marry the boss's daughter, he received other substantial blessings from white millionaires.

There were many signs of white approval, North and South, of Washington's racial leadership. Andrew Carnegie not only gave a large sum to Tuskegee Institute but also $150,000 to Washington himself and additional sums to aid several of Washington's black enterprises. John D. Rockefeller, Collis P. Huntington, Jacob Henry Schiff, and Julius Rosenwald, all "sainted philanthropists" in Washington's eyes, aided not only Tuskegee Institute but other schools and organizations Washington approved. Harvard University awarded him an honorary master's degree without noticing the irony of the title. Southern governors praised and consulted him. Queen Victoria served him tea. And he was the man who came to dinner with the Theodore Roosevelts in the White House. Washington hobnobbed with the wealthy and famous to a degree that no other black man of the segregation era achieved, and the reports of his life gave vicarious satisfaction to many humbler blacks. By a system of indirect rule, white Americans crowned Washington "king of a captive people." The price of his power, however, was acceptance of the overruling power of the whites. His public utterances were limited to what whites approved. He urged blacks to have faith that their rewards would come through the white man's Puritan ethic of work and striving, the conventional moral philosophy and economic thought of the day. He endorsed not only the beatitudes but all the platitudes—the Sunday school lesson, Polonius, Poor Richard, and the Gospel of Wealth.

While Washington publicly seemed to accept a separate and unequal life for black people, behind the mask of acquiescence he was busy with many schemes for black strength, self-improvement, and mutual aid. At his all-black school, Tuskegee Institute, and dozens of other schools under his influence, he promoted industrial education as the way to meet the practical needs of a depressed rural people. Farmers' conferences, land-purchase revolving funds, all-black towns, and countless speeches were his instruments for building black rural economic strength and his own leadership. Meanwhile, he also built what came to be called the Tuskegee Machine by methods similar to those of urban political bosses. Through the National Negro Business League he not only encouraged black businessmen but secured their organized support for his conservative faction in the northern cities.[2] He became Theodore Roosevelt's closest adviser on race matters and the black patronage broker for the Republican party. He dominated the black press by ownership of several leading newspapers and by advertising and subsidies to others. Partly through his power to dispense philanthropic funds but also through his close personal attention to every detail, Washington exerted a remarkable influence over black colleges and schools, church leaders, and even secret fraternal orders. Weaving many strands into an intricate web of influence and power, Washington became a minority-group boss whose power went beyond politics into almost every aspect of the life that black people were compelled to live in early twentieth-century America.

While Washington's staff of secretaries and ghost-writers operated his Tuskegee Machine, at a deeper level of secrecy his confidantes and spies helped him carry on a shadow life in which he was neither a black Christ nor an Uncle Tom but a cunning Brer Rabbit, "born and bred in the brier patch" of tangled American race relations. Here both white and black enemies were made to feel the secret stiletto of a Machiavellian prince.

It was in many ways unfortunate for Washington's historical reputation that he personally prospered in a time of black racial disaster. He was the Herbert Hoover of a black "Great Depression." Perhaps he could not have reached the top in any other time, and perhaps as he claimed, it was a world he never made. His militant black critics, nevertheless, deeply believed that his efforts at appeasement had led the whites to the very aggressions he was trying to check. This conviction gave a certain ruthlessness to the black infighting on both sides.

As a rural southern black man whose career had been based on compromise, Washington was less sensitive to racial slights than some northern blacks of the professional class, but he was appalled by the "final solution" approach of extreme white racists at the end of the nineteenth century. Yet an open and direct challenge to Jim Crow would wreck his precarious relationship with southern whites. Even the northern philanthropists who aided him would frown on tactics of social conflict. He had frequent reminders that the violent race relations of the era could touch him as well as others, and several times when racial tensions were high he employed private detectives as bodyguards. Washington in these circumstances decided to launch a secret but direct attack on racially restrictive laws. He secretly paid for an directed a succession of court suits against discrimination in voting, exclusion of blacks from jury panels, Jim Crow railroad facilities, and various kinds of exploitation of the black poor.[3] In all of this secret activism, it is clear that Washington was not merely trying to make a favorable impression on his militant critics or to spike their guns, for he took every precaution to keep information of his secret actions from leaking out. Only a handful of confidantes knew of his involvement.

The contrast between Washington's public stance and his private thought and behavior appeared first in connection with the issue of southern disfranchisement of blacks. As state after state placed property and educational restrictions on voting, he publicly pleaded with disfranchising conventions to apply the restrictions equally to both races. When the new constitutions protected the pedigreed white vote with grandfather clauses and other loopholes, however, Washington refused to fight openly against ratification of the new state constitutions. The registrars in his Alabama county gave him a special invitation to come in and awarded him a lifetime voting certificate, which he framed and proudly hung in his den at The Oaks.[4] He voted like a solid citizen and urged his faculty members to do likewise, but both publicly and privately he favored restrictions that would prevent the ignorant and propertyless of both races from voting.[5]

Secretly, meanwhile, Washington went to New Orleans to persuade black leaders there to launch a test case against the Louisiana grandfather clause.[6] To raise the money for court costs, Washington goaded into action the legal committee of the Afro-American Council, the leading black rights organization of that time. To help the committee's fund-raiser, he arranged for free railroad passes from philanthropist friends.[7] He himself gave some money and was listed as "X. Y. Z." in the council records; he also raised other money from white liberals, noted in the records as "per X. Y. Z."[8] Washington urged his co-workers never to use his name, and they reassured him that he could be of more service to them in a secret and advisory way than otherwise.[9] The outcome of the Louisiana case was disappointing. There was such endless wrangling over strategy between the local sponsors, the Afro-American Council lawyers, and the three white lawyers that the case was dropped without appealing to the federal courts after a four-year effort. Washington swore he would never work with a committee of lawyers again.[10]

Washington was more successful in two Alabama suffrage cases, *Giles v. Harris* (1903) and *Giles v. Teasley* (1904), both of which reached the United States Supreme Court. The plaintiff in both cases was Jackson Giles, a minor federal official in Montgomery. In this effort, Washington chose and paid the only lawyer involved, his friend and personal lawyer Wilford H. Smith of New York City. Washington doubly guarded his secrecy by having his private secretary Emmett J. Scott handle all the correspondence with Smith and by using code names to hide identities in case the letters were intercepted. Scott at first called Smith by the code name "Filipino," but Washington warned Scott: "It seems to me in case any of these communications were found, it would be less suspicious should some real name, such as 'John Smith' be found on the letters."[11] Scott could do better than "John Smith." He began a lively correspondence with Wilford Smith using the names R. C. Black and J. C. May, respectively, though Smith sometimes took the name "McAdoo" in telegrams. As the secret partners in the civil rights actions passed on money, news, and advice, they invented other code words also. Booker Washington was referred to as "His Nibs"; "D" stood for dollars, and "M" for Montgomery.[12]

The Giles cases in the end were as disappointing as the Louisiana case. Washington had hoped for a favorable decision from the local district judge, Thomas G. Jones, a southern conservative whom Washington had persuaded President Theodore Roosevelt to appoint. But Judge Jones ruled against Giles, as did the United States Supreme Court. Either because of Smith's carelessness or because of bias in the high court, or both, the Giles cases were thrown out on technicalities, the first because Giles had attacked the validity of the state constitution under which he sought to register and the second because he had failed to claim in the state courts that his rights as a United States citizen were denied, although that was the basis of his appeal. Smith wrote to Washington: "To my mind the Supreme Court took advantage of the only loop-hole in sight to get around the decision of a question fraught with so many important political consequences. We will have to find a way to hem them in as they do in playing checkers. . . . "[13] Washington urged Smith to press a new case, to, "at least, put the Supreme Court in an awkward position," but Smith and other lawyers convinced him it would be useless.[14]

Washington and Smith also collaborated successfully in a test of the exclusion of blacks from jury panels. With secret money from Washington, Smith carried the Dan Rogers case from Alabama to successful issue before the United States Supreme Court in 1904. They secured the freedom of a black man convicted in a criminal case because qualified blacks were excluded from the jury.[15]

Washington fought the unfairness of the Jim Crow railroad cars both openly and secretly. Publicly, he protested only against unequal facilities rather than separation itself. For example, in a national magazine article in 1912, he quoted another southern black man approvingly: "I pay the same money, but I cannot have a chair or a lavatory and rarely a through car. I must crawl out at all times of night, and in all kinds of weather, in order to catch another dirty 'Jim Crow' coach to make my connections. I do not ask to ride with white people. I do ask for equal accommodations for the same money."[16]

Behind the scenes, however, Washington was more militant. When the state of Georgia segregated sleeping cars in 1900, Washington urged Georgia black leaders to protest and also sought the help of William H. Baldwin, Jr., a railroad president who was chairman of the Tuskegee Board of Trustees. Through Baldwin, Washington secured a private conference with the president of the Pullman Company, none other than Abraham Lincoln's son Robert Todd Lincoln.[17] When Lincoln refused to join a black group in protesting the Georgia law, Baldwin advised Washington to look for "a light mulatto of good appearance, but unquestionably colored" for a test case.[18] But going to court is not a philanthropist's way of accomplishing an object, and Baldwin soon began to urge that Washington "let the matter drift a little longer" on the dubious ground that "if a test case is not made it will soon become a dead letter."[19]

Washington ignored Baldwin's advice. He and Wilford H. Smith secretly assisted W. E. Burghardt Du Bois of Atlanta in a case against the Georgia law in 1902, and though Du Bois rather clearly broke with Washington with the publication of his *Souls of Black Folk* in 1903, Du Bois and Washington were secretly cooperating as late as December 1904 in an effort to test the Tennessee Jim Crow law. Later, Emmett Scott criticized the militant Du Bois for not pushing these cases vigorously enough.[20] Washington also persuaded Giles B. Jackson of Richmond to begin a similar suit in 1900 against the Virginia railroad segregation law.[21] He talked another friend, James C. Napier, into a suit in Tennessee against a Pullman segregation law. When the man chosen for the Tennessee test case lost his nerve, Washington tried another round of conferences with the Pullman officials. This time the son of the Great Emancipator refused even to reply to the letters of the Great Accommodator. [22]

Washington was caught on both horns of the "separate but equal" dilemma, as was shown in 1906 by his agents' secret lobbying during the congressional debate on the Hepburn railway rate bill. Senators William Warner of Missouri and Joseph B. Foraker of Ohio proposed amendments that would guarantee equal railroad passenger facilities for blacks. Washington at first lobbied for the Warner-Foraker amendment, apparently being as insensitive as its sponsors to the implicit approval of separate facilities that such a guarantee carried. Through black friends in Washington, the Tuskegee educator paid $300 to Henry W. Blair, former senator from New Hampshire, to lobby for the amendment. Then he learned that militant blacks who were more sensitive to the implied racial exclusion were on their way from Boston to fight the amendment. Always alert to even the most subtle challenge to his power, Washington sent word to Blair to reverse himself and lobby against the amendment. [23] When it was defeated, Washington urged his secret black collaborators to claim the credit, but he personally was still undecided about the merits of the case. As in the Atlanta Compromise speech, social-equality abstractions had for him a low priority. He wrote to one of his collaborators: "In fact the more I think of it the more I am convinced that the Warner Amendment would have been a good measure, and very helpful."[24]

Washington also championed the rural black poor in their enjoyment of the most basic right of all, the right to live and to labor in their own behalf. He responded warmly and effectively, for example, to the predicament of Pink Franklin, an illiterate South Carolina farmer. Franklin shot and killed two white men in 1910 when they broke into his cabin before daylight without announcement of their purpose to arrest him for violating a state peonage statute already declared unconstitutional by the South Carolina Supreme Court. After the United States Supreme Court refused to reverse Franklin's conviction for murder, Oswald Garrison Villard, an officer of the newly formed National Association for the Advancement of Colored People, enlisted Washington's help in seeking a commutation of the sentence. Washington suggested two courses: (1) to employ a leading South Carolina white lawyer to go directly to the governor and (2) to ask Reverend Richard Carroll to intercede with a plea for clemency. An ultraconservative and rather sycophantic black man, Carroll had "many qualities that neither you nor I would admire," Washington wrote, but he had "tremendous influence with the white people of South Carolina."[25]

Villard replied that he had no money to pay a lawyer, but he urged Washington to do all he could through Carroll. Whether it was Carroll's influence, a persuasive letter from Washington's friend Robert C. Ogden, a Tuskegee trustee, or possibly a letter from President William Howard Taft that tipped the balance, the South Carolina governor did commute Pink Franklin's sentence to one of life imprisonment.[26]

The most significant example of Washington's secret aid to southern blacks threatened with peonage, however, was the Alonzo Bailey case, which Washington secretly aided all the way to its success in the United States Supreme Court. A farmworker in Montgomery County, Alabama, Bailey had signed a year contract with a corporate farm to work for $12 a month. When he borrowed $20 against his future wages and then left the farm without repaying, he was tried and convicted under the Alabama peonage statute, not in a civil suit for debt but in a criminal suit for signing a contract with intent to defraud. Washington and some of his upper-class southern white friends had long sought such a test case to prove the benevolence of their leadership, as had agents of the Justice Department under Roosevelt's attorney general Charles J. Bonaparte. Washington sent a discreet Tuskegee instructor, Ernest T. Attwell, to contact his secret collaborators in the Bailey case, Judge W. H. Thomas of the Montgomery city court and United States district judge Thomas G. Jones. The two judges secretly gave counsel in the case, but because of their judicial position they were barred from being the lawyers of record. With Washington's secret encouragement and financial assistance, therefore, they persuaded two local white lawyers to take the Bailey case without fee. Washington raised the other court costs from northern liberal friends, and Attorney General Bonaparte submitted an *amicus curiae* brief. Washington may have viewed the Bailey case as evidence of the viability of the bargain he had made with the southern white elite in his Atlanta Compromise speech, but his circumstances made it necessary to keep his part in the case hidden from public view. The Supreme Court in 1911 declared that peonage was involuntary servitude and that the Alabama law was therefore unconstitutional. Peonage continued illegally in Alabama, but, as Pete Daniel has shown, it was less common than in other southern states where contract labor laws were enforced. Alonzo Bailey soon unheroically found employment in a local country club, and Washington could take no public credit for this rare legal victory in an era when the whites were winning most of the power and the glory.[27]

In his personal conduct Booker T. Washington could never allow himself to forget that he represented his race and that any breach of decorum on his part would be blamed on his race. For this reason, and because he had been trained at Hampton Institute by straitlaced New Englanders, Washington lived a life of scrupulous puritanism. He avoided even such minor vices as tobacco and gave earnest public support to all the tenets of Sunday school morality. Despite all the honors heaped upon him, his demeanor was one of incorrigible humility. His life was the very model of the way white men wished to see black men behave. His secret actions against his black opponents, however, showed little forbearance and drew less from the teachings of Jesus than from those of Machiavelli.

When Washington said in his Atlanta Compromise address in 1895 that whites and blacks could be "as separate as the fingers," he set the teeth of some blacks on edge. Because they challenged his conservative doctrines, his opponents came to be known as "radicals," though in a later day their tactics would seem moderate. These men fairly gnashed their teeth when Washington won white applause and laughter by stories in which black men, chickens, and mules figured prominently, when he flattered or amused whites by making blacks the scapegoats of their own misfortunes, when he pointed the finger of scorn at what he considered the pretensions of educated, middle-class, urban blacks.

The first to challenge Washington's leadership and philosophy was a nervous young Harvard graduate, William Monroe Trotter, whose outspoken weekly newspaper, the Boston *Guardian*, trod the border line between personal journalism and libel. When Washington spoke in 1903 at a black church in Boston before a tightly packed audience of two thousand, Trotter dramatized his disagreement with Washington by disrupting the meeting. Standing on a chair, he read off nine accusatory questions in a high, shrill voice that pierced the hubbub. The police finally made their way to him and evicted him and nine others for disorderly conduct. The meeting continued, but Trotter had achieved his purpose, for the incident appeared on the front pages of the white press as "the Boston riot," penetrating Washington's news screen and letting the country know all blacks were not behind him.[28] Washington's lawyer promised to "put them in the jug";[29] and after a trial which Washington's Boston friends pushed vigorously, Trotter and one cohort served thirty days in jail. The incident drove a wedge between the two factions. A final effort to settle their differences, the Carnegie Hall Conference in 1904, was unsuccessful, largely because Washington insisted on a more conservative line than the militants could accept. The militant minority survived in the Niagara Movement after 1905 and grew more rapidly with the aid of white liberals in the NAACP after 1909.

Washington viewed this black criticism through a distorted personal lens. In his own eyes he was a heroic, constructive racial statesman beset by yapping dogs. He believed he had won leadership by open means and that his enemies were trying to wrest it from him by underhanded methods of distortion and innuendo. Washington egocentrically exaggerated the personal element in the opposition. It seemed to him mere jealousy of his standing and achievements. He felt justified in using ruthless means to retain his power; and those means were at hand. About the time of the Boston Riot, Washington employed a spy to help him outwit his enemies.

About a week before the Boston affair, a plump, possum-shaped young Texan, Melvin J. Chisum, offered Washington his services. An old friend of Emmett Scott, Chisum was then editing a shaky little black magazine, the *Impending Conflict*, in partnership with John E. Bruce. "I don't think Chisum is a very brainy man," Scott commented, "but I do know he is resourceful and I think at the same time honorable. . . . Our New York friend can use Chisum in any way that we desire."[30] Washington's faction soon found work for Chisum when they learned Trotter and his followers were planning to disrupt another Washington speech, this time in a black church in Cambridge. At a final meeting in Trotter's home Chisum was present. His report later mysteriously disappeared from Washington's files, but it was the basis of Emmett Scott's account two years later:

> . . . it was finally decided in Trotter's home that when the meeting should be in full sway one of their number would light a bonfire in a near-by vacant lot, that another in the church should yell "fire" and that a third should cut the electric wire, thereby throwing the church into darkness and confusion. This program of wrath, disorder and possibly murder, which Trotter and his gang had planned came near succeeding. At their final meeting to perfect their arrangements a colored attorney of Boston, who had learned of their scheme, threw open the door, walked into the midst of the band and gave them to understand in no Sunday-School language that he had the names of every man and knew all the details of their plans. He further told them that if a single one of them attempted to carry out the plan, he would have them all in a jail in a few hours. At this revelation the little gang was thunderstruck and scattered in every direction; not one of them dared to show his face at the meeting.[31]

Washington wanted to publicize what he called a "dastardly attempt on the part of that Boston crowd to disgrace the race,"[32] but William H. Lewis, the Boston lawyer who had burst into the meeting, said: "I rather prefer to hold it as a club over their heads." He warned that Chisum's unsupported affidavit would be insufficient safeguard against a libel suit. "Besides I am not inclined to believe absolutely the story of our confidential friend. I think he has overdrawn it somewhat, and I am not sure that he did not himself make some of the propositions purporting to have been made by others."[33]

Washington publicly ignored Trotter but secretly seized the first opportunity to counterattack. For months he and Scott combed the *Guardian* for evidence of libel, not against Washington but against someone else.[34] Using their findings, they persuaded William Pickens, a black student at Yale whom Washington had befriended, to sue Trotter and his coeditor George R. Forbes for libel. Washington and Wilford Smith gave Pickens financial and legal aid, and when the case was settled out of court, Washington gleefully reported to friends "the apology made by Trotter and Forbes so as to prevent wearing stripes."[35] The pro-Washington faction in Boston meanwhile sought to have Forbes removed from his job at the Boston Public Library.[36]

The next time Washington's New England black friends honored him, in Cambridge in 1904, they chose a banquet for which tickets would have to be purchased rather than risk an open meeting. Not to be outdone so easily, Trotter and his group schemed to hold an anti-Washington indignation meeting on the same night. They hired a hall and secretly printed advertising circulars for their rally. Once again, however, they had in their midst an unsuspected spy, Clifford H. Plummer, who had begun negotiating with Washington a year earlier while he was serving as lawyer for one of the Boston rioters.[37] Forewarned by Plummer, Washington's friends went to the owner of the hall and got the reservation for their enemies' meeting place canceled, while Plummer quietly gathered up and destroyed the circulars. Plummer succeeded in concealing his clandestine partnership with Washington. "I informed 'the gang' that I do not expect to attend the dinner," he wrote Washington, "which declaration by me made me eligible to any office within their gift, from the presidency of the United States, to a member of the common council from any ward in Boston or Cambridge."[38]

Hearing rumors in the summer of 1905 of a new national black protest organization, Washington through his secretary Emmett Scott sent Plummer fifty dollars and orders by telegram to "go to Buffalo . . . ostensibly to attend Elks convention but to report fully what goes on at meeting to be held there Wednesday and Thursday. Get into meeting if possible but be sure name of all who attend and what they do. "[39] This was the first meeting of the Niagara Movement, so named because the group crossed to Niagara Falls, Canada, after discrimination at a Buffalo hotel. Plummer went to the Associated Press to prevent publicity about the meeting. "Few of them here," he wired Washington from Buffalo, "nothing serious so far[,] will try to stop their declaration of principles from appearing."[40] Washington and Scott meanwhile wired all the black and white newspapermen they could absolutely trust, urging them to ignore the Niagara meeting. In this and subsequent years the silence of the press was effective in limiting the influence of the Niagara Movement.

When the Niagarites met the following year at Harpers Ferry, Washington had a new agent to report on their affairs, Richard T. Greener, first black graduate of Harvard and onetime professor of law at the University of South Carolina. Greener in 1906 was an old, broken, out-of-office politician. After a distinguished career as dean of the Howard University Law School, he sought a consular post. The State Department assigned him to Bombay, and when he complained of the climate there, they reassigned him to Vladivostok. Removed from office under circumstances which involved racial bias, he wrote Washington from Harpers Ferry, asking his help in regaining his office. "Here is a good chance to get a good friend into the inner portals of the Niagara meeting," suggested Emmett Scott. "I hope you will spare no pains to get on the inside of everything," Washington wrote Greener. He attributed motives to his opponents which help explain why he had few qualms about spying on them: "You will find, in the last analysis, that the whole object of the Niag[a]ra Movement is to defeat and oppose every thing I do. I have done all I could to work in harmony with DuBois, but he has permitted Trotter and others to fool him into the idea that he was some sort of a leader, consequently he has fritt[er]ed away his time in agitation when he could succeed as a scientist or Socologist [sic]."[41]

Other sleuths, paid and unpaid, also did Washington's bidding. Pinkerton detectives on a half-dozen occasions protected him or his distinguished guests from threatened attacks and eavesdropped on white conversations about him in hotel lobbies and trains.[42] He hired a white detective in Boston to find out whether Trotter's wife was employed as a domestic and, if so, for whom. Washington was probably disappointed to learn that Mrs. Trotter worked every day in her husband's office. Soon afterward the same detective was clumsy enough to be discovered as a Washington agent by the man he was shadowing.[43]

Washington had more success with the less professional black spies. His correspondence was filled with confidential information. Chicagoans and New Yorkers, for example, sent him lists of Niagara delegates from those cities.[44] Another agent searched the Atlanta tax records for evidence that Du Bois had failed to pay his poll tax.[45] Friends in New York, Washington, Boston, and Chicago transmitted Washington's bribes to black newspapers for favorable editorial treatment.[46] When a Tuskegee faculty member broke his contract, an agent of Washington stole the teacher's letters from his pastor's desk so as to embarrass the man with his new employer and force an apology. Such tactics, however, hardly disproved the teacher's assertion in the offending letters that Washington had "absolute control over his teachers" and kept them in "a modified form of slavery."[47] To promote Tuskegee, Washington paid a lecturer with stereopticon slides to tour the northern black churches, ostensibly presenting impartially the story of black education. "Of course the minute people get the idea that you are an agent of Tuskegee," Washington warned him, "that minute in a very large degree your influence would be modified."[48]

Washington's most active spy, however, was Melvin J. Chisum, whose Boston success naturally brought him to mind when the Niagara Movement posed a threat. Washington sought out Chisum again through Charles W. Anderson, collector of internal revenue in New York City, local black political boss, and Washington's intimate friend.[49] Chisum proved worthy of his hire. Securing a position as a reporter on the anti-Booker newspaper, the Washington *Bee*, he convinced its editor, W. Calvin Chase, that even though they both hated Washington as much as any other upstanding, race-loving black man, they should not let that stand in the way of profitable business dealings with him. Chisum persuaded Chase to accept a bribe offered at the strategic moment by two friends of Washington to pay for several pro-Washington editorials. "I have him, Doctor, I have him," Chisum almost crowed to Washington when Chase took the bait. "But, rest perfectly sure, that my plan is so carefully lain that he will not see."[50] After the editorials were written, the cream of the jest came when Chase's militant friends began criticizing him, and Chisum counted on Chase's hot temper to further his plan. Chisum wrote to Washington: "Now! The Bee will be a surprise to everybody that knows it the forthcoming week and the war is on between his highness bub Trotter and bub Chase. Are you willing that I remain here for a couple of weeks and make shure [*sic*] of Chase's broadsides being properly directed so as to put them beyond the point of repair, or reconnection? I know Trotter will fire on the

Bee, and I think I ought to be in the con[n]ing tower with Chase when he does."[51]

Chisum privately considered Chase "at heart, a vile, malicious, jealous—heartless 'cuss',", but in talking with Chase he was careful to knock Washington and then add, confidentially, "Mr. Chase, I would let no one but you hear me say this."[52] Chisum's scheme to trap Chase into dependency on Washington was successful, but in the years that followed Washington could not depend with certainty on Chase. Like many another impecunious black editor whose bondage was economic and whose real sympathy was with the other side, Chase was loyal to Washington only when paid. Washington, however, expressed himself as "most grateful" to Chisum, and Charles Anderson, who thought Chisum too expensive a luxury, grudgingly admitted that the spy had "his valuable points."[53]

Chisum obviously delighted in his work and in his closeness to the throne. "I am, Your obedient humble servant, Chisum," he ended one letter in picaresque style, "your own property, to use as your Eminence desires, absolutely."[54] He offered to go to Chicago and seek employment as a waiter in a black restaurant,[55] but Washington decided he would be more useful spying on the Brooklyn branch of the Niagara Movement.[56] "I am almost sure I will be able to attend the secret conference at the Convention," Chisum reported.[57] He shuttled between his Harlem residence and the Niagara meetings in Brooklyn Heights, often getting home long after midnight. His reports to Washington were usually oral, and their letters recorded only the times and places of meeting, usually on park benches in Manhattan. "I sat in the park today from 12:45 to now," he wrote Washington one day at 3:30, "and will be there near where we sat again tomorrow Friday at 1 sharp."[58] A few weeks later Washington wrote to Chisum: "I plan to be in New York about the 13th and shall hope to see you at the usual place at that time."[59] After 1906 Chisum engaged in a succession of small business enterprises, and his spying tapered off. "Questions are to be asked you tonight," he informed Washington on one occasion. "I will, I think, succeed in stopping them."[60] Chisum remained, as he said, Washington's "obedient, humble servant," but the master no longer rubbed the lamp.

While Washington both openly and secretly attacked the black radicals, some of his influential white supporters began to have doubts about his own effectiveness as a black leader. As segregation and race riots spread rather than diminished, it was increasingly clear that Washington's concessions and bland optimism were insufficient to bring racial harmony and justice. A race riot in Springfield, Illinois, in 1908 startled two of Washington's white liberal supporters into taking a leading role in founding the National Association for the Advancement of Colored People. These were Oswald Garrison Villard and Mary White Ovington. Grandson of the abolitionist William Lloyd Garrison and son of a railroad baron, Villard edited the influential *Nation* and the New York *Evening Post*. In the years of the Niagara Movement he raised $157,000 as chairman of the Tuskegee endowment committee, and for a decade he allowed Washington and Scott to help write his editorials on race matters. Villard became chairman of the board of the NAACP, and he continued to try to bring the organization and Washington together, but Washington refused to attend its meetings. Miss Ovington, a wealthy white settlement-house worker in the black slums of New York, had visited Tuskegee and had written articles favoring the school and its head. Persistent white racism turned her toward protest, however, and she became an NAACP staff member. One of Washington's principal critics, Du Bois, became the editor of the NAACP magazine, the *Crisis*.

Washington's response to the NAACP was more ambiguous than it had been in the cases of Trotter and the Niagara Movement. For a time he encouraged his friend Robert R. Moton to seek an accord with the NAACP group, but a sharply critical circular by Du Bois and others on stationery of "the National Negro Committee" angered him so that he broke off negotiations. Washington encouraged William H. Baldwin's widow to help found the National Urban League, an organization whose approach indirectly challenged that of the NAACP.

Toward the end of his life Washington seemed to move ideologically toward the NAACP position. He joined with it in protesting federal segregation in the Wilson administration, and he cooperated with it in efforts to ban the racist film *The Birth of a Nation*. Washington's posthumous article in the *New Republic*, entitled "My View of Segregation Laws," opposed residential segregation laws so forthrightly that the NAACP Board of Directors voted to reprint it as a pamphlet.[61] On the other hand, writing in 1914 to a Birmingham city official to argue against a proposed segregation ordinance, Washington warned that such legislation would "stir up racial strife and bring about bitterness to an extent that will result in discouraging a number of the best colored people in the state." He foxily suggested an alternative approach:

> Of course I do not know just in detail what the local conditions in Birmingham are, but I do know that taking the two races generally in the South that one

seldom buys property in a section of a community or city where he is not wanted. The general custom has settled the matter it seems to me, and custom in this case I sometimes think is stronger than a law. I believe if it were made known to a half dozen of the leading colored men in Birmingham that certain things were desired in reference to the purchase of property in the future that the same results could be obtained as by passing a law which I very much fear will be misunderstood throughout the country and, I repeat, stir up racial strife.[62]

During the formative years of the NAACP Washington launched a devastating secret attack on the white liberals who were working with his black enemies. This is illustrated by the Cosmopolitan Club dinner incidents in 1908 and 1911. A social club of liberal whites and members of the darker races, the Cosmopolitan Club was founded in Mary White Ovington's home in Brooklyn Heights and continued to meet quietly in private homes. In the spring of 1908, however, at Miss Ovington's suggestion they invited guests to meet with them at a midtown New York restaurant. About a hundred attended. Villard was one of the speakers, as was Hamilton Holt, editor of the *Independent*, a progressive weekly. About halfway through the dinner reporters entered the room, and a photographer stood on a chair to take flash pictures of the entire assemblage. The photographing was prevented after messages of protest were sent to the head table, but the New York *American,* a Hearst paper, reported next day: "Social equality and intermarriage between the races were advocated last night at a banquet . . . where twenty white girls and women dined side by side at table with negro men and women."[63] The New York *Times* denounced the affair as a "banquet, of which brotherhood was the 'note' and the promotion of Socialism the moving spirit and intent . . . ."[64] The publicity brought Miss Ovington such obscene mail that she was forced to have her letters opened by male relatives.[65]

Booker T. Washington was in New York at the time of the dinner, staying at the Manhattan Hotel. According to a newspaper report, "He sent word to the desk of the hotel that he was 'not to be disturbed,' and notified his two secretaries that he was 'not at home' to reporters."[66] As the news spread southward, suggestion became assertion, and the news became even more titillating as the sober diners were depicted as drinking and making love at a "Bacchanal feast." The incident reminded some southern newspapers of Booker Washington's dinner years earlier at the White House. One woman wrote him from Washington: "I think you better not try to see me as I asked you to, owing to the very strong race feeling here just now—some reporter might get hold of the fact that you called to see me, and misrepresent you. . . ." She felt that Washington's Atlanta address had done much to promote racial amity, "but temporarily this N. Y. episode has set things back greatly. I hope you will make another speech soon and reassure the public."[67]

Washington's secret cooperation with the racially biased white press in reporting another Cosmopolitan Club dinner in 1911 strongly suggests that he may have inspired the 1908 publicity also. In January 1911 Washington received from Charles W. Anderson a copy of an invitation to a Cosmopolitan Club dinner. "One needs only to glance over this invitation," Anderson commented, "printed as it is on yellow paper, and note the names of the speakers and the long-winded topics they are to discuss, to be convinced that they are a bunch of freaks."[68] Washington wired in reply: "Regarding black and white dinner be sure get hold of same reporter who reported for American year or two ago. Would see that copies of printed announcement reach all city editors in advance. Think New York Times will work in harmony with you."[69]

Anderson contacted not only the leading New York dailies but the City News Association and the Associated Press as well. He was disappointed that the story was crowded out of some local papers by other news. "The man who handled it last year could not be found," he wrote Washington, "but a 'good friend' on the Press took care of that end of it . . . and I hope the Associated Press did likewise."[70] The next day one edition of the New York *Press* carried the headline: "THREE RACES SIT AT BANQUET FOR MIXED MARRIAGE." Another edition carried the headline: "THREE RACES MIX AT BANQUET FOR MAN'S BROTHERHOOD/Fashionable White Women Sit at Board with Negroes, Japs and Chinamen to Promote 'Cause' of Miscegenation." In the text of the news story it was clear that miscegenation had not been advocated, but the *Press* reported: "White women, evidently of the cultured and wealthier classes, fashionably attired in low-cut gowns, leaned over the tables to chat confidentially to negro men of the true African type."[71] Even Washington's sharpest critics did not dream of his cooperation with the white reporters. Miss Ovington, a very proper old maid, was still upset by the incidents when she wrote her memoirs in 1947. Still wondering who had tipped off the reporters, she spoke of "the connivance of a few club members" and recalled suspiciously a Gallic twinkle in the eye of the club's treasurer, the Frenchman André Tridon.[72] She had no idea of Washington's secret role.

Washington's secret life is probably more significant as a revelation of his character than because of its effects. It did not change materially the shape of the Color Line, and he had other, more effective means to use against his black opponents. Washington's private papers afford a glimpse, however, behind his conventional mask of accommodation and morality, showing a man who, under trying circumstances, sought in his own peculiar way to play a more aggressive and manly role. In both his secret struggle against Jim Crow laws and his espionage among his black and white liberal critics he exhibited more of what the Mexicans call *machismo* than his public role allowed. It is also clear that he sometimes confused his own interests with those of the race, assuming that what was good for Booker Washington was good for "the brother." He illustrated the uneasiness of every head that wears a crown. He was sure that history would vindicate his actions when the whole tale was told. That verdict is uncertain, but there is no doubt that he was far more than a foot-dragging "Uncle Tom." He was a man, with all that the name implies of strength and weakness. Some will see him sympathetically as a Brer Rabbit moving adroitly through the brier patch. Others will view him unfavorably as a classical deep-dyed villain. Whatever the judgment that black history pronounces on Booker T. Washington, it is clear that black history, if it is to be more than a procession of cardboard figures, must like other history have its shades of gray, its villains as well as heroes, its imperfect human characters as well as saints.

1. The speech is quoted in full in Booker T. Washington (hereinafter cited as BTW), *Up from Slavery: An Autobiography* (New York, 1901), 218-25.

2. See "Booker T. Washington and the National Negro Business League," above.

3. This interpretation owes a debt to August Meier for his pioneer article, "Toward a Reinterpretation of Booker T. Washington," *Journal of Southern History*, XXIII (May 1957), 220- 27, and for his critique of the present article, read before the Association for the Study of Negro Life and History. BTW's motivation is more fully discussed in "Booker T. Washington in Biographical Perspective," above.

4. Emmett J. Scott to Richard W. Thompson, March 7, 1906 (34), BTW Papers (Manuscript Division, Library of Congress, Washington, D. C.) Manuscripts from this collection are cited with the container number in parentheses.

5. BTW to Roscoe Conkling Bruce, *ca.* April 1, 1906 (571); BTW to James B. Washington, May 5, 1910 (596), *ibid.*

6. Scott to BTW, June 21, 1900 (182); George W. Henderson to BTW, June 9, July 16, September 2, October 4, 17, 1900, and undated letter (174), *ibid.*

7. Giles B. Jackson to BTW, June 1, 12, 1900 (176); BTW to Scott, March 11, 1900 (186), *ibid.*

8. Jesse Lawson to BTW, July 30, 1901 (203), *ibid.*

9. Jackson to BTW, June 12, 1900 (176); Lawson to BTW, August 6, 1902 (1); Richard P. Hallowell to BTW, March 2, 1900 (199), *ibid.*

10. See report of *State* ex. rel. *Ryanes* v. *Gleason*, 112 La. 612 (1903); extensive correspondence on the case from 1899 to 1902 and occasional letters thereafter, BTW Papers (1, 46, 172-212, 215, 227, 233, 244, 246, 265, 271, 278, 281, 865).

11. Use of the code name Filipino is discussed in Scott to BTW, June 18, 1902 (45); June 23, 1902 (241); BTW to Scott, June 24, July 26, 1902 (247), BTW Papers.

12. Letters in 1903 and 1904 between R. C. Black (code name of Emmett J. Scott) and J. C. May (code name of Wilford H. Smith) were collected by Helene M. Hooker from several containers and placed in Container 25, *ibid.* "McAdoo," which appeared on some telegrams, was the name of Smith's stenographer. Scott to BTW, undated [1908] (582), *ibid.* For other information on the Alabama franchise cases, see *ibid.* (1, 20, 203, 214, 216, 220, 233, 239, 241, 246, 255, 276, 529); Montgomery *Advertiser*, 1902–1903; *Giles* v. *Harris*, 189 U. S. 475 (1903); *Giles* v. *Teasley*, 193 U. S. 146 (1904).

13. Smith to BTW, February 24, 1904 (25), BTW Papers.

14. BTW to Smith, February 24, March 3, 1904; Smith to BTW, February 26, March 1, 1904 (25), *ibid.*

15. *Rogers* v. *Alabama*, 192 U. S. 226 (1904). On BTW's role in the case, see the three-way correspondence of 1903-1904 among BTW, Scott, and Smith, sometimes using code names (25, 871); BTW to Charles W. Anderson, February 1, 1904 (19), BTW Papers.

16. BTW, "Is the Negro Having a Fair Chance?" *Century Illustrated Monthly Magazine*, LXXXV (November 1912), 51, quoting R. S. Lovinggood of Austin, Texas.

17. Henry H. Proctor to BTW, April 18, July 6, 1900 (181); Baldwin to BTW, January 24, 1900 (792); Lincoln to BTW, February 6, 1900 (177), BTW Papers.

18. Baldwin to BTW, January 24, 1900 (792), *ibid.*

19. Baldwin to BTW, March 19, 1900, *ibid.*

20. Du Bois to BTW, November 22, December 4, 1902 (225); January 24, 1904 (272); BTW to Du Bois, February 27, 1904 (20); June 4, 1904 (868); Scott to Richard W. Thompson, February 10, 1905 (31), *ibid.*

21. Jackson to BTW, October 5, 1900 (176); January 24, 1901 (201); Jackson as counsel of the Constitutional Rights Association of Richmond, *To the Board of Aldermen and Common Council of the City of Richmond, Va.*, undated leaflet [1900] (167), *ibid.*; James H. Brewer, "The War Against Jim Crow in the Land of Goshen," *Negro History Bulletin*, XXIV (December 1960), 53-57.

22. BTW to Lincoln, October 28, 1903 (249); BTW to Baldwin, October 28, 1903 (792); December 3, 1903 (792); December 4, 1903 (792); January 18, 1904 (18); BTW to Napier, November 2, 1903 (268); BTW to Du Bois, February 27, 1904 (20); Napier to BTW, May 30, 1904 (870), BTW Papers.

23. A detailed account using these and other sources is Daniel W. Crofts, "The Warner-Foraker Amendment to the Hepburn Act: Friend or Foe of Jim Crow?" (unpublished paper read at the annual meeting of the Association for the Study of Negro Life and History in October 1968). See correspondence between Washington and his secret go-betweens Kelly Miller, Archibald H. Grimké, and Whitefield McKinlay, March-June 1906 (3, 4, 33, 261, 328) and correspondence between BTW and Scott and T. Thomas Fortune, Richard W. Thompson, J. A. Lankford, S. Laing Williams, and Andrew B. Humphrey in 1906 (3, 32, 34), BTW Papers.

24. BTW to Miller, August 4, 1906 (328), BTW Papers.

25. Villard to BTW, August 4, 1910 (410); August 12, 1910 (51); BTW to Villard, August 9, 1910 (411), *ibid.*

26. A more detailed account of the Franklin case is in Charles Flint Kellogg, NAACP: *A History of the National Association for the Advancement of Colored People*, Vol. 1, 1909–1920 (Baltimore, 1967), 57-60.

27. For a fuller discussion of the Bailey case, see Pete Daniel, "Up from Slavery and Down to Peonage: The Alonzo Bailey Case," a Pelzer Prize essay, *Journal of American History*, LVII (December 1970), 654-70. *Bailey* v. *Alabama* is reported in 219 U. S. 219 (1911). BTW's negotiations with judges and lawyers in Montgomery and with the federal administration are shown in BTW to Judge W. H. Thomas, June 16, October 21, 1908, and undated replies (383); Ernest T. Attwell to BTW, June 24, 1908 (583); Attwell to Scott, July 6, 1908 (583); BTW to Charles J. Bonaparte, October 20, 1908 (365); undated letters from Thomas in 1909 (399, 900); Attwell to BTW, June 4, 1909 (590); brief and argument of Frederick S. Ball before the U. S. Supreme Court, 1909 (913); Scott to BTW, March 17, 1910 (596); correspondence with Thomas in 1910 (913); BTW to Charles W. Anderson, January 6, 1911 (52); BTW to George W. Wickersham, January 7, 1911 (445); BTW to Thomas, January 7, 1911; Thomas to BTW, January 9, February 9, 1911 (443); BTW to William Hayes Ward, January 18, 1911 (445), BTW Papers; Thomas to Theodore Roosevelt, January 20, 1911 (Container 155), Theodore Roosevelt Papers (Manuscript Division, Library of Congress). BTW applied a curious double standard, however, in the case of conviction of an Alabama white man for holding Italian immigrants in peonage. BTW sought clemency for the man from President Taft on the ground that "no man in Alabama has treated the colored workman better than he has." BTW to Charles D. Hilles, secretary to President Taft, undated [May 1911] (424), BTW Papers.

28. A thoroughly researched new biography of Trotter is Stephen R. Fox, *The Guardian of Boston: William Monroe Trotter* (New York, 1970), which was begun as a senior essay at Williams College in 1966.

29. J. C. May [Smith] to R. C. Black [Scott], September 4, 1903 (25), BTW Papers.

30. Chisum to Scott, May 18, 1903 (254); July 23, 1903 (252); Scott to BTW, July 28, 1903 (272), *ibid.* Chisum for several years had also conducted a training school for servants in New York City.

31. Drafts of an article, "Trotter and Trotterism," 1905, corrected in Scott's hand (308); on the disappearance from the files of Chisum's report, see Harry C. Smith to BTW, March 9, 1906 (334); BTW to Scott, July 5, 1906; Scott to BTW, July 9, August 9, 1906 (566), *ibid.*

32. BTW to T. Thomas Fortune, September 10, 1903 (290), *ibid.*

33. Lewis to BTW, September 11, 16, 1903 (265); BTW to Samuel E. Courtney, September 12, 1903 (253), *ibid.*

34. Search of the *Guardian* for libelous matter began months before the Boston Riot. "There has been nothing said in the Guardian respecting our friend [Robert W.] Taylor. They seem so circumspect here of late I am beginning to fear that they suspect something. We will continue to watch them however." J. C. May [Smith] to R. C. Black [Scott], March 2, 1903 (281), *ibid.*

35. BTW to Richard W. Thompson, November 12, 1903 (279); see also McAdoo [Smith], telegram to Scott, June 9 [1903] (266); J. C. May [Smith] to R. C. Black [Scott],

August 6, 1903 (25); BTW to Pickens, November 4, 1903 (261); BTW to Smith, November 4, 1903 (277); Pickens to BTW, November 8, 1903 (275), *ibid.*

36. Roscoe Conkling Bruce, soon to become head of the academic department at Tuskegee Institute, wrote to BTW as early as 1902 that in response to his private suggestion the head of the Boston Public Library, Dr. James L. Whitney, "promised to do whatever he could to shut Forbes mouth." Bruce to BTW, February 22, 1902 (221), *ibid.* Bruce concluded that it might be best for Forbes to remain "at the beck & call of Whitney."

37. On Plummer's double game see William H. Moss to BTW, June 9, 28, 1903 (268); Boston *Evening News*, July 31, 1903, clipping (1036), *ibid.*

38. Plummer to BTW, October [September?] 19, 1904 (870), *ibid.*; see also correspondence of September—October 1904 between BTW and W. W. Bryant and Robert W. Taylor in Cambridge (19, 25); Samuel E. Courtney to BTW, September 27, 1904 (286); letters and telegrams between BTW, Scott, and Plummer (4, 19, 24, 293, 870), *ibid.*

39. BTW to Julius R. Cox (two telegrams), July 10, 1905; Cox to BTW, July 6 (telegram), July 11, 1905 (556), *ibid.* BTW instructed Cox, one of his secretaries, to convey money and instructions to Plummer.

40. Plummer to BTW (telegram), July 13, [1905]; see also "C. S. P." to BTW (telegram), July 12, [1905]; "E. J. S." to Plummer (telegram), July 12, 1905; Plummer to BTW, July 16, September 25, 1905 (305), *ibid.*

41. Greener to BTW, July 31, 1906, and Scott's note attached, August 2, 1906 (33); BTW to Greener, August 11, 1906 (322), *ibid.* Greener rejected BTW's suggestion that he seek a consulate in the Congo Free State on the ground that the climate was too hot for his health. Some years later a BTW spy at an NAACP convention reported: "Prof. Richard T. Greener, late Consul to Russia, is about on the fence. He is just a little irritated at Dr. BTW because he didn't take him up and give him a job in or since 1906, during which year Mr. Greener lost his political post." C. B. Hosmer to Scott, April 20, 1912 (456), *ibid.*

42. See, for example, D. C. Thornhill, Pinkerton's National Detective Agency, to BTW, September 23, 1905 (5); reports of Pinkerton operative E. V. O., September 10-12, 1905 (30); Thornhill to Scott, October 17, 1905; reports of Pinkerton operative No. 58, October 22-24, 1905 (5); reports of Pinkerton operative J. F. P., November 14-24, 1905 (4); Thornhill to BTW, October 18, 1906 (33); reports of Pinkerton operative F. E. Miller, October 4-10, 1908 (379); Scott to Pinkerton office in St. Louis, November 16, 1912 (462); special memorandum [1912] reading: "Pay Pinkerton $80.55 in the name of Chas. W. Anderson." (626), *ibid.*

43. James R. Wood, Jr., to BTW, April 9, July 19, 1906; James R. Wood, Sr., to BTW, July 14, 1906; BTW to Wood, Sr., July 5, 18, 1906 (5); February 15, 25, 1907 (363), *ibid.*

44. S. Laing Williams to BTW, July 10, 21, 1905 (31); Fred R. Moore to BTW (telegram), August 17, [1906] (33), *ibid.*

45. BTW to Scott, May 3, 1910 (596), *ibid.*: "I want to take some measures to find out through a visit on the part of Mr. Attwell or somebody whether or not Dr. D. is actually a registered voter in Atlanta or not. I do not care to take the chances, I want to get the facts." On an earlier effort to get the information see BTW to Henry A. Rucker, March 20, 1906 (4); Rucker to BTW, n.d. [1906] (332); October 2, 1908 (380), *ibid.*

46. BTW's relations with the black press, including outright ownership, advertising subsidies, and bribes, are discussed in detail elsewhere. See August Meier, "Booker T. Washington and the Negro Press: With Special Reference to the *Colored American*

Magazine," *Journal of Negro History,* XXXVIII (January 1953), 67-90; Emma Lou Thornbrough, "More Light on Booker T. Washington and the New York Age," *ibid.,* XLIII (January 1958), 34-49; August Meier, *Negro Thought in America, 1880–1915: Racial Ideologies in the Age of Booker T. Washington* (Ann Arbor, 1963), 224-36.

47. G. David Houston to Reverend J. Henry Duckrey, September 28, 1906 (699), BTW Papers. See also Houston to Duckrey, September 28, 1904; July 31, August 13, 1906; March 3, 1907 (699); Samuel E. Courtney to BTW, June 15, 1907; BTW to Duckrey, June 18, 1907 (346); Houston to BTW, July 31, 1907 (350); August 4, 1907 (699); August 6, 1907 (6); BTW to Houston, August 5, 1907 (copies in 699 and 36); BTW to J. H. N. Waring, August 8, 1907; BTW to Scott (telegram), August 7, 1907 (574), *ibid.*

48. BTW to George F. Richings, January 25, 1905 [should be 1904] (23), *ibid.* For evidence of Richings's incidental espionage for BTW see Richings to BTW, December 15, 21, 1903 (273); January 1, 20, 23, 28, February 4, 15, 20, 25, 1904 (23); May 23, 1905 (30); March 22, 1907 (23); Scott to BTW, March 24, 1904 (549), *ibid.*

49. BTW to Anderson, December 30, 1905 (27); but see also Anderson to BTW, February 17, 1904 (551), *ibid.*

50. Chisum to BTW, February 16, 1906 (2), *ibid.* In his letter Chisum named John C. Dancy and Robert H. Terrell as those who were to pay $100 for the editorials, but he promised BTW he would "in no way connect your Excellence with my plans."

51. Chisum to BTW, February 19, 1906 (2); see also Chisum to BTW, February 17, 20, 27, 1906 (2); February 26, May 29, 1906 (318) *ibid.* Chisum so frequently asked BTW and Charles W. Anderson for money that Anderson concluded: "He is a much too expensive luxury for me." Anderson to BTW, March 5, 1906 (2), *ibid.*

52. Chisum to BTW, February 19, 1906 (2), *ibid.*

53. BTW to Chisum, February 24, 1906 (2); Anderson to BTW, February 21, 1906 (261), *ibid.*

54. Chisum to BTW, February 17, 1906 (2), *ibid.*

55. Chisum to BTW, March 21, 1906 (32), *ibid.*

56. Chisum to BTW, May 23, June 11, 1906 (2), *ibid.*

57. Chisum to BTW, June 16, 1906 (2), *ibid.*

58. Chisum to BTW, July 12 [1906] (2), *ibid.*

59. BTW to Chisum, August 4, 1906 (2), *ibid.*

60. Chisum to BTW, October 11, 1906 (2), *ibid.*

61. *New Republic,* V (December 4, 1915), 113-14; Minutes of the Meeting of the Board of Directors, March 13, 1916, National Association for the Advancement of Colored People Records (Manuscript Division, Library of Congress).

62. BTW to George B. Ward, president of Board of Commissioners, City of Birmingham, Alabama, July 13, 1914; Ward to BTW, July 16, 1914 (525), BTW Papers.

63. New York *American,* April 28, 1908.

64. Editorial in New York *Times,* April 29, 1908; see also news accounts and letters, *ibid.,* April 28-May 4, 1908.

65. Kellogg, NAACP, I, 71-72, gives a detailed account. "The Cosmopolitan Club Dinner taught me how to read the morning paper," Miss Ovington commented in her book *The Walls Came Tumbling Down* (New York, 1947), 46.

66. Norwalk (Conn.) *Evening Hour,* April 28, 1908, clipping (1050), BTW Papers.

67. Jane E. Thompson to BTW, May 11, 1908 (383), *ibid.*

68. Anderson to BTW, January 19, 1911 (52), *ibid.*

69. BTW to Anderson (telegram), January 21, 1911 (52), *ibid.*

70. Anderson to BTW, January 25, 1911 (52), *ibid.*

71. New York *Press*, January 25, 1911; also clipping of another edition of same date in Anderson to BTW, January 25, 1911 (52), BTW Papers.

72. Ovington, *The Walls Came Tumbling Down*, 43-47.

Booker T. Washington
and the *Voice of the Negro,* 1904-1907

Booker Taliaferro Washington dominated the black scene in America throughout the early years of the twentieth century not only in the South, where he presided over Tuskegee Institute, but also in the black ghettos of the leading cities of the North. Unlike the political bosses of the period, Washington sought to control both the actions and the thought and expression of the black community. Little that happened in black America escaped his watchful eyes or those of his lieutenants in every state and city. Much has been written about his partial ownership of the leading black newspaper of the time, the New York *Age,* and a Boston newspaper designed to compete with that of his chief critic in that city and of his subsidizing of other papers by cash contributions and advertising. His efforts to control and then to suppress the *Voice of the Negro,* however, offer fresh evidence of the totality of his power and the lengths he would go to hound a critic.

Magazines are important to many groups for the opportunity they provide for self-discovery and exploration of alternative policies, free of the haste and terseness of newspaper writing. In the first decade of the twentieth century a half-dozen black magazines appeared—*Howard's,* the *Colored American Magazine, Alexander's,* the *Horizon,* the *Moon*—but the most promising of those short-lived enterprises was the *Voice of the Negro.* As its name suggested, it attempted to be the voice, or at least the forum, for all black Americans. Its signed articles spanned the whole range of black ideology, from the back-to-Africa nationalists at one extreme to the immediate integrationists at the other, with all shadings of conservative and militant attitudes in between. Scorning serials and other fillers, the magazine had a monthly news review of all matters concerning the race, forthright editorials, and articles on such diverse subjects as the debate over the name "Negro," race relations in foreign countries, disfranchisement, peonage, black business advancement, and the rights of women. Its thoroughly professional editing was backed by the business skill of a subscription-book publishing house. In addition to the usual advertisements for patent medicines, books, and schools, it carried advertisements of railroad lines and Coca-Cola. Just before the *Voice* suspended publication in 1907 it had 12,000 subscribers. It was a patron of black artists, poets, and photographers. Far from being an instrument for Booker T. Washington's destruction, it began with a conscious effort to take a middle ground between Washington and his critics. Nevertheless, Washington first tried to force the *Voice* to sing his song and then tried to silence it.

A white publisher took the initiative in the creation of the *Voice of the Negro*. Austin N. Jenkins was vice-president of J. L. Nichols and Company, the firm that had published Washington's first autobiography, *The Story of My Life and Work*, in 1900 and had sold it door-to-door along with other black-oriented books in the black neighborhoods. In 1903, while visiting John A. Hopkins, one of the company's sales agents and a senior at Virginia Union University, Jenkins met Jesse Max Barber, editor of the student newspaper. The three made plans for a black magazine.[1]

Barber was then twenty-five years old. Born at Blackstock, South Carolina, he had secured a secondary education at Friendship Institute in Rock Hill and attended Benedict College for a time before enrolling at Virginia Union from 1901 to 1903.[2] J. L. Nichols and Company in the summer of 1903 made Hopkins head of its Negro department, with offices in Atlanta. In October 1903 the firm appointed John Wesley Edward Bowen as editor of the *Voice of the Negro* with nominal duties consisting largely of overseeing the managing editor, J. Max Barber, who assumed office in November. Bowen was a professor and later president of Gammon Theological Seminary, a Northern Methodist institution for blacks in Atlanta. Long an admirer of Booker T. Washington, Bowen supported both his accommodationism and the industrial education of the black masses.[3]

Washington's first knowledge of the new enterprise apparently was when Hopkins asked him for an endorsement of the magazine project. Washington responded: "A first class well edited and well printed magazine has been among the prominent wants of the Negro race for a number of years. . . ."[4] Sensing that because of its solid financial backing "this magazine is going to be a power and successful from the start," Washington wrote to Emmett Jay Scott, his private secretary: "I am very anxious that you have a good confidential talk with Hopkins and be very sure that we get an influence with this magazine that shall keep it working our way or at least not against us. Hopkins seems to be a very sensible fellow, but we want to be sure that he does not get under wrong influences, which is very easy to be done in Atlanta."[5]

Because of Washington's good relations with the publishers and Bowen, Scott established a liaison with the magazine as a part-time, salaried associate editor. After a trip to Atlanta, Scott reported to his chief "an amicable understanding all along the line." He found Bowen particularly congenial. "He more than ever before, is in accord with Tuskegee and its work," Scott wrote, "and was particularly anxious that you be represented in the first number, also to have your photograph in this first number, saying that a man so prominent should have his photograph accompany his article although it is not the purpose to do this with all the articles that appear."[6]

Washington and Scott apparently believed they could control the editorial course of the *Voice of the Negro* through Bowen's oversight and Scott's occasional review. Scott, however, was both absent and busy, and Bowen, though close by, was also busy and was more tolerant of diversity than the Tuskegeans. Besides, he liked young Barber personally and wanted to give him his head. So Barber soon became the dominant editor, and though he was cautious at first it soon became clear that he was idealistic, a hater of injustice, and a champion of civil rights. He also had a youthful, brash optimism that prompted him to take on a giant before ascertaining whether he himself was a giant killer.

The first number of the *Voice of the Negro* in January 1904 demonstrated the magazine's split personality. The issue included an article by Washington that Scott had edited from a previous publication, photographs of both Washington and Scott, and articles by other Bookerites. An unsigned editorial, almost certainly written by Bowen, promised that "it is our purpose to steer clear of the prophets, seers and visionaries who dream dreams and prophesy out of their lurid imaginations or unreasoning hopes." Instead, the journal was to be "a broad, sensible, practical magazine for all the people." In his own signed editorial, "The Morning Cometh," however, Barber dreamed dreams. He promised a muckraker's fearless exposure: "There may be times when literature we publish will rip open the conventional veil of optimism and drag into view conditions that shock."[7]

Barber lost no time in declaring his editorial independence, though his early numbers showed a moderate editorial tone and an openness to a variety of voices. The first of many misunderstandings arose when Washington met in Chicago the president of J. L. Nichols and Company, John A.

Hertel. Hertel asked Washington's candid opinion of the magazine, and Washington spoke disparagingly of the news review section written by Barber, the only part of the magazine in which Barber had an almost completely free hand. Hertel passed the criticism on to Barber without explaining that Washington had not volunteered it, and Barber exploded. He wrote Emmett Scott that "there is so much talk of Mr. Washington trying to get a hold on and dictate the policy of every colored interest in this country that such an incident as that . . . was likely to excite suspicion."[8] After Scott had explained the circumstances, Barber apologized but added: "Mr. Washington ought to let The Voice of the Negro severely alone and let us run it, or we could get out and let him run it."[9]

The back cover of the April 1904 issue had a full-page advertisement of Tuskegee's Phelps Hall Bible Training School. The May and August issues contained Scott's articles on the Tuskegee Negro Conference and on blacks at the Louisiana Purchase Exposition. Washington's wife wrote an article in the July issue. Scott sent Barber a mollifying note that "it pleases me very much indeed to drop entirely the unpleasant correspondence which we have lately carried on."[10]

Soon, however, the peppery Barber and the supercilious Scott found fresh occasion for quarreling. During the election campaign of 1904 Barber asked Scott to give him letters of introduction to President Theodore Roosevelt's campaign manager and other Republican officials in Washington. Scott rejected the request, saying "I happen to know of the plans, so far as the Negro end of the campaign is concerned,—plans which are not yet ready for divulgence, but which necessarily preclude my writing Mr. [George Bruce] Cortelyou, while possessed of that knowledge and information." Scott implied that Barber wanted the letters not to pursue a journalistic errand but to interfere in Booker T. Washington's confidential arrangements with Republican leaders.[11] Barber's reply does not survive in the Washington private papers, but one can imagine its tone of shrill outrage. Forwarding the letter to Washington, Scott observed: "You can catch the man's general disposition and character in the last paragraph of his letter. I do not think anything can be gained by my continuing in connection with the magazine. He is out of sympathy with you and Tuskegee, and, as I explain in the letter to him, is more like a baby than a man."[12] Scott wrote to Barber: "I could hardly believe that you would permit yourself to write a letter so contemptible in tone." He offered Barber his resignation as associate editor.[13] On reflection, he felt that "perhaps I sh'd not have answered a 'fool according to his folly' & ignored

Barber's foolish letter,"[14] but he had gone too far to retreat. In letters of resignation to Hertel and Jenkins, Scott praised the firm, now reorganized as Hertel, Jenkins and Company, "but the malevolent spirit of Barber, his nagging propensities, his studied affectation of superiority; the man's overweening egotism and acceptance of everything as an insult, have made my relations with him unbearable." Scott wrote that he had originally joined the magazine because of his faith in Bowen, "but his primacy has been disputed and disowned."[15]

Jenkins replied to Scott that he was glad that he had resigned, for otherwise he would have had to ask for his resignation on account of a conflict of interest. He had "quite definite information," Jenkins said, that Booker T. Washington and Doubleday, Page and Company jointly owned the *Colored American Magazine,* the principal rival of the *Voice of the Negro.* As Washington's private secretary, therefore, Scott could not serve impartially as an editor.[16] Washington was indeed part owner of the *Colored American Magazine,*[17] but he and Scott categorically denied such ownership to Jenkins. "I do not own one cent's worth of financial interest in any colored magazine or newspaper in this country," Washington wrote, "and have consistently and persistently refused to have any such investment."[18] Washington gently chided Scott for quarreling with Barber rather than dealing directly with the heads of the firm. "I do not think it ever pays to deal with a little man," he said. "I am determined to find a way, however, very soon to show him his place."[19]

Scott's resignation ended the ambiguity of the Tuskegee connection, and the magazine soon felt the force of Washington's disapproval. Bowen tried to reassure Scott that the angry words between him and Barber "need never cut a feathers weight with me" and that he continued a friend of Tuskegee.[20] But neither the Tuskegeans nor Barber needed a go-between now. In December 1904 Barber published a list of mock definitions of "What Is a Good Negro?" that unmistakably satirized Booker T. Washington. He wrote: "'A good Negro' is one who says that his race does not need the higher learning; that what they need is industrial education, pure and simple. He stands up before his people and murders the truth and the Kings English in trying to enforce upon them the evils of a College Education and the beauties of the plow."[21] In the next issue Barber published William Edward Burghardt Du Bois's charge that "'$3000 of 'hush money'" had been spent in the past year "to subsidize the Negro press in five leading cities."[22] Again Washington's name was not mentioned, but the meaning of the charge was clear.

Scott took a characteristically undercover course of retaliation. He called the offending editorials to the attention of his friend Wilford H. Smith of New York, Washington's personal attorney and a fellow investor with Scott in the block-busting Afro-American Realty Company in Harlem, and urged Smith to withdraw the company's advertisement from the *Voice of the Negro*. "Please do not dictate a reply to this letter," asked Scott, "and please be good enough to respect my confidence to the extent of not placing this letter on file but destroying it." Scott did not destroy his own copy, however, but filed it routinely at Tuskegee. Smith agreed "immediately [to] write them cancelling everything."[23] On further reflection, however, Scott shrewdly suggested that the company's letter of withdrawal refer to a disparaging editorial in an earlier number on the National Negro Business League and conclude: "Business enterprise is the thing for which we stand and we think it rather anomalous to continue our advertisement in a magazine which editorially opposes the very thing we so heartily favor."[24]

Washington meanwhile bitterly complained of the editorial to his friend Bowen and asked if it meant a change in Bowen's attitude toward him. "Do you know a single Negro in the history of the whole South," he asked, "who has for two years, borne the curses of the entire Southern white people for standing up for principal [*sic*] and asserting his rights as a citizen in accepting the hospitality when offered, of a gentleman with whom he had a right to dine?" Then he hinted at his secret civil rights activities, saying: "My check book will show that I have spent at least four thousand dollars in cash, out of my own pocket, during this same period, in advancing the rights of the black man. If necessary, I could give you the details as to the expenditure of this money."[25]

The manager of the Afro-American Realty Company, Philip A. Payton, Jr., sent a withdrawal letter worded as Scott had suggested. Barber replied that the claim that his magazine opposed the National Negro Business League was "utterly without foundation." Only once had it commented on the league and that was praise "but with discriminating language." The magazine had given much attention to news of black businessmen and had put out a special Negro Business League number in August. "If you discontinue your advertisement, you will not do so because we are editorially opposed to The Negro Business League—for we are not," he wrote. "There must be some other reason." He assured Payton that the magazine heartily favored all legitimate black enterprise. He added, however, that the magazine could not allow advertisers to control editorial policy. "We wear no man's yoke. We will remain independent and jealously guard the interests of the Negro race if every advertiser withdraws from our pages."[26] Payton stood firmly by his decision to withdraw the advertisement, however, and Scott in an appreciative letter said: "It rather shows them that 'The Wizard' has friends who resent the untoward position of that publication."[27]

In the spring of 1905 Washington personally directed a many-pronged campaign to change the ideological orientation of the *Voice of the Negro*. He urged his friend Timothy Thomas Fortune of the New York *Age* to stop giving editorial attention to the magazine on the ground that "paying attention to them only advertises them all the more," and he wrote to Scott that "this ought to be observed in all the rest of the Afro-American papers excepting the local papers in Atlanta."[28]

As Hertel, Jenkins and Company was advertising Washington's forthcoming book, *The Negro in Business*, Washington wrote to Jenkins that, "with your firm praising and selling my books on the one hand and your magazine doing all it can to destroy the effect of my books on the other hand," he found the arrangement almost intolerable. Two editorials in the March number, he complained, were "wholly directed toward me." "My first impulse," he wrote Jenkins, "was to write Bowen a strong letter, regarding his hypocricy [*sic*], but on further consideration I have decided to be patient and leave the whole matter in your hands, for the present, believing you will find a wise way to remedy present conditions."[29] Jenkins evidently passed Washington's letter on to Hertel, for Washington wrote Hertel three days later insisting that "it is not a matter between your firm and Mr. Scott, but between your firm and myself." "Every thing you say in praise of my works is slandered by your editors," he added. "I am deeply interested in your magazine and will do all I can to help it if it pursues the policy of upholding the race instead of tearing it down." He said he would "leave the matter to you for solution believing you will solve it in the wisest way."[30] Hertel replied that he would discuss the whole matter with Jenkins at the company's annual stockholders' meeting. "I am also writing to the editors of the Voice," he said. "I cannot understand why the editors of our magazine are not in sympathy with your work. I have said it repeatedly and believe it sincerely, that you are doing more for the elevation of the Negro Race than any living man, white or black, and we certainly want to have your interest and co-operation in making our magazine a power for good."[31]

The Reverend Henry Hugh Proctor of Atlanta, a member of the board of editors of the *Voice of the Negro*, meanwhile visited Tuskegee. Scott took him for a long buggy ride and later reported Proctor's remarks to Washington: "He complained rather strongly that though he had insisted upon it, no meetings of the Board of Editors has been called since he first agreed to act with it. . . . He is not at all in accord, he says, with the general attitude of the magazine with reference to its treatment of racial conditions and thinks of serving notice upon them to that effect. I do not know whether he will stand for this or not, but he voluntarily offered that assurance while we were talking."[32]

These pressures from Tuskegee on the young editor seemed for a while to produce the desired effect, though a fire of rebellion continued to smolder in Barber's heart. Washington thanked Bowen for an appreciative article in the April number, "Doing Things at Tuskegee Institute," on the Tuskegee Negro Conference.[33] "I feel sure, Mr. Washington," Hertel wrote, "everything will come around all right in time. Both Mr. Jenkins and myself have had this matter up. Of course we must work along pleasantly and judiciously. I wish, however, to state confidentially that I am assured by both our editors they are not going out of the way in any manner to criticize you or your work. On the other hand, you are to a very great extent a public man and, as is the custom with magazines a man *who does things* not only receives commendation but also comes in for some criticism."[34] A few weeks later, however, Scott complained to Barber that an article he had submitted "has been emasculated,"[35] but Washington was so pleased with recent issues of the *Voice of the Negro* that he wrote to Scott that Barber "is a young fellow that can be educated into something good, but the question is, how?"[36]

Washington apparently was unaware that Barber was a participant two weeks earlier in the first meeting of the Niagara Movement, a group of about thirty black intellectuals dedicated to civil rights and to militant methods of racial advancement. Washington considered the Niagara Movement a conspiracy against himself and, forewarned of their plans, sent a spy to Buffalo to observe them and to prevent publicity of their meeting from going to the daily newspapers over the Associated Press wires.[37] The spy apparently missed their adjourned session at Niagara Falls, Canada, after discrimination against the participants at a Buffalo hotel, but he did prevent national publicity of their meeting.

Barber published in the August number of the *Voice of the Negro* a news item on the Niagara Movement, which included a veiled reference to Booker T. Washington. "The conference was called," he wrote, "for the purpose of beginning organized, determined, aggressive action to oppose certain underhanded methods of strangling honest criticism, manipulating public opinion and centralizing political power by means of improper and corrupt use of money and influence. . . ."[38] Washington immediately wrote a "Personal & Confidential" letter to Hertel, saying: "The enclosed clipping from a Buffalo paper, where the meeting was held, will give you the true aim of the persons in it. I have found out definitely that not over 12 or 15 persons were in the meeting, and as I said to you, you will find that they attempt to use your magazine as a propaganda, and if permitted, you will find that Barbour [Barber] will show his hand more fully in the September number."[39] "As stated to you verbally several days ago," Hertel replied, "I shall keep an eye on the magazine, and you can count on me to always stand for fair play. . . . I must, however, handle our young editor very carefully and very diplomatically. I cannot place the magazine under censorship, but I will be on the alert and endeavor to put in the proper word at the proper time. Everything will come out all O. K. if you are patient and keep me informed."[40]

Despite Hertel's assurances, Barber did make his magazine the voice of the Niagara Movement. An editorial in the next issue declared: "We wish to go on record as not in sympathy or harmony with the efforts of certain temporizers and compromisers to make for the whole Negro race in the country, one leader, one policy and one kind of education."[41] Du Bois replaced Washington as the official hero of the journal. Photographs and pen sketches of him appeared in almost every number. In November 1905 the magazine unfavorably reviewed Tuskegee's annual report, remarking that Washington was "too anxious to please the white people" by making black education of the practical sort. "Why don't the white people ask when our education is going to reach the point where we shall have our own professional and mercantile classes?" Barber asked. "They don't want us to have them."[42] He continued to solicit articles from Washington and his faction, however, perhaps at the insistence of Jenkins and Hertel. "We want to give all sides free scope in our Magazine to discuss the questions," Barber wrote Washington. "It is not our desire—and never has been—to appear one-sided and narrow."[43] Washington made clear, however, that he was too busy to write for the *Voice of the Negro*.[44]

Washington's lieutenants meanwhile launched a new under-cover attack on the magazine. Emmett Scott sent anonymous editorials to friendly black newspaper editors, ridiculing the *Voice of the Negro* and finding a vulnerable spot in the segregated conditions under which the magazine was forced to conduct business. In one press release Scott gleefully reported: "The pounding of the Afro-American press seems to have been effectual in forcing the editors of *The Voice of the Negro* to move their headquarters from the Austell Building, where the aforesaid editors and all of their friends had to ride in freight elevators, to 68½ Alabama St., its present location." Since there had been no newspaper notice of the move, however, the mail still went to the Austell Building, where the white owners opened it. "If any proof were needed that the colored men who have been parading themselves as owners of the magazine, were nothing but employees, it is clearly shown in this: that financial receipts and all mail intended for the firm, must pass through the hands of the white owners before reaching the colored editorial employees." Scott took delight in pointing out "the inconsistency of men posing as valiant 'manhood' defenders, while accepting 'Jim crow' privileges in freight elevators!"[45]

Other Bookerites joined in heaping hot coals on Barber. Frederick Randolph Moore of the *Colored American Magazine* proved his loyalty to Washington by not advertising in the *Voice of the Negro*.[46] When Barber's magazine joined with the Niagara Movement and the Constitution League, an interracial civil rights organization, in urging a reduction of representation of the southern states in Congress because of disfranchisement, he correctly identified Washington as the leader of opposition to the proposal. A *Voice of the Negro* cartoon showed Washington with a padlock on his mouth, and the key that hung from the lock was labeled "Southern White Supremacy." T. Thomas Fortune, however, wrote Barber that he was "shocked by the brutal coarseness and vulgarity of your treatment of the question of those who think differently from you." "If Dr. Washington's mouth is padlocked on the question of Southern representation," he added, "it was padlocked by me, as he came over to my view of the matter reluctantly after I had shown him the danger which lurked in that proposition." Fortune complained that the Niagara leaders "appear to run riot in defamation of character and misrepresentation of fact."[47] Fortune's letter may have been part of a systematic letter-writing campaign, for Scott wrote another Bookerite in Chicago urging him and his friends to write to Hertel or Jenkins complaining of Barber.[48]

Apparently chastened by these complaints, Barber spent two days at Tuskegee during its twenty-fifth anniversary in 1906. He "pretended to be greatly interested," Washington reported to Fortune, "but I have little faith in him."[49] Barber claimed to have been greatly impressed by the school.[50] In a conciliatory reply, Washington could not resist giving some fatherly advice. He hoped eventually to achieve an atmosphere of completely free discussion at Tuskegee, he wrote Barber. "In pursuing this policy, however, I am not unmindful of the fact that in this critical period we shall have to be very careful to guard against expressions that might prove harmful, by placing the race in a false position, and making its upward march the more difficult."[51]

In his seven-page report of the anniversary Barber expressed approval of its industrial-education program but not of Washington's race-leadership role. The money-worshipping speakers, he said, urged blacks to "join in the mad race for the current coin of greatness—money—and overtake it." The anniversary revealed "not only the massing of great wealth in the hands of one man for the propagation of an idea, but also the unprecedented concentration of all the political power and destiny of a race in the hands of a single man." Washington was a great student of human nature, said Barber, and had "won his way up largely by cajolery." Barber thought Washington should stay in his place as promoter of economic efficiency and not assume the position of race leader, political adviser, or supervisor of black education.[52] As Scott sized up the issue, "In the first part of the magazine Barber tries to damn everything as far as he can with faint praise," and an editorial in the back by Bowen "unstintedly praises everything."[53]

The Atlanta race riot in September 1906 dealt a fatal blow to the *Voice of the Negro* and to Barber's career as a black leader. When the racial extremist John Temple Graves, editor of the Atlanta *Georgian*, wrote to the New York *World* that "a carnival of rapes" of white women by black men had caused the riot, Barber replied anonymously as "A Colored Citizen." Repeating hearsay that some of the alleged assault attempts were by white men with blackened faces, who were trying to win votes for Hoke Smith for governor by arousing race antipathies, Barber alleged that blood-hounds on several occasions had led pursuers to the houses of white men, but no arrests were made. He concluded that "sensational newspapers and unscrupulous politicians" caused the riot and that the remedy was "impartial enforcement of the laws of the land."[54]

The day after the letter was published, while the riot atmosphere still pervaded Atlanta, the city police commissioner, Captain James Warren English, summoned Barber to a conference. English urged Barber to clear himself of the charge that he had maligned the whites of Atlanta by writing the telegram to the *World*. Surmising that the telegraph operator had informed on him, Barber did not admit responsibility but asked what the penalty would be in case he had written it. "I was told," he wrote later, "that that letter was a vile slander on Atlanta and that the man who wrote it would serve a sentence on the Georgia chain gang or leave the town." Barber concluded that "the only alternative I had was to get out of Atlanta," but he vigorously denied that he lacked courage. "For the information of the public," he wrote from Chicago, "I beg to state that I was at my office every day during the riot, including Sunday while most of the other Negroes were hugging their homes; that nobody else mentioned dared to send such a letter to the press as I sent and that none of them were asked to leave town. What is more, I went back to Atlanta twenty-four hours after I left and found my office watched by policemen. I was approached, rudely handled and abused by these policemen."[55]

Washington was proud that he went to Atlanta at considerable personal risk to aid in restoring racial peace while Barber was fleeing from the city. Of course, others, including Du Bois, also came swiftly to the aid of the beleaguered black community of Atlanta, and Washington was only one of many peacemakers. Washington sensed correctly, however, that Barber was vulnerable to implications of desertion under fire. Either Washington or Scott wrote an anonymous letter to the New York *Age*, dating it at Atlanta on October 1 so as to disguise its source. "There is a rumor to the effect that J. Max Barber, the editor of the Voice of the Negro, has left Atlanta because of some threats against him," said the letter. It noted other blacks in Atlanta who stood their ground in spite of threats. "We all will be disappointed in Mr. Barber's bravery and sense of loyalty to the race if he deserts us in this trying hour. . . . If Mr. Barber, however, does leave us and go North, we very much hope that he will not follow the example of so many others, that is, after fleeing himself, spend his time in giving advice to the Negro from a long distance how he should conduct himself in the South."[56] Scott said privately that "there was no reason whatever for Barbour to get scared and leave Atlanta as he did. Bowen, [William H.] Crogman and others were persecuted but yet they stood their ground. It would seem that a man who claimed to partake of the spirit of John Brown would face the enemy instead of flying at the first rumor of danger."[57]

The implications of cowardice and personal failure, whether fair or not, overshadowed all of Barber's efforts to reestablish his standing as a journalist in Chicago. "I came to Chicago to avoid the chain gang, which you know is worse than death," Barber wrote in a printed circular seeking new subscribers. "No, no, I am not a coward. I am not afraid to die for a righteous cause. . . . Now I am here in Chicago to stay, and to fearlessly edit and send out the 'Voice,' if my people will stand by me."[58] Washington's disapproval, however, was unrelenting. "It is pitiful to find a man of Barber's education who seems to succeed so well in being a failure," he commented to a friend.[59]

Even before Barber moved to Chicago his magazine fell on hard times, which did not improve in his new headquarters. The previous summer Washington had received confidential information that Hertel and Jenkins had lost so much money on the *Voice of the Negro* that they were not speaking to each other. This was confirmed a few months later when Hertel said his firm had sold its branch office in Atlanta, including the magazine, to Jenkins. Washington concluded that "The magazine made a mistake, so they realize, in fighting the forces in existence instead of cooperating with them."[60] Barber proclaimed from Chicago that "The Voice Still Lives." He omitted "of the Negro" from the title. He had found, he said, that in dealing with white businessmen as potential advertisers the name "Negro" was as serious a handicap as dark skin color. Furthermore, "A large class of colored people object to the word 'Negro.' "[61]

Soon after Barber left for Chicago, Washington mysteriously invited James A. Woodlee, circulation manager of the magazine, to come from Atlanta to Tuskegee at his expense. They may have discussed Washington's possible purchase of the *Voice.*[62] Both Jenkins in Atlanta and Hertel in Illinois claimed to own the *Voice,* and both offered to sell a share of it to Washington and Scott.[63] Scott asked Hertel: "Would it help matters for Mr. B. to be given employment as editor or one of the editors by those who bought the magazine? It would not be the policy to throw Mr. B. overboard but to let him remain as one of the editors, giving him an opportunity to make a career for himself, but it would be the policy to gradually change the policy of the magazine in constructive directions and cease the policy of merely calling attention to the faults of white people and condemning people right and left. It would be the policy to see that more can be accomplished in race building by actually doing something than by merely whining and complaining."[64] Hertel agreed to this and expressed himself as "heartily in sympathy with Dr. Washington's educational policy,"[65] but nothing came of the offer.

In the fall of 1907 T. Thomas Fortune arrived in Chicago with money he had received from selling his stock in the New York *Age,* ostensibly to Fred R. Moore but actually to Booker T. Washington and others. Fortune used this money to buy a controlling interest in the *Voice,* while Barber and his

Niagara Movement friends owned the remaining shares. Fortune found, however, that the *Voice* was heavily in debt, and he and Barber had no money with which to publish the magazine. Fortune appealed to Washington in vain.[66] Barber had a conspiracy theory about the failure of the *Voice*. He later wrote: "Tom Fortune and Booker Washington conspired together, got control of the majority stock of the company and put me out. They then put the Voice to sleep."[67] Fortune actually was far from conspiring with Washington at this period, however, for he blamed Washington for his ouster from the New York *Age* and believed that it was a result of his own refusal to support President Roosevelt after his dismissal of the black soldiers in the Brownsville affair. He hoped to use the *Voice* to criticize Washington and Roosevelt and to promote Charles Evans Hughes as a candidate for President.[68] Fortune and Barber also considered buying or starting a weekly newspaper with aid from the Constitution League, but nothing came of it, and Fortune returned to New York.[69]

To Washington's surprise, in January 1908 Barber became editor of the Chicago *Conservator*. "I don't think he will last long," Samuel Laing Williams wrote complacently to Washington. "His special fatuity is that he thinks himself a great editor. Under his management as editor, he takes more editorial space than the Tribune. His sputterings are so stale and so musty that no one cares to read them."[70] The paper's chief stockholder was a staunch Bookerite, Sandy W. Trice, a department store owner and member of the National Negro Business League. Trice assured Washington that "I will see to it that it will not be antagonistic to you."[71] Soon afterward, however, Barber wrote an anti-Washington editorial, and Trice wrote to the Tuskegean: ". . . all that I can say to you is, that I had this gentleman understand that if anything like that happened again he could no longer hold that position."[72] Two other friends of Washington thought Barber was doing serious harm, writing: "We *must* and by acting promptly, put an end to the papers career if it is to allow this man to go on as he is at present."[73]

There is no direct evidence that Washington urged the dismissal of Barber, but Washington did write to Trice: "As I said to you when I saw you, the party that you write about is wholly dependent upon the position which he now holds. I happen to have inside information that he was to the point of nearly starving when you gave him something to do."[74] Two days later Trice telegraphed Washington: "Barber no longer editor conservator."[75] Williams reported to Washington after a talk with Barber: "I learn that he does blame you for his present predicament. The fact that the

Conservator did not print the report of the Tuskegee Conference is, in his opinion, the cause for his being let out." Williams thought Trice had not been sufficiently tactful about Washington's connection with his dismissal of Barber. Williams wrote to Washington: "I protested to Barber that he was going a long way about to connect you with the matter of his separation from the paper, but he insists that 'you have been pursuing him for several years trying to make it impossible for him to succeed in any thing, etc.' "[76] Barber tried to start another Chicago paper, and Du Bois sought to help him by securing funds from the sponsors of Charles Evans Hughes for the Presidency in 1908. This was unsuccessful. [77]

Barber moved to Philadelphia in search of sanctuary from Booker T. Washington. He secured a position as a teacher in the Berean Manual Labor School, headed by Dr. Matthew Anderson, a black admirer of Washington. "Again the same sinister influence passed me on," Barber wrote some years later. [78] Barber could not prove the charge, but he was right. Washington picked up his trail when, soon after Barber was employed, a white trustee of the school wrote for Washington's opinion of Barber. Washington replied that Barber was "about as unfitted for such work as is needed to be done in Dr. Anderson's school, as any man that I can think of." Having known Barber for a number of years, he could not think of a single qualification Barber had. "He has failed at everything that he has undertaken, besides he has a bad influence," wrote Washington. "He stirs up racial strife wherever he goes, teaching colored people to hate white people. Aside from this, he has been connected with a number of newspapers and magazines, and in one of them he has most heartily and inconsistently opposed industrial and manual training in every conceivable way. He is now seeking a position in a manual training school because he cannot get anything else to do, and is forced to do that or starve. Aside from the matters which I have mentioned, he is a pessimist, and I do not believe that any pessimist can properly lead and inspire young people." Washington added that he took it for granted that his name would not be used unless absolutely necessary, and his correspondent assured him that he would tell only a few influential board members, who would keep it in confidence. [79]

It is a measure of Washington's power and ruthless use of it that Barber, who had been editor of the leading black magazine and one of the founders of the Niagara Movement, could be driven completely out of work for his race. "After all of my prominence I went back to the hotels and 'slung hash' to study dentistry so as to get where I could not be passed on,"

Barber later recalled with understandable bitterness. In the innocuous profession of dentistry he finally achieved a modest success. After graduation from the Philadelphia Dental School (of Temple University) in 1912 until his death in 1949 he developed a substantial practice and became president of the Negro Professional Club of Philadelphia and president of the St. Marks Building and Loan Company.[80]

Not all of the crusading spirit that had marked the young editor was crushed out of the middle-aged dentist. He was an early member and a director of the National Association for the Advancement of Colored People and was a charter member of the Philadelphia branch in 1913. He was the first black president of the branch, serving from 1917 to 1921. Under his leadership the branch succeeded in ending racial segregation in the mess halls of military bases near Philadelphia. From 1919 to 1921 he was on the NAACP national executive committee and from 1921 to 1924 he was on the Philadelphia branch's executive committee. Leadership of the branch soon passed to others, but he remained a dues-paying member at least until the 1930s.[81]

Though his own life became less adventurous, Barber continued to admire the fiery militant figures of history. He believed as he had years earlier in Atlanta that W.E.B. Du Bois was "the greatest Negro of modern times."[82] John Brown was another of his heroes, and Barber organized and led a pilgrimage in 1922 and annually for several years thereafter to the grave of Brown at Lake Placid, New York. In an oration before a crowd of about one thousand Barber declared that Brown "really had more to do with the emancipation of the Negro than even Abraham Lincoln; for in the final analysis, public opinion and that alone—counts in settling great national questions."[83] Barber was right, but in his own day it was Booker T. Washington, not the militants, who was the real master of public opinion. Contrary to the fable, the giant overcame the would-be giant killer.

1. "Who Founded the Voice?" *Voice of the Negro,* II (March 1905), 192-93.

2. William Pickens, "Jesse Max Barber," *ibid.,* III (December 1906), 483-88.

3. August Meier, *Negro Thought in America, 1880-1915: Racial Ideologies in the Age of Booker T. Washington* (Ann Arbor, 1963), 211-12.

4. Washington (hereinafter abbreviated as BTW) to Hopkins, November 2, 1903, Container 261, Booker T. Washington Papers (Manuscript Division, Library of Congress,

Washington, D. C.). Unless otherwise noted, all further manuscript references are to this collection, and only the container number will be given.

5. BTW to Scott, November 4, 1903 (275).

6. Scott to BTW, December 10, 1903 (274).

7. *Voice of the Negro,* I (January 1904), 33, 37-38. A detailed review of the topics and authors in the four volumes of the magazine is in Penelope L. Bullock, "Profile of a Periodical: The 'Voice of the Negro,'" *Atlanta Historical Bulletin,* XXI (Spring 1977), 99-110.

8. Barber to Scott, April 18, 1904 (26).

9. Scott to Barber, April 14, 1904 (26); Barber to Scott, April 27, 1904 (26).

10. Scott to Barber, May 3, 1904 (26).

11. Scott to Barber, July 20, 1904 (26).

12. Scott to BTW, July 23, 1904 (24).

13. Scott to Barber, July 23, 1904 (26).

14. Scott to BTW, undated, *ca.* August 5, 1904 (24).

15. Scott to Hertel, Jenkins and Company, August 4, 1904 (21).

16. Jenkins to Scott, August 5, 1904 (21).

17. See August Meier, "Booker T. Washington and the Negro Press, with Special Reference to the *Colored American Magazine,*" *Journal of Negro History,* XXXVIII (January 1953), 68, 75-76.

18. BTW to Jenkins, August 10, 1904 (261); Scott to Jenkins, August 9, 1904 (21); Jenkins to BTW, August 10, 1904 (21).

19. BTW to Scott, August 9, 1904 (24).

20. Bowen to Scott, August 20, 1904 (26).

21. *Voice of the Negro,* I (December 1904), 618.

22. *Ibid.,* II (January 1905), 677.

23. Scott to Smith, December 22, 1904 (24); Smith to Scott, December 26, 1904 (24), handwritten.

24. Scott to Smith with enclosure, December 31, 1904 (25).

25. BTW to Bowen, December 27, 1904 (26).

26. Payton to Publishers of *Voice of the Negro,* January 4, 1905 (307); Barber to Payton, January 5, 1905, copy (305).

27. Payton to *Voice of the Negro,* January 20, 1905, copy (305); Scott to Smith, January 25, 1905 (307).

28. BTW to Scott, March 11, 1905 (557).

29. BTW to Jenkins, March 12, 1905 (29).

30. BTW to John A. Hertel, March 15, 1905 (29).

31. Hertel to BTW, March 22, 1905 (29).

32. Scott to BTW, March 22, 1905 (556).

33. *Voice of the Negro,* II (April 1905), 249-53; BTW to Bowen, April 11, 1905 (27).

34. Hertel to BTW, April 19, 1905 (29).

35. Scott to Barber, May 5, 1905 (26). The article was not published.

36. BTW to Scott, July 24, 1905 (556).

37. See "The Secret Life of Booker T. Washington," above.

38. *Voice of the Negro,* II (August 1905), 522-23.

39. BTW to Hertel, August 7, 1905 (29).

40. Hertel to BTW, August 8, 1905 (29).

41. *Voice of the Negro*, II (September 1905), 648.

42. *Ibid.* (November 1905), 801; (December 1905), 873.

43. Barber to BTW, November 29, 1905 (27); see also "The National Negro Business League," *Voice of the Negro*, II (October 1905), 723-24.

44. BTW to Barber, December 1, 1905 (27).

45. Typescript press release, undated (27).

46. Moore to BTW, September 21, 1905 (29).

47. *Voice of the Negro*, III (March 1906), 243; Fortune to Barber, April 5, 1906 (3).

48. Scott to S. Laing Williams, April 15, 1906 (34).

49. BTW to Fortune, April 10, 1906 (32).

50. Barber to BTW, April 6, 1906 (32).

51. BTW to Barber, April 14, 1906 (32).

52. *Voice of the Negro*, III (May 1906), 315-22.

53. Scott to BTW, May 3, 1906 (566).

54. Copy of the letter in J. Max Barber, "Why Mr. Barber Left Atlanta," *Voice*, III (November 1906), 470. A scholarly study of the riot confirms Barber's interpretation. Charles Crowe, "Racial Massacre in Atlanta, September 22, 1906," *Journal of Negro History*, LIV (April 1969), 150-73.

55. Barber, "Why Mr. Barber Left Atlanta," 471.

56. Unsigned letter to the editor of the New York *Age*, October 1, 1906 (330).

57. Scott to S. Laing Williams, October 19, 1906 (34).

58. Barber to "Dear Brother," October 20, 1906 (316).

59. BTW to Williams, March 16, 1908 (42).

60. BTW to Scott, July 24, 1906 (566); Hertel to Whom It May Concern, September 6, 1906 (885).

61. Editorial, *Voice*, III (November 1906), 463-64.

62. BTW to James A. Woodlee, October 14, 1906, telegram (338).

63. Jenkins to BTW, April 4, 1907 (351); Hertel to Scott, April 10, 1907 (36).

64. Scott to Hertel, May 29, 1907 (36).

65. Hertel to Scott, June 1, 1907 (36).

66. Emma Lou Thornbrough, *T. Thomas Fortune, Militant Journalist* (Chicago and London, 1972), 307-13.

67. Barber to Walter White, June 14, 1918 (G186), Records of the National Association for the Advancement of Colored People (Manuscript Division, Library of Congress).

68. S. Laing Williams to BTW, November 2, 1907 (37).

69. Barber to Mary Church Terrell, November 26, 1907, Mary Church Terrell Papers (Manuscript Division, Library of Congress); Williams to BTW, December 20, 1907 (37); Barber to Fortune, January 6, 1908 (365). W. E. B. Du Bois sought to secure financial aid for Barber from the Hughes presidential campaign. Du Bois to John E. Milholland, March 20, 1908, W. E. B. Du Bois Papers (University of Massachusetts, Amherst, Mass.).

70. Williams to BTW, January 30, 1908 (42).

71. Trice to BTW, February 3, 1908 (383).

72. Trice to BTW, February 24, 1908 (383).

73. Amos E. Wilson and R. B. Montgomery to BTW, March 2, 1908 (582).

74. BTW to Trice, March 2, 1908 (383).

75. Trice to BTW, March 4, 1908, telegram (383).

76. Williams to BTW, March 10, 1908 (42).

77. Du Bois to John E. Milholland, March 20, 1908, Du Bois Papers.

78. Barber to Walter White, June 14, 1918 (G186), NAACP Records.

79. BTW to John T. Emlen, June 13, 1908; Emlen to BTW, June 19, 1908 (370).

80. Barber to Walter White, June 14, 1918 (G186), NAACP Records; Bullock, "Profile of a Periodical," 99.

81. May Childs Nerney to Mrs. S. W. Layten, July 31, 1913; Isadore Martin to James Weldon Johnson, December 25, 1917; Barber to Walter White, April 20, 1918 (G186); Isadore Martin to White, May 18, 1930 (G187), NAACP Records.

82. Barber to Mary White Ovington, January 10, 1918 (G186), *ibid.*

83. Copy of the address (G186), *ibid.*

Booker T. Washington's Discovery of Jews

Booker T. Washington in his struggle up from slavery learned many things the hard way, through experience. His discovery of and understanding with American Jewry was no exception. It began with a faux pas. In an early article in a black church magazine, Washington told the success story of a Jew, only a few months from Europe, who had passed through the town of Tuskegee, Alabama, four years earlier with all of his earthly possessions on his back. Settling at a crossroads hamlet, the Jew had hired himself out as a laborer, soon rented land to sublet to others, opened a store, and bought land; "and there is not a man, woman nor child within five miles who does not pay tribute to this Jew." What Washington assumed to be the unexceptionable moral of this story was that "the blackest Negro in the United States" had the same opportunity to succeed in business, pure and simple, as "a Jew or a white man." He added, "Of course the black man, like the Jew or white man, should be careful as to the kind of business he selects." Washington's article, entitled "Taking Advantage of Our Disadvantages," suggested that blacks should enter the occupations that white prejudice had left to them.[1]

Washington's expression "a Jew or a white man" aroused the wrath of Rabbi Isaac Mayer Wise of Cincinnati, editor of the *American Israelite* and one of the founders of Reform Judaism. Wise was particularly sensitive on this point, for he had been an apologist for Southern slaveholders and a Copperhead during the Civil War. What Washington needed was "a lesson in primary ethnology," wrote Wise. Assuming that Washington was a clergyman because his article appeared in a church periodical, Wise added, "All Jewish Americans are Caucasians and when the Rev. Prof. uses such an expression as 'a Jew or a white man' he commits a scientific blunder." Wise then committed his own racist blunder: "Possibly, how-
152 ever, the Rev. Prof. is only exhibiting the secret malice that invariably

marks a servile nature seeking to assume a feeling of equality with something higher, which it does not possess."[2]

Fortunately, this contretemps with Rabbi Wise following Washington's first known reference to a Jew was only the prelude to his gradually unfolding knowledge and his fruitful collaboration not with Wise himself but with many other American Jews. Washington was not unique in bridging the cultural gap between these ethnically diverse peoples who shared a common experience of defamation, discrimination, and segregation. Many other black spokesmen, for example, suggested the Jewish model for the rising black businessman,[3] the Jewish demonstration of the value of group solidarity,[4] and the common black and Jewish experience of proscription, suffering, and achievement. The National Association for the Advancement of Colored People also represented a collaboration of Jews with blacks and other Gentiles. Washington's experience, therefore, is significant chiefly because it was representative, because it was an early example of collaboration between the two groups, and because Washington's Tuskegee Institute was unique among black educational institutions of his time in seeking and securing substantial aid from Jewish philanthropy.[5] As we shall see, Washington also encouraged Jewish millionaires to contribute to black public schools and smaller industrial institutes founded by Tuskegee graduates.

Washington's growing involvement with Jews was also a voyage of discovery. What began in the embarrassment of his exchange with Isaac Wise became a pragmatic alliance for the endowment of his school with the Jewish millionaires, mostly of German origin, and gradually grew into a sympathetic identity with the poor Jewish immigrants of the Lower East Side and the victims of the violent pogroms of Eastern Europe in the late nineteenth and early twentieth centuries. The richness of detail in Washington's voluminous private papers affords the reader a glimpse of the beginnings of a collaboration between blacks and Jews that later flowered in the civil-rights movement of the 1960s.

In addition to his confusion about the racial identity of Jews, Washington shared with other rural and small-town Americans of his day a rhetorical anti-Semitism that identified Jews with the crossroads storekeepers who exacted high prices for goods bought on credit and charged usurious interest for crop mortgages. The Populist movement that dominated farm politics in the South and West in the 1890s also in some degree partook of anti-Semitism.[6] Unfavorable references to Jews apparently colored some of Washington's early speeches, but in his effort to secure donations to his school in the Northern cities, it was in his interest to drop his prejudice. "I would leave out the Jew as distinct from others in cheating the people," his close white adviser, the Reverend Robert C. Bedford, wrote him as he planned a fund-raising effort in Chicago. "He [the Jew] may have started it but others were quick and eager learners. I have always admired your addresses because of their freedom from any personal or race attack. This little tradition about the Jew I notice once in a while creeps in."[7]

Washington had no particular love for the imigrants who poured into the United States during his lifetime, regarding them as labor competitors of blacks, and also perhaps unconsciously as threats to the stability of a society dominated by the rich donors to Tuskegee. He made an exception of Jews, however, particularly of Jews with money. Since these wealthier Jews were usually the settled and culturally assimilated German Jews rather than the newly arrived, more "Jewish" Jews from Eastern Europe, it was easier for Washington to see them as potential benefactors of his school than as potential competitors of his race. Despite their foreign tongue, religion, and habits, Jews symbolized to Washington a shrewd attendance to business instead of politics and abstract rights. When Simon Marx, a Tuskegee merchant, ran for county sheriff, Washington and other Tuskegee Institute faculty members voted for him and rejoiced in his election.[8] "The Jew that was once in about the same position that the Negro is to-day has now complete recognition," Washington observed, "because he has entwined himself about America in a business or industrial sense. Say or think what we will, it is the tangible or visible element that is going to tell largely during the next twenty years in the solution of the race problem."[9]

Blacks had a more compelling reason, however, to emulate the Jews in their group solidarity and pride. In *The Future of the American Negro* (1899), which was the closest he ever came to expounding a coherent racial philosophy, Washington wrote, "We have a very bright and striking example in the history of the Jews in this and other countries. There is, perhaps, no race that has suffered so much, not so much in America as in some of the countries in Europe. But these people have clung together. They have had a certain amount of unity, pride, and love of race; and, as the years go on, they will be more and more influential in this country—a country where they were once despised, and looked upon with scorn and derision. It is largely because the Jewish race has had faith in itself.

Unless the Negro learns more and more to imitate the Jew in these matters, to have faith in himself, he cannot expect to have any high degree of success."[10]

As news of the Russian pogroms filled the newspapers, Washington sympathized with Jews as victims of persecution. "Not only as a citizen of the American Republic, but as a member of a race which has, itself, been the victim of much wrong and oppression," he said in a statement for the Kishineff Relief League of Chicago in 1904, "my heart goes out to our Hebrew fellow-sufferers across the sea."[11] Washington could always find a cheerful aspect of any situation, however. Speaking to a mixed audience in Little Rock in 1905, he noted, "In Russia there are one-half as many Jews as there are Negroes in this country, and yet I feel sure that within a month more Jews have been persecuted and killed than the whole number of our people who have been lynched during the past forty years, but this, of course, is no excuse for lynching."[12]

Jews frequently reminded Washington of their common bond of victimization. Rabbi Alfred G. Moses of Mobile, who was spellbound by one of Washington's speeches, sent him works on Jewish history to give him "a new conception of the Jews."[13] The rabbi's brother in New York invited Washington to dinner at the East Side settlement house where he lived and worked at problems similar to those Washington was meeting in the South. "We have people here whose faults and peculiarities are the result of persecution, as is the case with the Negro," wrote J. Garfield Moses. "So surely as the Negro is persecuted and dealt unfairly with, so surely will the status and the security of the Jews be the next object of attack."[14]

Louis Edelman, a Jewish physician in Huntsville, Alabama, befriended Washington and Tuskegee Institute in a variety of ways. Spending two days on the campus in 1903, he worked with the school physician to treat, free of charge, all students with eye, ear, or nose troubles, his specialty. He gave a lecture to an audience of a thousand in the chapel on "The Jew: His Persecutions and Achievements."[15] Edelman also defended the school against its Southern detractors in letters to the editor of Southern newspapers, but in conservative terms that suggested that a Southern attack on Tuskegee would lead to Northern interference. When Washington sent a copy of one of Edelman's letters to the chairman of the Tuskegee trustees as an example of Southern white support, the trustee replied, "Glad to see the courage of the man, and of the paper to print it. Is he an American, or Hebrew?"[16]

Tuskegee Institute attracted many Jewish supporters, partly because of

Washington's aggressive canvass for funds among them and his persuasiveness as an intergroup diplomat. The nondenominational character of the institution also, no doubt, appealed to Jews of goodwill who would hesitate to aid black schools affiliated with Protestant denominations. With Jews as with Unitarians, Washington never allowed his own nominal affiliation with the Baptist faith to inhibit his active cultivation of millionaires. For whatever reasons, Jewish commitment to Tuskegee grew, both among Southern Jewish neighbors and those in the Northern cities. By Washington's own account, in 1911 "the majority of white people who come here for commencement are composed of Jews."[17] Two Jewish merchants of nearby Montgomery who did business with the school, Selig Gassenheimer and Charles F. Moritz, donated small prizes to be awarded to students at commencement, and Gassenheimer also gave money for the erection of a small building on the campus.[18] In 1905 a rabbi for the first time delivered the commencement sermon.[19]

Tuskegee originally modeled itself after Hampton Institute, where Washington had received his own education, and appealed to the old Protestant wealth and the Sunday-school collections of New England for its support. Around the turn of the twentieth century, however, Washington shifted his Northern fund-raising headquarters from Boston to New York and came into closer contact with the new wealth of industry and finance. In the same period Jewish bankers and merchants began to figure more prominently among the donors. In 1904 the idea occurred to Washington of "inviting Mr. [Paul M.] Warburg or some Hebrew of his standing" to join the board of trustees. "I feel that we need to put new life into the Board," he wrote the board chairman. He thought of two New Englanders, one a small businessman and the other a retired clergyman, who "in some way ought to be gotten rid of," as "Neither of these are of very much value to us."[20] Washington persuaded the two New Englanders to resign for the good of the school and proposed Paul M. Warburg, the New York investment banker. He was unanimously elected, and took his seat on the board.[21]

At about the same time as Warburg's election, other wealthy Jews began or increased their support of Tuskegee. Jacob and Mortimer Schiff, James Loeb, and Felix Warburg, all members of Kuhn, Loeb and Company, Paul Warburg's banking firm, gave donations. So did the Seligmans, the Lehmans, Joseph Pulitzer, Jacob Billikopf, and Julian Mack. Even Joel E. Spingarn, a founder and officer of the NAACP, made a small annual contribution to Washington's school while opposing Washington's race leadership.[22] The immensely wealthy Jacob H. Schiff, another early supporter of the NAACP, had such confidence in Washington that in 1909 he made him his almoner for other black schools. Schiff wrote to Washington that he felt "entirely at a loss to know where to contribute properly and justly," and put $3,000 at Washington's disposal, one-third to go to Tuskegee, smaller amounts to four other schools, and the remainder to schools of which Washington approved.[23] He annually sent Washington a list of the schools he had aided the preceding year on Washington's advice and asked him to make any changes he desired. The contributions, mostly of $100 or less, went principally to industrial schools on the Tuskegee model.[24] Schiff continued this practice until Washington's death in 1915, when his total contributions had increased threefold. He said of Washington soon after the latter's death: "I feel that America has lost one of its great men, whose life has been full of usefulness—not only to his own race, but to the white people of the United States."[25]

Though Paul Warburg resigned from the Tuskegee board of trustees in 1909, two years later Julius Rosenwald, president of Sears, Roebuck and Company, was profoundly moved by reading Washington's autobiography. He visited Tuskegee and a few months later agreed to become a trustee.[26] Rosenwald promoted the school with the same enthusiasm that he simultaneously showed in conditional grants for constructing black YMCA buildings in several major cities. He interested members of his family, friends, and other Chicago capitalists in Tuskegee, brought several parties of distinguished and wealthy visitors to the school in his private railroad car, and annually sent to Washington lists of wealthy men, many of them Jews, whom he should approach for contributions. The most imaginative of Tuskegee's philanthropists, Rosenwald gave bonuses to the Tuskegee faculty, and even sent surplus and defective Sears shoes and hats to be sold at low rates to students.[27]

Rosenwald's enthusiasm spread to some of Washington's other interests. In celebration of his fiftieth birthday in 1912 he gave $25,000 to be distributed by Washington on a matching basis to schools that had grown out of Tuskegee or were doing similar work.[28] At Washington's urging he aided the all-black town of Mound Bayou, Mississippi, by investing in its most ambitious enterprise, a cotton-oil mill, and lending money to its bank, both of which failed in the hard times of 1914.[29] Rosenwald's most ambitious philanthropic enterprise, however, involved a plan Washington had presented to him for aid to country public schools for blacks. Washington suggested that Rosenwald offer a small amount of money if patrons of a school would match it in money, materials, or labor for the construction of a small schoolhouse.[30] Under this program, which was institutionalized under the Rosenwald Foundation after Washington's death, hundreds of Rosenwald schools sprang up in places where white school authorities had refused to provide school facilities for blacks, and ever since freedom the black rural schools had met on weekdays in the single rooms of black country churches. Washington's close personal partnership in philanthropy with Rosenwald was the high point of his efforts to enlist the support of wealthy Jews.

Washington was always the realist. Despite his growing regard for individual Jews, both Northern millionaires and the Southern middle class, he told Tuskegee's business agent to buy supplies for the school whenever possible from Gentiles. "In looking over our bills from Montgomery," he wrote, "I very much fear that we are getting our trade too much centered in the hands of a few Jews. Wherever we can get equally fair treatment in prices and quality of goods from persons other than Jews, I prefer to have our trade scattered among them. In creating public sentiment in favor of the institution the Jews cannot be of much service. . . ." That this was a realistic business judgment rather than anti-Semitism, however, is suggested by an exception he made. He told the business agent, "Where all things are equal with our giving trade to Jews, I hope you will bear in mind Mr. J. Loeb. Quite a number of years ago when other wholesale merchants refused absolutely to deal with us and were threatened by boycott by the town merchants in case they did deal with us, Loeb paid no attention to our want of money and threatened boycott in town and stood by us and sold us goods at wholesale prices. Of course, after he was brave enough to stem the tide for several months, others fell in line, but we owe him a great deal for helping us out in this way in our earlier days."[31]

Washington found parallels in the historical experiences of blacks and Jews that bound the two peoples together more deeply than did either Jewish philanthropy or the Jewish example of self-help. In his early childhood Washington's favorite part of the Bible was the story of Moses leading the children of Israel out of the house of bondage, through the wilderness, and into the promised land. He had first heard that story from his mother when they were both slaves. "I learned in slavery to compare the condition of the Negro with that of the Jews in bondage in Egypt," he wrote in 1911, "so I have frequently, since freedom, been compelled to compare the prejudice, even persecution which the Jewish people have had to face and overcome in different parts of the world, with the disadvantages of the Negro in the United States and elsewhere." He had seen the poor Jews of New York and London, but it was not until his tour of the Continent in 1910 that he learned how life in the ghetto really was. He had thought he knew Jews on the sidewalks of New York, but after seeing those of Poland he decided that the Jews he had known were already halfway toward being Americanized. Polish Jews had lived for a thousand years, Washington observed, "as exiles and, more or less, like prisoners. Instead of trying to become like the other people among whom they lived, they seemed to be making every effort to preserve and emphasize the ways in which they were different from those about them."[32]

Washington was puzzled by the changing character of anti-Semitic prejudice from place to place and by its often religious rather than racial nature.[33] In a book about his European tour, *The Man Farthest Down*, he took the rather complacent view that, compared with the other downtrodden peoples of the earth, blacks in the United States and especially in the South were better off.[34] On the other hand the Jews, who in America and Western Europe were often wealthy, were in Russia and parts of Austria-Hungary among the poorest of civilized people. The Jews showed superiority not in wealth but in education. Not only in America did Jews rival the recently freed blacks in their "yearning for learning," but even in Russia, where they were burdened with educational restrictions, they outdid the rest of the population in literacy.[35]

Near the end of his life, when asked by the New York *Times* to name his favorite Shakespearean passage, Washington chose Shylock's speech in *The Merchant of Venice* that begins "I am a Jew."[36] Washington had begun his career full of misunderstandings about Jews, as illustrated by his controversy with Isaac M. Wise of the *American Israelite*. By the end of his life he had come to understand and appreciate Jews not only as exemplars of self-help and mutual help but as companions in travail and striving. "Hath not a Jew eyes? Hath not a Jew hands, organs, dimensions, senses, affections, passions? Fed with the same food, hurt with the same weapons, subject to the same diseases . . . ?" This passage from Shylock's speech was a parallel to the black man's plea to be treated as "a man and brother."

Through Washington's ceaseless journeys across the color line, many Jews learned to appreciate a black man's personal qualities. Rabbi Stephen S. Wise of the Free Synagogue in New York City, where Washington had spoken several times, wrote to Washington's widow on news of his death, "He was not only the guide and friend of one race but the servant and benefactor of two races."[37] In an obituary address at his synagogue, Wise said of the Black Moses: "He was more concerned about the Negro doing justice to himself than securing justice from the white race." Wise urged whites, however, to deal more justly with blacks than they had done, concluding with a statement that went to the heart of the race problem in America: "The inward memorial to Booker Washington lies in a new and heretofore untried justness of attitude toward the Negro in remembering that he is not a problem but a man, that the Negro is not a racial question but a fellow human to be accepted and honored in the spirit of that justness which is faith."[38]

Like Columbus, who discovered a new world but never reached the mainland and died thinking it was Asia he had reached, Washington died unaware that he and Rabbi Stephen Wise were present at the birth of brotherhood week. In his pursuit of the rich Jew, Washington also never fully understood the masses of the new immigrant Jews. He showed no awareness of Zionism, of the sectarian rivalries within Judaism, of the tension between Jewish assimilationism and nationalism, of the hold of unionism and socialism on the Jewish working class, or even of the lynching of Leo Frank, a Southern Jew.[39]

If Washington never reached the promised land, however, he did move the blacks and the children of Israel far down the road to the full partnership of the civil-rights movement. Even while he was still alive, Jewish donors to Tuskegee found no inconsistency in also being the angels of the early NAACP. As Washington groped, through contacts with Jews, toward an understanding of both their differentness and their common humanity, so many key figures in American Jewry in the early twentieth century found in Booker T. Washington a bridge to understanding of America's deepest social problem. Paradoxically, it was because of Washington's ordinariness—his conventional attitudes, his intellectual mediocrity, his penchant for cliché—that he could explain each group to the other in terms each could understand.

1. Booker T. Washington (hereafter cited as BTW), "Taking Advantage of Our Disadvantages," *A.M.E. Church Review*, 10 (1894), 478-83, reprinted in Louis R. Harlan and Raymond W. Smock, eds., *The BTW Papers* (Urbana, Ill., 1972–), III, 408-12.

2. *American Israelite*, 41 (July 26, 1894), 4. A sympathetic review of Wise's views on slavery, abolitionism, and the Civil War is in James G. Heller, *Isaac M. Wise: His Life, Work, and Thought* (New York, 1965), pp. 331-49.

3. This theme is developed in detail by Arnold Shankman, "Friend or Foe? Southern Blacks View the Jew 1880-1935," in Nathan M. Kaganoff and Melvin I. Urofsky, eds., *Turn to the South; Essays on Southern Jewry* (Charlottesville, 1979), pp. 109-14.

4. Ibid., pp. 115-16; "A Fellow Feeling Makes Us Wondrous Kind," editorial in Washington *Colored American*, May 6, 1899, p. 4; "A Few Lessons from Jews," Indianapolis *Freeman*, September 5, 1891, p. 1.

5. Lenora E. Berson, in *The Negroes and the Jews* (New York, 1971), pp. 63-79, noted that BTW made "the earliest recorded attempt" at active partnership with an American Jew, Julius Rosenwald. A more successful treatment of Jewish attitudes toward blacks, however, is Hasia R. Diner, *In the Almost Promised Land: American Jews and Blacks, 1915-1935* (Westport, Conn., 1977), which despite the dates of its title has much information on BTW's era. See also Robert G. Weisbord and Arthur Stein, *Bittersweet Encounter: The Afro-American and the American Jew* (Westport, Conn., 1970); Leonard Dinnerstein and Mary Dale Palsson, eds., *Jews in the South* (Baton Rouge, 1973).

6. On the historiographical controversy over the extent of Populist anti-Semitism, see particularly Oscar Handlin, "American Views of the Jew at the Opening of the Twentieth Century," *Publications of the American Jewish Historical Society*, 40 (1951); C. Vann Woodward, "The Populist Heritage and the Intellectuals," *American Scholar*, 29 (winter 1959-60), 55-72; Norman Pollack, "The Myth of Populist Anti-Semitism," *American Historical Review*, 68 (1962), 76-80; Norman Pollack, "Handlin on Anti-Semitism: A Critique of 'American Views of the Jew,'" *Journal of American History*, 51 (1964), 391-403; and Walter T. K. Nugent, *The Tolerant Populists: Kansas Populism and Nativism* (Chicago, 1963).

7. R. C. Bedford to BTW, January 14, 1896, Container 114, BTW Papers, Library of Congress. Documents from this collection will be referred to hereafter only by the container number, in parentheses.

8. William Jenkins to BTW, August 7, 1896, G. W. A. Johnston to BTW, August 13, 1896 (118).

9. BTW, "Industrial Training for the Negro," *Independent*, 50 (February 3, 1898), 146, in Harlan and Smock, eds. *BTW Papers*, IV, 373.

10. Reprinted in Harlan and Smock, eds., *BTW Papers*, V, 369-70. The Cleveland lawyer John P. Green expressed in 1895 a common black attitude in "The Jew and the Negro," Indianapolis *Freeman*, December 21, 1895, p. 3. He wrote, "We feel and think our lot in this so-called 'white man's country,' is a hard one; and in very truth it is . . . but when we scan the blood stained recitals of what the Jews have passed through since the destruction of Jerusalem, during the first century of our Christian era, and then note how conspicuous they are in all civilized communities for their real attainments along the lines of science, art, literature and finance, we may well cheer up and persevere along the same lines until victory crowns our efforts."

11. BTW to Mrs. A. F. D. Grey, ca. June 5, 1903, in Harlan and Smock, eds., *BTW Papers*, VII, 169. See also Arnold Shankman, "Brothers Across the Sea: Afro-Americans on the Persecution of Russian Jews, 1881-1917," *Jewish Social Studies*, 37 (1975), 114-21.

12. Excerpt of address in Boston *Transcript*, December 4, 1905, clipping (27).

13. Alfred G. Moses to BTW, January 2 and 8, 1906 (328).

14. J. Garfield Moses to BTW, January 14, 1906 (809).

15. *Tuskegee Student*, 15 (May 9, 1903), 2; typescript of lecture, May 5, 1903 (257).

16. Birmingham *News*, September 5, 1903 (clipping), BTW to W. H. Baldwin, Jr., September 11, 1903, and Baldwin's marginal note (257).

17. BTW to Robert H. Terrell, April 4. 1911 (443).

18. A. R. Stewart to BTW, June 14, 1909, BTW to Selig Gassenheimer, June 16, 1909 (734).

19. A. J. Messing of Montgomery, Ala., in *Tuskegee Student*, 17 (June 17, 1905), 1.

20. BTW to W. H. Baldwin, Jr., May 20, 1904 (18). See also BTW to Baldwin, June 2, 1904 (18).

21. Marcus M. Marks to BTW, May 24, 1904, in Harlan and Smock, eds., *BTW Papers*, VII, 512; minutes of adjourned meeting of the Tuskegee Institute board of trustees, June 23, 1904 (18).

22. Spingarn to BTW, December 24, 1909 (736).

23. Schiff to BTW, June 16 and July 7, 1909 (47).

24. BTW to Schiff, March 6, 10, 16, and 17, 1910 (51).

25. Schiff to W. H. Holtzclaw, in Cyrus Adler manuscript, microfilm reel 677, Jacob H. Schiff Papers, American Jewish Archives, Hebrew Union College.

26. BTW to Ruth S. Baldwin, January 25, 1912 (916).

27. Julius Rosenwald to BTW, May 31, 1912 (56); William C. Graves to BTW. December 30, 1912 (66); BTW to Rosenwald, February 8, April 2, and September 19, 1913 (66); Morris S. Rosenwald to BTW, April 2, 1912 (755); BTW to Julius Rosenwald, undated draft, ca. May 1915 (78). For a survey of Jewish philanthropy and Tuskegee, see Diner, *In the Almost Promised Land*, pp. 166-72.

28. Rosenwald to BTW, August 5, 1912 (56).

29. A detailed account is August Meier, "Booker T. Washington and the Town of Mound Bayou," *Phylon*, 15 (1954), 396-401, reprinted in Meier and Elliott Rudwick, *Along the Color Line* (Urbana, Ill., 1976), pp. 217-23.

30. BTW outlined his plan in letters to Rosenwald, June 21 and September 12, 1912 (62).

31. BTW to Lloyd G. Wheeler, October 17, 1904 (551). BTW also urged a liberal order of stationery from one of the school's Jewish benefactors, Selig Gassenheimer. BTW to E. T. Attwell, April 4, 1911 (610).

32. BTW, "Race Prejudice in Europe," typescript, December 5, 1911 (957).

33. Actually, racial anti-Semitism, as represented by the writings of Houston Stewart Chamberlain, was on the increase in Europe and the United States in the late nineteenth and early twentieth centuries.

34. (New York, 1912), with Robert E. Park.

35. See Meyer Weinberg, "A Yearning for Learning: Blacks and Jews Through History," *Integrated Education*, 7 (1969), 20-29.

36. Later he changed his favorite quotation to the passage in *Julius Caesar* that begins "There is a tide in the affairs of men." BTW to the editor of the New York *Times*, April 15, 18, 1914 (525).

37. Stephen S. Wise to Margaret M. Washington, November 15, 1915 (952).

38. Stephen S. Wise, "Booker Washington: American," *Southern Workman*, 45 (1916), 382-83, an abstract of his address.

39. BTW's silence may be explained by the fact that a black janitor testified he had

helped Leo Frank to remove the body. If the Jew was found innocent, the black man was the logical suspect. Jonah Wise, who succeeded his father, Isaac M. Wise, as editor of the *American Israelite*, at first thought Frank guilty because he doubted that a Southern white jury would convict on the "unsupported testimony of a low type of negro," but after Frank was lynched he concluded that the real murderer was "the vicious and criminal negro." Wise's only consistency was his racism. Quoted in Eugene Levy, " 'Is the Jew a White Man?': Press Reaction to the Leo Frank Case, 1913-1915," *Phylon*, 35 (1974), 218-19.

Booker T. Washington
and the Politics of Accommodation

█t is ironic that Booker T. Washington, the most powerful black American of his time and perhaps of all time, should be the black leader whose claim to the title is most often dismissed by the lay public. Blacks often question his legitimacy because of the role that favor by whites played in Washington's assumption of power, and whites often remember him only as an educator or, confusing him with George Washington Carver, as "that great Negro scientist." This irony is something that Washington will have to live with in history, for he himself deliberately created the ambiguity about his role and purposes that has haunted his image. And yet, Washington was a genuine black leader, with a substantial black following and with virtually the same long-range goals for Afro-Americans as his rivals. This presentation is concerned with Washington's social philosophy, such as it was, but it also addresses his methods of leadership, both his Delphic public utterances that meant one thing to whites and another to blacks and his adroit private movements through the brier patch of American race relations. It does not try to solve the ultimate riddle of his character.

Washington's own view of himself was that he was the Negro of the hour, whose career and racial program epitomized what blacks needed to maintain themselves against white encroachments and to make progress toward equality in America. The facts of his life certainly fitted his self-image. He was the last of the major black leaders to be born in slavery, on a small farm in western Virginia in 1856. Growing up during the Reconstruction era in West Virginia, he believed that one of the lessons he learned was that the Reconstruction experiment in racial democracy failed because it began at the wrong end, emphasizing political means and civil rights acts rather than economic means and self-determination. Washington learned this lesson not so much through experience as a child

worker in the salt works and coal mines as by what he was taught as a houseboy for the leading family of Malden, West Virginia, and later as a student at Hampton Institute in Virginia. Hampton applied the missionary method to black education and made its peace with the white South.

After teaching school in his home town, Washington briefly studied in a Baptist seminary and in a lawyer's office. But he soon abandoned these alternative careers, perhaps sensing that disfranchisement and the secularization of society would weaken these occupations as bases for racial leadership. He returned to Hampton Institute as a teacher for two years and then founded Tuskegee Normal and Industrial Institute in Alabama in 1881. Over the next quarter of a century, using Hampton's methods but with greater emphasis on the skilled trades, Washington built up Tuskegee Institute to be an equal of Hampton.

Washington's bid for leadership went beyond education and institution-building, however. Symbolic of his fresh approach to black-white relations were a speech he gave in 1895 before a commercial exposition, known as the Atlanta Compromise Address, and his autobiography, *Up from Slavery* (1901). As Washington saw it, blacks were toiling upward from slavery by their own efforts into the American middle class and needed chiefly social peace to continue in this steady social evolution. Thus, in the Atlanta Compromise he sought to disarm the white South by declaring agitation of the social equality question "the merest folly" and proclaiming that in "purely social" matters "we can be as separate as the fingers, yet one as the hand in all things essential to mutual progress." These concessions came to haunt Washington as southerners used segregation as a means of systematizing discrimination, and northerners followed suit. And they did not stop at the "purely social."

Washington's concessions to the white South, however, were only half of a bargain. In return for downgrading civil and political rights in the black list of priorities, Washington asked whites to place no barriers to black economic advancement and even to become partners of their black neighbors "in all things essential to mutual progress." Washington saw his own role as the axis between the races, the only leader who could negotiate and keep the peace by holding extremists on both sides in check. He was always conscious that his unique influence could be destroyed in an instant of self-indulgent flamboyance.

Washington sought to influence whites, but he never forgot that it was the blacks that he undertook to lead. He offered blacks not the empty promises of the demagogue but a solid program of economic and educational progress through struggle. It was less important "just now," he said, for a black person to seek admission to an opera house than to have the money for the ticket. Mediating diplomacy with whites was only half of Washington's strategy; the other half was black solidarity, mutual aid, and institution-building. He thought outspoken complaint against injustice was necessary but insufficient, and he thought factional dissent among black leaders was self-defeating and should be suppressed.

Washington brought to his role as a black leader the talents and outlook of a machine boss. He made Tuskegee Institute the largest and best-supported black educational institution of his day, and it spawned a large network of other industrial schools. Tuskegee's educational function is an important and debatable subject, of course, but the central concern here is Washington's use of the school as the base of operations of what came to be known as the Tuskegee Machine. It was an all-black school with an all-black faculty at a time when most black colleges were still run by white missionaries. Tuskegee taught self-determination. It also taught trades designed for economic independence in a region dominated by sharecrop agriculture. At the same time, by verbal juggling tricks, Washington convinced the southern whites that Tuskegee was not educating black youth away from the farms. Tuskegee also functioned as a model black community, not only by acquainting its students with a middle-class way of life, but by buying up the surrounding farmland and selling it at low rates of interest to create a commuity of small landowners and home-owners. The Institute became larger than the town.

Washington built a regional constituency of farmers, artisans, country teachers, and small businessmen; he expanded the Tuskegee Machine nationwide after the Atlanta Compromise seemed acceptable to blacks all over the country, even by many who later denounced it. His first northern black ally was T. Thomas Fortune, editor of the militant and influential New York *Age* and founder of the Afro-American Council, the leading forum of black thought at the time. Washington was not a member, but he usually spoke at the annual meetings, and his lieutenants so tightly controlled the council that it never passed an action or resolution not in Washington's interest. Seeking more direct allies, Washington founded in 1900 the National Negro Business League, of which he was president for life. The league was important not so much for what it did for black business, which was little, but because the local branch of the league was a stronghold of Washington men in every substantial black population center.

Other classes of influential blacks did not agree with Washington's stated philosophy but were beholden to him for the favors he did them or offered to do for them. He was not called the Wizard for nothing. White philanthropists who approved of him for their own reasons gave him the money to help black colleges by providing for a Carnegie library here, a dormitory there. Through Washington Andrew Carnegie alone gave buildings to twenty-nine black schools. Not only college administrators owed him for favors, but so did church leaders, YMCA directors, and many others. Though never much of a joiner, he became a power in the Baptist church, and he schemed through lieutenants to control the secret black fraternal orders and make his friends the high potentates of the Pythians, Odd Fellows, and so on. Like any boss, he turned every favor into a bond of obligation.

It was in politics, however, that Washington built the most elaborate tentacle of the octopus-like Tuskegee Machine. In politics as in everything else, Washington cultivated ambiguity. He downgraded politics as a solution of black problems, did not recommend politics to the ambitious young black man, and never held office. But when Theodore Roosevelt became president in 1901 and asked for Washington's advice on black and southern appointments, Washington consented with alacrity. He became the chief black adviser of both Presidents Roosevelt and William Howard Taft. He failed in his efforts to liberalize Republican policy on voting rights, lynching, and racial discrimination, however, and relations between the Republican party and black voters reached a low ebb.

In patronage politics, however, Washington found his opportunity. For a man who minimized the importance of politics, Washington devoted an inordinate amount of his time and tremendous energy to securing federal jobs for his machine lieutenants. These men played a certain role in the politics of the period, but their first obligation was to the Tuskegean. Washington advised the presidents to replace the old venal officeholding class of blacks with men who had proven themselves in the independent world of business, but in practice it took only loyalty to Washington to cleanse miraculously an old-time political hack.

Washington also used high political office in the North to win the loyalty of key figures in the legal profession whose ideology and natural bent were usually in the direction of more outspoken protest. A notable example was William H. Lewis of Boston, a graduate of Amherst College and Harvard University Law School, who had been an outspoken critic of Washington. President Roosevelt had long admired Lewis's all-American prowess on the football field as much as his professional attainments, and when

Washington began talking of raising the quality of the black civil service, Roosevelt brought up Lewis. Washington was skeptical, but as soon as possible he met with Lewis and made a deal with him. As Lewis wrote, there were "many things about which we might differ, but that we had the same aims and the same end in view." Lewis became, with Washington's blessing, the assistant U.S. district attorney in Boston, and a few years later Taft appointed him assistant attorney general of the United States, the highest appointive federal post held by a black man up to that time—and for decades afterward.

In another sphere also Washington spread the web of his Tuskegee Machine over the several hundred black weekly newspapers and half-dozen magazines through which the black community communicated with itself. W.E.B. Du Bois tried in 1903 to prove that Washington's "hush money" controlled the black press through subsidies and outright ownership. Challenged, Du Bois could not prove his case, but when Washington's papers were opened forty years later, they revealed the essential accuracy of the charge. The question of how *much* control is complicated, however, by the willing complicity of the editors in this domination. The editors were themselves small businessmen who generally agreed with Washington's economic orientation and the conventional wisdom of a commercial age. Furthermore, Washington's small subsidies, except in a few instances, were only a minor part of the operating funds of these newspapers.

Washington's outright critics and enemies were called "radicals" because they challenged Washington's conservatism and bossism, though their tactics of verbal protest would seem moderate indeed to a later generation of activists. They were the college-educated blacks, engaged in professional pursuits, and proud of their membership in an elite class—what one of them called the Talented Tenth. The strongholds of the radicals were the northern cities and southern black colleges. They stood for full political and civil rights, liberal education, free expression, and aspiration. They dreamed of a better world and believed Booker T. Washington was a menace to its achievement.

The first to challenge Washington and all his works was a young Harvard graduate, William Monroe Trotter, who founded in 1900 a newspaper, the Boston *Guardian*. Trotter not only differed with the Tuskegean on every conceivable subject but engaged in personal abuse. He spoke of Washington's "crime of race ridicule and belittlement." He called him Pope Washington, the Black Boss, the Benedict Arnold of the Negro race, the

Exploiter of Exploiters, the Great Traitor, and the Great Divider. In reporting a speech by Washington in Boston in 1902 Trotter described him thus: "His features were harsh in the extreme. His vast leonine jaws into which vast mastiff-like rows of teeth were set clinched together like a vise. His forehead shot up to a great cone; his chin was massive and square; his eyes were dull and absolutely characterless, and with a glance that would leave you uneasy and restless during the night if you had failed to report to the police such a man around before you went to bed." That this yellow journalism was far from an accurate description of Washington's modest and reassuring appearance was beside the point. In Trotter's vendetta against Washington no charge, true or false, was too big or too petty to use.

Trotter seized the chance to confront Washington directly when the black leader spoke at a Boston church in 1903 under sponsorship of the local branch of the National Negro Business League. Trotter stood on a chair to interrupt Washington's speech with nine questions that were actually challenges. Quoting from a Washington speech, for example, Trotter asked: "When you said: 'It was not so important whether the Negro was in the inferior car as whether there was in that car a superior man not a beast,' did you not minimize the outrage of the insulting Jim-crow car discrimination and justify it by the 'bestiality' of the Negro?" The final provocative question was: "Are the rope and the torch all the race is to get under your leadership?"

The police moved through the crowd to arrest Trotter for disorderly conduct, and Washington proceeded with his speech as though nothing had happened, but Trotter had achieved his purpose. The incident appeared next day in all the newspapers as the Boston Riot, penetrating Washington's news screen to show that not all blacks approved of Washington's leadership. Washington publicly ignored the affair, but his Boston lieutenants made a martyr of Trotter by vigorous prosecution of his case, forcing him to serve thirty days in jail.

Perhaps the most important effect of the Boston Riot was that it forced Du Bois, the leading black intellectual and now the leading civil rights champion of his generation, off the fence. A Harvard Ph. D. with German university training, Du Bois was never even considered for tenure in any leading American university, and in 1903 he was a professor at Atlanta University. In *The Souls of Black Folk*, published before the Boston Riot, he had criticized Washington in a searching but moderate way, in no way comparable with Trotter's cry that the emperor had no clothes. Believing that Trotter was being victimized, Du Bois wrote Trotter a private letter of sympathy, which Trotter promptly published, and this started Du Bois's movement out of academe into the arena of racial politics.

Washington had a chance in January 1904 to heal the wounds of dissidence that the Boston Riot had opened. With the consent and cooperation of Du Bois, Washington convened the Carnegie Hall Conference, a three-day secret meeting of about thirty black leaders, excluding Trotter. But Washington with his penchant for bossism torpedoed his own effort at rapprochement by packing the meeting with his own lieutenants to such a degree that Du Bois and his adherents resigned from the organization that was created at the conference.

The following year, Du Bois and Trotter formed their own organization, the Niagara Movement, dedicated to "persistent manly agitation" for civil rights, voting rights, job opportunities, equal educational opportunities, and human rights in general. The Niagara Movement is an important link in the historical development of the civil rights movement, but here we are concerned with its role in the minority-group leadership struggle with Washington. This small band of intellectuals, hurling their manifestos, was no match for the political skill and marshaled power of the Wizard of Tuskegee. They themselves limited their membership to the small black professional class, insisted on an ideological "likemindedness" that few could achieve, and had no white allies. By contrast, Washington had a broader base and a commoner touch. Though Washington proposed the leadership of another elite class, the black businessmen, he kept in close touch with the black masses and directed his program to their immediate needs. Furthermore, he fished for allies wherever he could find them, among whites and even among the professional men who would ordinarily be expected in the Niagara Movement. He cared little about the ideology of a lieutenant, as long as the man did what Washington wanted done.

The Niagara Movement called Washington, in effect, a puppet of the whites, who thrust him into prominence because he did not challenge their wrongdoing. According to the Niagarites, Washington needed to mollify the whites in behalf of his school to such an extent that he was rendered unfit for black leadership, that instead of leadership he gave them cowardice and apology. Furthermore, his critics charged that Washington was a half-educated southerner whose control over black affairs was stifling an emergent black educated elite, the Talented Tenth, the logical leaders. Because of his own class orientation he was trying to change the social position of blacks through the acquisitive propensities and the leadership of businessmen instead of through political and civil rights agitation, which the Niagara men saw as the need of the hour. Extremists among them called Washington an instrument of white indirect rule, like the slave drivers of the old days. Even the moderate Kelly Miller of Howard University observed in 1903 that Washington was "not a leader of the people's own choosing." Though they might accept his gifts, said Miller, "few thoughtful colored men espouse what passes as Mr. Washington's policy without apology or reserve."

Washington dismissed his black critics by questioning their motives, their claim to superior wisdom, and—the politician's ultimate argument—their numbers. Washington understood, if his critics did not, that his leadership of the black community largely depended on his recognition by whites as the black leader. If he did not meet some minimal standards of satisfactoriness to whites, another Washington would be created. He obviously could not lead the whites; he could not even divide the whites. He could only, in a limited way, exploit the class divisions that whites created among themselves. He could work in the cracks of their social structure, move like Brer Rabbit through the brier patch, and thus outwit the more numerous and powerful whites.

While Washington recognized the centrality of black-white relations in his efforts to lead blacks, he was severely restricted by the historical context of his leadership. It was an age of polarization of black and white. The overheated atmosphere of the South at the turn of the century resembled that of a crisis center on the eve of war. Lynching became a more than weekly occurrence; discrimination and humiliation of blacks were constant and pervasive and bred a whole literature and behavioral science of self-justification. Race riots terrorized blacks in many cities, and not only in the South. It would have required not courage but foolhardiness for Washington, standing with both feet in Alabama, to have challenged this raging white aggression openly and directly. Even un-qualified verbal protest would have brought him little support from either southern blacks or white well-wishers. Du Bois took higher ground and perhaps a better vision of the future when he urged forthright protest against every white injustice, on the assumption that whites were rational beings and would respond dialectically to black protest. But few white racists of the early twentieth century cared anything for the facts. And when Du Bois in his Atlanta years undertook to implement his protest with action, he was driven to the negative means of refusing to pay his poll tax or refusing to ride segregated streetcars and elevators.

Instead of either confronting all of white America or admitting that his

Faustian bargain for leadership had created a systemic weakness in his program, Washington simply met each day as it came, pragmatically, seeking what white allies he could against avowed white enemies. A serious fault of this policy was that Washington usually appealed for white support on a basis of a vaguely conceived mutual interest rather than on ideological agreement. For example, in both the South and the North Washington allied himself with the white upper class against the masses. In the South he joined with the planter class and when possible with the coal barons and railroad officials against the Populists and other small white farmer groups who seemed to him to harbor the most virulent anti-black attitudes born of labor competition. Similarly, in the North, Washington admired and bargained with the big business class. The bigger the businessman, the more Washington admired him, as the avatar and arbiter of American society. At the pinnacle in his measure of men were the industrialists Carnegie, John D. Rockefeller, and Henry H. Rogers and the merchant princes Robert C. Ogden and Julius Rosenwald. To be fair to Washington, he appreciated their philanthropic generosity at least as much as he admired their worldly success, but his lips were sealed against criticism of even the more rapacious and ungenerous members of the business elite.

Washington made constructive use of his philanthropic allies to aid not only Tuskegee but black education and black society as a whole. He guided the generous impulse of a Quaker millionairess into the Anna T. Jeanes Foundation to improve the teaching in black public schools. He persuaded the Jewish philanthropist Julius Rosenwald to begin a program that lasted for decades for building more adequate black schoolhouses all over the South. Washington's influence on Carnegie, Rockefeller, Jacob Schiff, and other rich men also transcended immediate Tuskegee interests to endow other black institutions. In short, Washington did play a role in educational statesmanship. There were limits, however, to his power to advance black interests through philanthropy. When his northern benefactors became involved in the Southern Education Board to improve the southern public school systems, for example, he worked repeatedly but without success to get this board to redress the imbalance of public expenditures or even to halt the rapid increase of discrimination against black schools and black children. He had to shrug off his failure and get from these so-called philanthropists whatever they were willing to give.

Having committed himself to the business elite, Washington took a dim view of the leaders of the working class. Immigrants represented to him, as to many blacks, labor competitors; Jews were the exception here, as he held them up to ambitious blacks as models of the work-ethic and group solidarity. He claimed in his autobiography that his disillusionment with labor unions went back to his youthful membership in the Knights of Labor and stemmed from observation of their disruption of the natural laws of economics. In his heyday, however, which was also the age of Samuel Gompers, Washington's anti-union attitudes were explained by the widespread exclusion of blacks from membership in many unions and hence from employment in many trades. There is no evidence that Washington ever actively supported black strikebreaking, but his refusal to intervene in behalf of all-white unions is understandable. It was more often white employees rather than employers who excluded blacks, or so Washington believed. He worked hard to introduce black labor into the non-union, white-only cotton mills in the South, even to the extent of interesting northern capitalists in investing in black cotton mills and similar enterprises.

Washington was a conservative by just about any measure. Though he flourished in the Progressive era it was not he, but his opponents who were the men of good hope, full of reform proposals and faith in the common man. Washington's vision of the common man included the southern poor white full of rancor against blacks, the foreign-born anarchist ready to pull down the temple of American business, and the black sharecropper unqualified by education or economic freedom for the ballot. Though Washington opposed the grandfather clause and every other southern device to exclude the black man from voting solely on account of his color, Washington did not favor universal suffrage. He believed in literacy and property tests, fairly enforced. He was no democrat. And he did not believe in woman suffrage, either.

In his eagerness to establish common ground with whites, that is, with some whites, Washington often overstepped his purpose in public speeches by telling chicken-thief, mule, and other dialect stories intended to appeal to white stereotypes of blacks, and he occasionally spoke of the Afro-American as "a child race." No doubt his intent was to disarm his listeners, and before mixed audiences he often alternately addressed the two groups, reassuring whites that blacks should cooperate with their white neighbors in all constructive efforts, but saying to blacks that in their cooperation there should be "no unmanly cowering or stooping." At the cost of some forcefulness of presentation, Washington did have a remarkable capacity to convince whites as well as blacks that he not only understood them but agreed with them. It is one of Washington's intangible qualities as a black leader that he could influence, if not lead, so many whites. The agreement that whites sensed in him was more in his manner than in his program or goals, which always included human rights as well as material advancement for blacks.

In his constant effort to influence public opinion, Washington relied on the uncertain instruments of the press and the public platform. A flood of books and articles appeared over his name, largely written by his private secretary and a stable of ghostwriters, because he was too busy to do much writing. His ghostwriters were able and faithful, but they could not put new words or new ideas out over his signature, so for the crucial twenty years after 1895, Washington's writings showed no fresh creativity or real response to events, only a steady flood of platitudes. Washington's speeches generally suffered from an opposite handicap, that he was the only one who could deliver them. But he was too busy making two or three speeches a day to write a new one for each occasion, so the audiences rather than the speeches changed. But everywhere he went, North, South, or West, he drew large crowds ready to hear or rehear his platitudes.

Washington did try to change his world by other means. Some forms of racial injustice, such as lynching, disfranchisement, and unequal facilities in education and transportation, Washington dealt with publicly and directly. Early in his career as a leader he tried to side step the lynching question by saying that, deplorable though it was, he was too busy working for the education of black youth to divide his energies by dealing with other public questions. Friends and critics alike sharply told him that if he proposed to be a leader of blacks, he was going to have to deal with this subject. So he began an annual letter on lynching that he sent to all the southern white dailies, and he made Tuskegee Institute the center of statistical and news information on lynching. He always took a moderate tone, deplored rape and crime by blacks, but always denied that the crime blacks committed was either the cause of or justification for the crime of lynching. He tried to make up for his moderation by persistence, factual accuracy, and persuasive logic. Disfranchisement of black voters swept through the South from Texas to Virginia during Washington's day. He publicly protested in letters to the constitutional conventions and legislatures in Alabama, Georgia, and Louisiana and aided similar efforts in several other states. He failed to stop lynching, to prevent the loss of voting rights, and to clean up the Jim Crow cars or bring about even minimal standards of fairness in the public schools. But he did try.

As for social segregaton, Washington abided by southern customs while in the South but forthrightly declared it unreasonable for white southerners to dictate his behavior outside of the South. His celebrated dinner at the White House in 1901, therefore, though it caused consternation and protest among white southerners, was consistent with his lifetime practice. Tuskegee Institute underwent an elaborate ritual of segregation with every white visitor, but the man who came to dinner at the White House, had tea with the queen of England, and attended hundreds of banquets and private meals with whites outside the South certainly never internalized the attitudes of the segregators.

What Washington could not do publicly to achieve equal rights, he sought to accomplish secretly. He spent four years in cooperation with the Afro-American Council on a court case to test the constitutionality of the Louisiana grandfather clause, providing funds from his own pocket and from northern white liberal friends. In his own state of Alabama, Washington secretly directed the efforts of his personal lawyer to carry two grandfather-clause cases all the way to the U.S. Supreme Court, where they were lost on technicalities. He took the extra precaution of using code names in all the correspondence on the Alabama cases. Through private pressure on railroad officials and congressmen, Washington tried to bring about improvement in the Jim Crow cars and railroad waiting rooms. He had more success in the Dan Rogers case, which overturned a criminal verdict against a black man because blacks were excluded from the jury. He also secretly collaborated with two southern white attorneys to defend Alonzo Bailey, a farm laborer held in peonage for debt; the outcome here was also successful, for the Alabama peonage law was declared unconstitutional. These and other secret actions were certainly not enough to tear down the legal structure of white supremacy, but they show that Washington's role in Afro-American history was not always that of the accommodationist "heavy." He was working, at several levels and in imaginative ways, and always with vigor, toward goals similar to those of his critics. If his methods did not work, the same could be said of theirs. And he did not take these civil rights actions as a means of answering criticism, because he kept his part in the court cases a secret except to a handful of confidants, a secret not revealed until his papers were opened to historians in recent decades.

There was another, uglier side of Washington's secret behavior, however—his ruthless spying and sabotage against his leading black critics. Washington never articulated a justification for these actions, perhaps because, being secret, they did not require defense. And yet Washington and Emmett Scott left the evidence of his secret machinations undestroyed in his papers, apparently in the faith that history would vindicate him when all the facts were known. Then, too, Washington was not given to explaining himself.

Espionage became an important instrument of Washington's black leadership—or bossism—a few days before the Boston Riot in 1903, when he hired a young black man, Melvin J. Chisum, to infiltrate the inner councils of Trotter's anti-Washington organization in Boston. Chisum later spied on the Niagara Movement's Brooklyn branch, arranged to bribe an opposition newspaper editor in Washington, D.C., and reported these and other clandestine actions to the Wizard on a park bench in New York City. Washington also used Pinkerton detectives and other paid and unpaid secret agents on a variety of errands, to infiltrate the inner councils of the Niagara Movement, to repress newspaper reporting of Niagara meetings, to find out if Trotter's wife worked as a domestic, to research the tax records of Atlanta to get evidence that Du Bois, a champion of black political action, had not paid his poll tax. When a young black magazine editor, J. Max Barber, began to criticize him, Washington tried to muzzle Barber through his publisher and advertisers, then hounded Barber not only out of his magazine but out of job after job until Barber retired from race work to become a dentist. Even the white liberals who joined with the Niagara Movement to form the interracial National Association for the Advancement of Colored People in 1909 were not immune from Washington's secret attacks. Washington arranged with the racially biased New York newspaper reporters to cover—in a sensational fashion—a dinner meeting of the Cosmopolitan Club, an interracial social group to which a number of the NAACP leaders belonged. Even they never guessed that Washington had done this in collusion with white racists.

The Booker T. Washington who emerges into the light of history from his private papers is a complex, Faustian character quite different from the paragon of self-uplift and Christian forbearance that Washington projected in his autobiography. On the other hand, there is little evidence for and much evidence against the charge of some of his contemporaries that he was simply an accommodationist who bargained away his race's birthright for a mess of pottage. Nor does he fit some historians' single-factor explanations of his career: that he offered "education for the new slavery," that he was a proto-black-nationalist, that he was or must have been psychologically crippled by the constraints and guilt feelings of his social role.

Washington's complexity should not be overstressed, however, for the more we know about anybody the more complex that person seems. And through the complexity of Washington's life, its busyness and its multiple levels, two main themes stand out, his true belief in his program for black progress and his great skill in and appetite for politics, broadly defined, serving both his goals and his personal power.

First, let us look closely at Washington's industrial education and small business program. It may have been anachronistic preparation for the age of mass production and corporate gigantism then coming into being, but it had considerable social realism for a black population which was, until long after Washington's death, predominantly rural and southern. Furthermore, it was well attuned to the growth and changing character of black business in his day. Increasingly, the nineteenth-century black businesses catering to white clients surrendered predominance to ghetto businesses such as banks, insurance companies, undertakers, and barbers catering to black customers. These new businessmen, with a vested interest in black solidarity, were the backbone of Washington's National Negro Business League. Washington clearly found congenial the prospect of an elite class of self-made businessmen as leaders and models for the struggling masses. There was also room for the Talented Tenth of professional men in the Tuskegee Machine, however. Washington welcomed every college-educated recruit he could secure. Directly or through agents, he was the largest employer in the country of black college graduates.

Second, let us consider Washington as a powerful politician. Though he warned young men away from politics as a dead-end career, what distinguished Washington's career was not his rather conventional goals, which in public or private he shared with almost every other black spokesmen, but his consummate political skill, his wheeling and dealing.

Du Bois spent much of his long life puzzling over the phenomenon of Washington, a man who did not seem to have an abstraction about him. But toward the end of his life, in 1954 in an oral history memoir at Columbia University, Du Bois said of his old rival dead almost forty years: "Oh, Washington was a politician. He was a man who believed that we should get what we could get." Du Bois, who himself found the political part of his race work the least agreeable, went on to say of Washington: "It wasn't a matter of ideals or anything of that sort. . . . With everybody that Washington met, he evidently had the idea: 'Now, what's your racket? What are you out for?' " Du Bois was a shrewd observer, but what he saw in Washington as a lack—of ideals, of principles, of vision—was his great and almost unique gift as a black political leader. Washington could almost immediately, intuitively, and without formal questioning see through the masks and intellectual superstructure of men to the mainsprings of their behavior. Then he imaginatively sought to bend their purposes to his own. Du Bois said that Washington had no faith in white people but that he was very popular among them because, whenever he met a white man, he listened to him until he figured out what that man wanted him to say, and then as soon as possible he said it. Washington did not always get his way, of course, but he always understood, as his more doctrinaire critics did not, that politics was the art of the possible. What was surprising about Washington was the number and diversity of those he enlisted in his coalition.

Washington's program was not consensus politics, for he always sought change, and there was always vocal opposition to him on both sides that he never tried to mollify. Denounced on the one hand by the Niagara Movement and the NAACP for not protesting enough, he was also distrusted and denounced by white supremacists for bringing the wooden horse within the walls of Troy. All of the racist demagogues of his time—Benjamin Tillman, James Vardaman, Theodore Bilbo, Thomas Dixon, and J. Thomas Heflin, to name a few—called Washington their insidious enemy. One descriptive label for Washington might be centrist coalition politics. The Tuskegee Machine had the middle and undecided majority of white and black people behind it. Washington was a rallying point for the southern moderates, the northern publicists and makers of opinion, and the thousands who read his autobiography or crowded into halls to hear him. Among blacks he had the businessmen solidly behind him, and even, as August Meier has shown, a majority of the Talented Tenth of professional men, so great was his power to reward and punish, to make or break careers. He had access to the wellsprings of philanthropy, political preferment, and other white sources of black opportunity. For blacks at the bottom of the ladder, Washington's program offered education, a self-help formula, and, importantly for a group demoralized by the white aggression of that period, a social philosophy that gave dignity and purpose to lives of daily toil.

It could be said with some justification that the Tuskegee Machine was a stationary machine, that it went nowhere. Because the machine was held together by the glue of self-interest, Washington was frequently disappointed by the inadequate response of his allies. The southern upper class did not effectively resist disfranchisement as he had hoped and never gave blacks the equal economic chance that he considered an integral part of the Atlanta Compromise. Washington's philanthropist-friends never stood up for equal opportunity in public education. Black businessmen frequently found their own vested interest in a captive market rather than a more open society. And Washington himself often took the view that whatever was good for Tuskegee and himself was good for blacks.

To the charge that he accomplished nothing, it can only be imagined what Washington would have answered, since he did not have the years of hindsight and self-justification that some of his critics enjoyed. He would probably have stressed how much worse the southern racial reaction would have been without his coalition of moderates, his soothing syrup, and his practical message to blacks of self-improvement and progress along the lines of least resistance. Washington's power over his following, and hence his power to bring about change, have probably been exaggerated. It was the breadth rather than the depth of his coalition that was unique. Perhaps one Booker T. Washington was enough. But even today, in a very different society, Washington's autobiography is still in print. It still has some impalpable power to bridge the racial gap, to move new readers to take the first steps across the color line. Many of his ideas of self-help and racial solidarity still have currency in the black community. But he was an important leader because, like Frederick Douglass before him and Martin Luther King after him, he had the program and strategy and skill to influence the behavior of not only the Afro-American one-tenth, but the white nine-tenths of the American people. He was a political realist.

The Booker T. Washington Papers
With Raymond W. Smock

When the Booker T. Washington Papers project originated in 1967 it was the first project of its kind that dealt with the letters of a black person. Subsequently, John Blassingame has launched the Frederick Douglass Papers, Herbert Aptheker and the University of Massachusetts Press are engaged in the publication of the W. E. B. Du Bois Papers, and projects to microfilm the papers of John Hope, George Washington Carver, and Mary McLeod Bethune are underway. These projects are an attempt to recover the black past through its documents and to make the record of that past more available to scholars and the general public. They represent an important step toward correcting an imbalance in historical editing, which has traditionally been concerned with the papers of the great white founding fathers. We hope that these projects will open other new fields of historical editing that will include the papers of other blacks as well as of women, workingmen, and other groups who have been neglected by historians in the past.

Surely, qualified editors can be found willing to edit documentary selections from scattered sources illustrating historical topics and themes that interest them. For example, a documentary history of factory working conditions in the nineteenth century could draw on labor archives, state bureaus of labor statistics, and private letters to present a poignant chapter in our history. Similarly, documentary studies of the prison experience, of the teaching and learning experience of the classroom, of public health, or of sexual experience in the American past might convey the sense of our national history as a people better than overconcentration on national political leaders.

The problem and rewards of each editing project are unique because of the different natures of the subjects and of the manuscript collections. For the Booker T. Washington Papers the greatest reward and the greatest **180** problem stem from the same fact—the bulk and richness of the Washington Papers. Nearly a million items are in the main collection at the Library of Congress, and thousands more at Tuskegee Institute, Hampton, Fisk, Howard, Chapel Hill, the Schomburg Collection, and elsewhere.

At the height of Washington's power and influence, everything of his private correspondence was carefully saved by his faithful secretary, and that made possible a unique opportunity to learn of the private man of infinite complexity who stood behind the public mask of convention, accommodation, and platitude. In the case of only very few black men is such a rich private record available. Editing the Washington Papers in fourteen volumes provides an opportunity to present one of the founding fathers of black history in the full detail that used to be reserved for the founding fathers of the nation. We do not suggest that Washington was unique in his psychological complexity or his elaborate private intrigues to accomplish what he could not do publicly. We have seen evidence that Richard Nixon, for example, was not what he seemed to millions who thought they had observed him closely. Of course, the Washington Papers like other editing programs is history, not biography, at least equally as concerned with the times as with the man. The focus on a single collection inevitably causes some distortion of the total past. Washington was at one pole of the black ideology of his time, and William Monroe Trotter and W. E. B. Du Bois were at the other. Naturally Washington's friends and those who agreed with him wrote him more letters than his critics. We balance the picture that the documents convey as best we can by annotation, but we cannot do it completely. That is why we welcome the appearance of the Du Bois Papers, Douglass Papers, Hope Papers, and others to help keep balance and perspective on the documented past.

This same richness of resources, on the other hand, creates our major problem, how to select out of a million items the documents that will fill the fourteen volumes projected for the series. We still believe fourteen is a suitable number. For most people interested in the subject, fourteen volumes is all they ever wanted to know about Booker T. Washington, and weren't afraid to ask. For the others, there are still the originals in the Library of Congress and elsewhere.

To select for publication only about one percent of the total available documents, however, puts a heavy burden of decision on the editors. In several rounds of decision-making, the three editors argue out the relative historical value of various documents, their literary quality, and the possibility of using one letter in the annotation of another. The criteria determining selection are all-important, but they do not lend themselves to a single formula. For example, a long letter may have one paragraph of historically interesting matter surrounded by two or three pages of dull and trivial information. We tend to omit the letter, but quote or paraphrase the paragraph in annotation of a more interesting letter on the same subject. After all, we are preparing these volumes to be read.

Another problem that looms large for any editor is authentication of the text. We have an obligation to be as accurate as humanly possible in reproducing the document. At the same time we try to set it up in type in as readable a manner as is consistent with its original form. To guard against error, the editorial staff has read the original aloud against the typed version, and read it aloud a second time against the galley proof. There is much drudgery in editing work, but is also carries with it the reward of feeling that we are providing the kind of fuller knowledge of the Afro-American past that has long been available for white Americans.

The form of publication of the records of our history is a significant matter. We believe that letterpress publication is far more available and readable than microfilm reproduction, and this is especially important when historical editors are breaking ground in areas that have not been amply documented. The Washington Papers can be viewed as an aid to scholarship in so far as it makes some documents more easily accessible to scholars who cannot get to the originals in the Library of Congress, but more significantly the project is a form of scholarship in its own right. The selection of documents calls for the same kinds of informed judgment that writers of monographs use in deciding on the significance of their data. The annotation research necessary to illuminate the document and the proper names and events mentioned in it adds flesh to the bare bones of the past. This is especially true in black history, where it is often difficult even to find "the invisible man," much less understand the meaning of his life.

Microfilm publication, on the other hand, unless it is done in conjunction with systematic annotation research, coupled with editorial aids that guide the reader to significant topics, does not add substantially to our body of knowledge of the past. Microfilming only makes more readily available a source of raw material. In these days of inflation and cut-backs in federal and academic spending, microfilm seems to some funding agencies an attractive substitute for letterpress publication, but we believe that fully annotated letterpress publications in the field of black history will render a far greater service to scholars and the general public. Considering the distinguished and valuable contributions that the major letterpress publications regarding whites have made to our historical past, it would also be unfair to relegate new fields of inquiry such as black history or women's history to microfilm publication alone.

While the Booker T. Washington Papers deal with the life and times of a black man, it would be incorrect to assume that this is the only focus of the papers, or that the only value of the volumes will be for specialists in black history. Washington's world included wealthy white philanthropists, political leaders, and celebrities as well as poor black farmers in the Black Belt of Alabama. Persons interested in women's history will find many letters to and from black and white women such as Emily Howland, Mary Stearns, Ednah D. Cheney, Olivia Egleston Phelps Stokes, Halle Tanner Dillon, Julia S. Tutwiler, Margaret Murray Washington, Ida B. Wells-Barnett, Frances A. Kellor, Jane Addams, Hallie Q. Brown, and many others. Students of American literature will find correspondence with some of the leading editors, newspapermen, and writers of the period such as William Dean Howells, Lyman Abbott, Charles W. Chesnutt, Paul Laurence Dunbar, and Walter Hines Page.

Another significant way that the papers of black Americans can be used is in the classroom both at the undergraduate and graduate levels. For example, Stuart Kaufman at the University of Maryland plans to have students in a seminar in historical editing read volume 1 of the Woodrow Wilson Papers in conjunction with volume 2 of the Booker T. Washington Papers. These volumes, covering approximately the same period in the lives of these men, offer rich contrasts in the experiences of two southerners, one white and the other black, who were born in the same year. The use of documents in the classroom offers undergraduates a refreshing sense of discovering history in its raw state.

The first documentation of Wilson's existence was in a page of a family Bible, where the time of his birth was recorded down to the very minute. Washington, on the other hand, was never sure of the year of his birth and did not even know who his father was. He first appeared in a document far less personal than a family Bible, the 1860 census, as an anonymous four-year-old mulatto slave. Though he later achieved distinction, Booker T. Washington clearly began his history "from the bottom up." From these beginnings the two men went on to lead remarkable careers as educators and politicians. It is improbable that for the period of the late nineteenth and early twentieth centuries we will ever see two such contrasting lives so amply documented.

With all the concern in the history profession in the last few years for "bottoms up" history, we on the Washington Papers project are often amused that even Booker T. Washington is occasionally lumped with the elite of American society or that the project represents an elitist approach to history. Because Washington internalized many "white" values and was a conservative who represents an outmoded social philosophy, a few historians have criticized the project because it does not meet their own more "radical" version of the past. How far "down" do we have to go to pull Booker T. Washington up from slavery and the West Virginia coal mines and salt furnaces? How great does the contrast have to be between a favored son like Woodrow Wilson, who as a teenager dreamed about being commander-in-chief and invented elaborately detailed fantasies where he was the Duke of Eagleton or the Marquis of Huntington, and Booker T. Washington who at the same time was pondering the fate of his race and asking himself "can we not improve?"

Certainly the white, the wealthy, and the powerful have dominated the interests of historians as well as the general public, and the call for writing the history of the less powerful, the inarticulate, and the dispossessed groups in American life is legitimate. At this stage we need to continue the dialogue begun several years ago by Jesse Lemisch on just what history from the bottom up really is, and we also need some concrete documentary editing proposals to represent this new dimension of historical inquiry.

Perhaps we have been asking the wrong questions in our search for a new more democratic and comprehensive view of the American people. We should be asking ourselves how we can add richness and depth to our understanding of our heritage. In the future this means more energy should be directed toward individuals, groups, and topics that have been generally neglected in the past. This does not mean, however, that there is something sinister in learning more about the founding fathers, the wealthy, or the powerful. Until historians can change their vision of the past to include a wider horizon, most historians and editors will continue to rely on traditional forms of documentation.

We can learn, however, how to read the documents we have more carefully, and also learn how to glean from traditional sources more information about the inarticulate. American historians who want to specialize in the history of the inarticulate will probably have to learn the tools of the anthropologist, and the tools used by historians of preliterate peoples in Africa and elsewhere, such as oral history, folklore, and linguistics. There is plenty for all of us to do without quarreling over which end is up.

Sympathy and Detachment: Dilemmas of a Biographer

I hope that under the circumstances you will allow me to begin autobiographically. I was born in Mississippi but left there when I was three and learned to read and write. I grew up in the South, but it was the urban South, a suburb of Atlanta, where the commercial spirit and bourgeois liberalism were tainted by racism but not completely overwhelmed by it. It was, it seems to me, a right background though certainly not the only right background for a biographer of Booker T. Washington. I was in the South but not completely of it, as a suburban dweller and as a displaced person—that is, not of the local families, born in Mississippi of Tennessee parents and growing up in Georgia. The sense of displacement probably allowed me to think in ways that diverged from the received opinions and conventional wisdom of the community. But living in the South was in some important respects an advantage. It is an article of Southern faith that only white Southerners understand the Negro—the Nigra. This is manifestly a myth, and a dangerous one. As blacks have been telling us for a long time and finally shouting at us, none of us whites can completely understand blacks because we can't share the same experiences. But within the myth there is, as with many myths, a grain of truth. The Northerner thinks, reasons, abstracts, even quantifies. The Southerner, closer to the earth, feels, responds emotionally to a challenge, personalizes. This direct emotional response by white Southerners has led as often to race riots and demagoguery as to racial liberalism, of course, but a white Southerner purged of his arrogance and delusions is capable of looking on blacks as fellow-humans, as many an ex-soldier who has fought side by side with blacks can tell you. And the Southern white who goes all the way from extreme race prejudice to civil rights advocacy has an emotional experience not as easy to forget as for someone who never had a strong bias to begin with.

When did I become interested in Booker T. Washington? It was when I **185** was in graduate school at Johns Hopkins, a school with one foot in the Ivy League and the other foot in the South. I had married a West Virginia girl from a little coal-mining town where you couldn't tell black men from white until the Saturday night bath. She taught me a racial liberalism that had nothing to do with abstractions but a lot to do with common humanity. And I studied at Johns Hopkins under C. Vann Woodward, the great Southern liberal historian, then a young man with only his biography of Tom Watson behind him and his major works, *Origins of the New South* and *The Strange Career of Jim Crow*, ahead of him. Woodward taught me almost nothing directly—in fact, he believed that the lecture method had been made obsolete by the invention of printing. But he taught me much by example, the example of history as literature, the example of an ironic approach to Southern history, and his personal example, as when he brought John Hope Franklin, then a young professor at Howard University, to our seminar. It was the first time I had seen a black man in a role of distinction and authority.

It was in 1949 or 1950 that I first saw the huge mountain of documents, nearly a million pages, that make up the Booker T. Washington Papers. The Library of Congress had acquired them in 1943 from Tuskegee Institute. Apparently neither institution realized their historical value, or Tuskegee would never have let them go, and the Library of Congress would at least have catalogued them and prepared them for use. When I saw them they were stacked in confusion in unlabeled boxes deep in the recesses of the Library's Manuscripts Division. In those easy-going days before tight security regulations, the authorities let me go into the stacks and poke around among the boxes for what I wanted. It was like discovering a new world, the private world of the black community hidden behind the veil and mask that protected blacks from the gaze of whites. Washington and his private secretary, particularly in the fifteen years from 1900 until his death, saved every scrap of incoming and outgoing correspondence, as though they had decided that he was a great man whose life and work, and even his dirty tricks, would be vindicated by history when the whole truth was known. I am not able to say what history's final verdict on Booker T. Washington will be—the jury is still out—but from the viewpoint of biography I must say I am grateful. Even when much of it deals with the commonplace daily affairs that don't deserve a place in history, the sifting and winnowing of this material often yields meaningful information to the biographer. This collection, the richest in the whole field of black history, I have been privileged to be able to use. Thank you, Booker T. Washington, for the egotism or sense of history that caused you to save it all.

That first discovery of the Washington Papers was exhilarating, because I had never before seen a collection of documents so full of social history, the stuff of life itself. But Washington had directly only a peripheral connection with the subject of my doctoral dissertation, which eventually became my first book. So I briefly sampled it and left, but with a half-submerged feeling that here was the appropriate subject for my next book, if there ever would be any next book, or even a first book, for I had the usual self-doubts of the graduate student, said to be the lowest form of academic life. It was five years more before I got my Ph. D., and more than ten years before I got back to Booker T. Washington. Meanwhile I published and perished. I say that jokingly. I was a missionary in a small college in East Texas for nine years, among the culturally deprived white rural people of that area, and there was considerable resentment of the form my enlightenment took, a book on the history of Southern racial injustice. But I gained something valuable from those nine years of immersion in a little town of 5,000, an understanding of the life of rural Southerners that was almost totally foreign to my earlier life in the suburbs. If my treatment of Booker T. Washington's rural outlook has any authenticity, it comes from that experience. It may all sound like *Middletown Revisited* to you, but experiences often have an unseen value.

Another delaying factor was that, before I could turn to Booker T. Washington, I found that another biographer was already at work on the subject with a $100,000 research grant and three or four assistants. However, Marquis James died after he had completed his basic research and written a chapter or two. After more delay, I took the plunge. I began to spend first summers and then all year, spending my retirement money, borrowing, and finally getting some grant money, exploiting my wife as a typist, digging deeper and deeper into the same huge mound of material until I disappeared underground. In the process of coming across this and that scrap of meaningful detail, gradually and imperceptibly I came to know the character I was studying.

Before I began serious study of Washington I thought of him entirely in terms of the Uncle Tom stereotype—a stereotype I might add, with many elements of truth. I had read his main autobiography, *Up from Slavery*, and most of his principal public speeches, and I correctly thought I knew the public man pretty well. I believed he betrayed the black race and the cause of equal justice by his compromises with segregation and with the millionaires—the robber barons—who misruled American society. I still believe that this picture is largely accurate. He made peace with the white racist, looked up to Carnegie and Rockefeller and Huntington, and frowned upon labor unions, higher education for blacks, woman suffrage, and even manhood suffrage. That *was* the public man. And furthermore, he was the most peripatetic public purveyor of platitude before Spiro T. Agnew. But I found in his private papers that he was playing other roles than Uncle Tom, dancing another dance than Jump Jim Crow. I had a more interesting and more manly character on my hands than I had at first supposed, not necessarily always on the right side, but more complex, more human, and more worthy of respect and interest.

Deeply hidden from the gaze of whites, below his public life and known to only a handful of his closest friends, Washington carried on a secret life. He clandestinely financed and directed a number of court suits challenging the grandfather clause, the denial of jury service to blacks, Jim Crow railroad cars, and peonage. Thus, Washington secretly and directly attacked the racial settlement that he publicly accepted. There was another phase of his secret life, however, that could best be described as "dirty tricks." He employed spies to infiltrate all of the organizations of his black opponents, the New England Suffrage League, the Niagara Movement, and the NAACP. They not only forwarned him of what the opposition was planning, but engaged in sabotage and provoked these groups into actions that would get them in trouble. In sharp contrast to his public submission and Sunday school morality, then, Washington was secretly fighting for civil rights and knifing his opponents.

Perhaps psychoanalysis or role psychology would help us solve Booker T. Washington's behavioral riddle, if we could only put him on the couch. If we could remove those layers of secrecy as one peels an onion, perhaps at the center of Washington's being would be revealed a person with a single-minded concern with power, a minotaur, a lion, a fox, or Brer Rabbit, some frightened little man like the Wizard of Oz, or, as in the case of the onion, nothing—a personality that had vanished into the roles it played. Seeking to be all things to all men in a multifaceted society, Washington "jumped Jim Crow" with the skill of long practice, but he seemed to have lost sight of the original purposes of his motion. To treat a character of such complexity, I had to abandon my original plan of an ironic or satirical biography, and deal with the whole man.

What is biography, anyhow? It all began, at least in modern times, with the court historians, whose history was all the biography and genealogy of the reigning monarch and his house, and with the church historians, the hagiographers, who wrote of the history of the faith as a succession of the lives of saints. The court historians attributed all significant achievements casually to the king or some member of his family. The classic example is that of Prince Henry the Navigator of Portugal, who never went to sea in his life except once when he was about twenty to Ceuta, just across the Strait of Gibraltar. Yet, because nearly all the records we have are those of the court scribes, Henry the Navigator gets the credit for what others did, exploring far down the coast of West Africa, the beginning of the expansion of Europe and the modern world. Since those days, biography has matured and become more democratic, of course. In the nineteenth-century climate of romantic individualism Thomas Carlyle went so far as to assert that history was made by heroes, a handful of heroic individuals, not kings this time, necessarily, but men especially marked by genius and force of will, men of mark, who left their footprints in the sands of time. This view still survives in popular culture, in Superman comics, juvenile biographies, "This Is Your Life," and TV documentaries on deceased presidents. But serious biography moved on in the nineteenth century to the "life and letters" style, or literary entombment.

Then came Lytton Strachey to liberate biography from its elegiac role. His book, *Eminent Victorians,* appeared in 1918 and held the previous generation up to public ridicule. His biographies read almost like novels, so carefully did he select his facts to heighten the drama. The only trouble was that he omitted a lot of the whole truth, but he lived in a cynical age. Henry Ford put it briefly. "History is more or less bunk" was one of the few wise things Ford said, though he didn't understand it himself. Much of history as written, and particularly as taught and learned, *is* bunk. Strachey and his many imitators in America did not write great biography, but they did clear the air considerably. Since then, particularly in the last quarter-century, we have seen the art of biography come of age. Much scholarly effort has gone into many-volume biographies of the founding fathers and national leaders—Washington, Jefferson, Lincoln, Wilson, Roosevelt, and even Robert E. Lee—men whose lives are supposed somehow to reveal to us our American national character. This form of biography may go out of style, as recent events have shaken our faith that we have a national character, or at any rate a very good one. But I am more interested in the recent biography whose virtue is in depth, not length, going behind the masks and conventions of the public figure to the private man, and showing also the broad relationship between the man and his times. More penetrating and well-written biography is being written in your lifetime than ever before. It is a good time to be at work on the first major biography of a black American, with available documentary sources that unfortunately don't exist for most of the black participants in our history.

Six years ago, as I was completing my research on the biography, one way out of my dilemma of how to treat Washington's complexity and contradictions presented itself. The National Historical Publications Commission and the National Endowment for the Humanities offered to join with the University of Maryland in supporting a multi-volume selection of Washington's papers, under my editorship. This includes mostly his letters, both incoming and outgoing, as well as speeches, articles, and even books. Three volumes of this series are now published, and others are partially completed. Thus, without cramming all the details into the framework of a biography, I can do full justice to the range and complexity of Washington's life, at all the different levels of public, private and secret.

Meanwhile, back at the slave cabin. . . In the belief that "the child is father to the man," that the complexities of the mature man could best be understood by a study of the early experiences that had shaped him, I began to try to explore his childhood and youth—not in a Freudian way, for I had neither the information nor the inclination for that, but simply making the best use I could of traditional methods.

The trouble was that Washington's papers contained almost nothing on his early life. Washington's origins are shrouded in mist. Origins can't get to be more obscure than to be born a slave. The federal census of 1860 did not even list slaves by name. Washington's birth was unrecorded, and he never knew when his birthday was, though after his death the Tuskegee trustees assigned him a birthday from a family Bible of his master that nobody has seen before or since, so they could celebrate Founder's Day. His white father he never knew, and I was unable to find out, though my biography does discuss all the possibilities.

Not being able to find out much about Washington's early life directly, I studied and presented it indirectly. I gathered all the information I could about everything that surrounded him—the family that owned him, the small farm he lived on, and the way of life in that part of western Virginia. In this technique, which may be compared with pointillism in painting, I was greatly helped by the National Park Service historians at the national monument at his birthplace, one of the least visited monuments in America. The manuscript census records were also invaluable. The census taker not only counted all the people but all the livestock, all the acres in this or that crop, the little tobacco factories and gristmills down the road, the churches, the schools. Through such means, and through tantalizing scraps from his autobiography and later letters, I was able to recreate the world he lived in, and even learned something of the later lives of his aunt and uncle and cousin Sally. For his life in West Virginia, where his family moved as soon as they were free, I used scraps of data from the local newspapers and some long letters from a boyhood friend. His education at Hampton Institute, his early work as a teacher, and his floundering about in search of a career I was able to piece together from a small but revealing file of his letters at Hampton.

I concluded that, if we read Washington's life from front to back instead of focusing only on the mature man, we can find a consistency in what appears at first to be a fragmented personality. Perhaps because there were few black models in his life who had the charisma of success, Washington from early life became inordinately attached to a succession of fatherly white men, and I might add, motherly white women. They were all white racists, but relatively mild and benevolent in their racism. General Lewis Ruffner was the first of these, and his Yankee wife Viola Knapp Ruffner. Though a slaveowner before the Civil War, Ruffner opposed secession, became a Union Army general, and joined the Republican party. Booker T. Washington became their houseboy, and Mrs. Ruffner taught him his first lessons in industriousness and personal pride. At Hampton Institute another general, Samuel C. Armstrong, literally transformed Washington. Washington was "born again" at Hampton with Armstrong figuratively as the father he had never had. Armstrong, the son of missionaries in Hawaii, believed that people of the dark, tropical races needed to have their character strengthened, their languor quickened, by inculcation of the Puritan virtues of hard work, thrift, and moral earnestness. He considered Booker T. Washington the best product of his lifetime of effort. When Armstrong died, Washington made William H. Baldwin, a railroad president, chairman of his board of trustees and his closest adviser white or black. Finally, there was Theodore Roosevelt, Washington's political patron and confidant.

All his life, Washington followed the precepts that Hampton Institute taught and all these white benefactors subscribed to: a nineteenth-century faith in individual initiative and self-help, an accommodationist strategy toward Southern whites, and a faith that these men could be his effective partners in counteracting Southern proscription and discrimination and advancing the black race. As he became a leader instead of a follower, however, Washington found that his identity with the black community or his own interest frequently impelled him to actions of which these white counselors and benefactors would not approve. He then resorted to secrecy, with some resulting contradictions and inner tensions.

It is hard to see how Washington could have become anything but a "white man's black man," considering the circumstances and experiences of his youth. I ended the first volume of my biography, published last year, on an inconclusive note. I showed how, through his Atlanta Compromise speech and dinner at the White House and the aid of Northern philanthropists he had become by 1901 "the king of a captive people." I suggested, though I did not say outright, that the young Moses of his race had become the old Pharaoh. I could not make the final judgment of the man, could not say the final word, when only halfway through his career. Otherwise, the second volume would be anticlimactic.

Now, however, I confront the old minotaur himself. Booker T. Washington, like any other man, looks better while struggling to reach the top than he does on the top and trying to stay there, impelled by his situation to prevent others from climbing up to displace him. Washington at the height of his power and influence did much that was designed to further racial justice and black advancement. On the other hand, he did much that was designed, however much he disguised the fact, to keep him in power.

My task as a biographer is to try to understand the character and to write about him in such a way that the reader can understand him. It is not my task to impeach Booker T. Washington or to defend him either. It has been said that the historian must in the final analysis, after weighing all the factors and modifying all the sweeping assertions, be a judge, and if necessary a hanging judge. Perhaps it is the biographer's role and duty also, in the final analysis. But in the meanwhile, the biographer's duty is to keep everything in balance so that he and the reader can understand the character and the events in which he lives his life. There must be a balance between life and times, that is, we need to avoid the egocentric fallacy that the man—any man, even Napoleon or Hitler—causes the events that occur around him. History does not move in that simple a way. On the other hand, by studying a man's life we can learn the effect rather than the cause of events that swirl around him in his lifetime. Thus, through biography, we can give a human dimension to history. We see historical causation as stemming from impersonal forces, but we see history happening to an ordinary human being like ourselves. Thus,

Booker T. Washington, by his compromises with American white racism, did not *cause* the wave of race riots, segregation, and other racial aggressions of his day, the worst era of race relations since Reconstruction. But we can see in Washington the kind of black leader that such an era would throw to the top.

The most important balance that a biographer can bring to his subject, however, is a balance between sympathy and detachment. The reason why there has never been a great satirical biography is that the satirist looks at the subject entirely from the outside, making no effort to try to understand why he behaves as he does. Sympathy, on the other hand, opens the door to understanding motives, impulses, and attitudes that would otherwise be complete mysteries. "A fellow-feeling makes one wond'rous kind." But, carried too far, sympathy can lead to identity with the character, seeing the whole world through his eyes, and thus entrapment in his egocentric belief that the world revolves about him. Sympathy, then, needs the counterweight of detachment to keep the proper emotional and aesthetic balance. Detachment, the cool, critical eye of the uninvolved bystander, not the stern pointing finger of the moralist, is the right counterbalance.

As the biographer of Booker T. Washington, therefore, I must keep my heart open but also keep my eyes open. I can sympathize with his struggle up from slavery, the tragic death of his first two wives, his faithful devotion to his extended family, his constructive work of education at Tuskegee, and his efforts to uplift the crop-mortgaged black tenant farmers of the South from their poverty and frequent misery. I can appreciate his efforts, quietly and moderately in public and directly in secret, to work for civil rights and justice, the end to lynching, the equal right to vote, and the outlawing of peonage. I can even find in my heart some sympathy for Washington's less decorous private attacks on his enemies as part of his humanness, although his public image required him to behave in public like a Sunday school teacher. And I must say, I admire him for resolutely enjoying life in an era when hateful whites wanted to victimize him and even the friends of the black man insisted that the black person play the role of victim so they could feel sorry for him. Washington was, it is fair to say, the least victimized black man of his time.

On the other hand, a detached view of Washington's life and his era compels the biographer to deal with the less savory aspects of his career. In his effort to be practical, and in his effort not to give offense to the Southern whites, Washington emphasized the most basic schooling, the humbler trades and occupations, and deferential behavior, at the expense of college training, the professions, and higher aspirations. In this he behaved as he thought the circumstances made necessary rather than as someone a thousand miles or a hundred years away would have had him act. When others criticized him for this, however, he took the criticisms not as legitimate intellectual disagreement but as personal attacks on him. Thus much of his energy was spent in thwarting the black colleges or diverting them from their original ends. When William Monroe Trotter, a Harvard graduate, in his newspaper the *Boston Guardian* began to pepper Washington with criticisms and insults, Washington went to inordinate lengths to silence or crush him. When the black intellectuals under Du Bois' leadership formed the Niagara Movement for black civil rights, Washington outgeneraled it at every turn and prevented its full development. When the National Association for the Advancement of Colored People was formed in 1909 by a merger of the Niagara Movement blacks with liberal whites, Washington refused to join it and fought it both openly and secretly. Obviously, Washington was among the less lovable major figures in American black history. But if we muster some sympathy and balance it with detachment, we can see that he was neither the black superman nor a moral monster, but, like the rest of us, somewhere in between.

Booker T. Washington:
The Labyrinth and the Thread

I am living proof that an editor *can* be a biographer. Whether an editor *should* be a biographer, or vice versa, depends on the person and the subject. I cannot speak for everyone faced with that dilemma, but for me as editor and biographer the double life proved that much richer. As a biographer focusing on the thread of biographical narrative I had the advantage of collaborating with an editor, a co-editor, and a corporal's guard of editorial researchers who explored the geography of the labyrinth—the historical context, the principal associates of my central figure, and even what Tom Clark called "the once-at-bat characters" in my story. Colleagues surrounded me who knew the meaningful—and sometimes the meaningless—details as well as I did. Academia these days is such a lonely crowd of specialists that it is a real pleasure to be in such a workshop. As a biographer, I could shed light on the behavior and unfolding character of my protagonist which the editing project could use and had to consider. Editors tend to assume that their own steady focus on the documents and their more exhaustive annotation research give them more complete and certain knowledge than any biographer. It is harder to be smug in that assumption when a biographer is in the house. He knows where the thread leads, which is also crucial knowledge.

It was biography rather than editing that I had in mind at first. While I was a graduate student doing research for my doctoral dissertation I got my first exciting look at the huge mound of Washington's papers, recently acquired by the Library of Congress from Tuskegee Institute. It was a remarkable treasure of black history and American social history: more than a million items of correspondence, speeches, writings, inter-departmental memos, minutes of the faculty council, thirty-nine scrapbooks of newspaper clippings, and many items of dubious biographical importance, such as a daily report of the menu of students and faculty for twenty years, daily reports of a swine herd and poultry yard, a tomato label from the Tuskegee cannery, a package of dried beans from a black farmer, and a letter from Jesus Christ from his temporary headquarters in upstate New York—he said he wrote in English as it was the language of the Hebrews before the tower of Babel.

It was by far the largest record of any black individual in American history, and it still is so with the possible exception of Martin Luther King. Equally to the point, it revealed a much more complex character than historians had imagined, and opened a window through the veil that had always screened the private lives of blacks from white view. For the last twenty years of Washington's life, he and his shrewd, faithful private secretary Emmett Scott saved every scrap of the record, apparently in the conviction that when it was all revealed, even including his dirty tricks, history would vindicate him. Despite my biography, or maybe because of it, the jury is·still out on Booker T. Washington. But the biographer must be grateful for the sense of destiny or whatever motive that caused them to save everything, and also for the reasons, whatever they were, that caused those in charge of Tuskegee Institute in the 1940s to let the papers go to one of the great manuscript repositories.

It was more than ten years after the first glimpse before I returned to Booker T. Washington. Thereby hangs another long tale that I'll forbear telling here, except to say that I spent nine years in cultural exile in a teachers' college in a small Texas town that resembled Tuskegee. Having grown up in the Atlanta suburbs, I needed that long immersion in the rural South before I could have understood Washington's experience and the outlook that grew out of that experience. I began serious work on a Washington biography in 1961, spending my retirement money one summer, then getting summer grants and finally a fellowship for a whole year, exploiting my wife as a research assistant, and digging away at the mound of evidence until I gradually distinguished the meaningful details from the trivia. I came to know the man I had been studying. All this was taking years, because although I was obsessed by my subject I was not driven. As my notes piled up, I began to realize that only a small part of the life and times of Booker T. Washington could be incorporated into the themes of a biography.

At this moment Oliver W. Holmes of the National Historical Publications Commission approached me with an invitation to edit Washington's papers. He had his own reasons for the suggestion, stemming at least partly from a growing criticism of his federal agency from American historians who called for history "from the bottom up" and decried the elitism of the NHPC's almost exclusive focus on the Founding Fathers. Bottoms-up history has been demanded more often than it has been written or edited over the past twenty years. But Ira Berlin's Freedom History project, David Katzman and William Tuttle's *Plain People,* and Thomas Frazier's *The Underside of American History* are a few recent indications of an emerging history of the American people. At any rate, Dr. Holmes thought an edition of Washington's papers would help move American historical editing away from concentration on the Great White Fathers. Of course, Washington was another elite character, one of the great black fathers of black history. Maybe I did not sufficiently clarify that fact for Dr. Holmes, for I was already thinking how an edition—a highly selective edition—of Washington's papers would solve some of my dilemmas as a biographer.

Washington was a challenge to the biographer not merely because his private papers were so voluminous but because he was so complex, and it seemd to me in 1966 when I began the editing project that it would be a good showcase for illustrating this complexity. Washington was not complex the way I imagine an intellectual is, with most of the contradictions ultimately resolvable into some sort of unity, intellectual integrity, or consistent outlook. Maybe I have inaccurately idealized the intellectual by that description, but my purpose is to show what Washington was not. He was a man of action and a politician, not an intellectual, and he both despised and feared the black intellectuals of his day. His contradictions were unresolvable because they represented the various roles an all-purpose black leader had to play in white America.

Given such a complex character, and given the biographer's obligation to tell the truth—the whole truth—about his subject, it seemed to me and still seems to me that one of the best ways to do it would be to present the documentary evidence, not merely cite the evidence. Publicly Washington acquiesced in the disfranchisement and segregation of blacks, whereas his private papers make clear that he initiated, guided, and secured financing for court cases challenging the grandfather clause, denial of jury service to blacks, Jim Crow railroad cars, peonage, and other forms of black subordination that he publicly accepted. He did all of this subversion of white supremacy in the deepest secrecy, and only a handful of intimates had any idea of it during his lifetime.

There was also a less attractive, more feral side to Washington's secret life. He presented himself to the world in his autobiography and other writings and speeches as a social pacifist who turned the other cheek and adjured blacks to prepare themselves for future opportunities by self-improvement. In fact, most of his public utterances were grab bags of Sunday-school platitudes. In secret, however, he treated his black and white critics as enemies and used ruthless Machiavellian methods against them. He hired spies to infiltrate all the organizations of his opponents and not only forewarn him of their actions but serve as provocateurs and saboteurs of their plans. He bought black newspapers to sing his song, and publicly lied about it. He secretly hounded some of his more vulnerable opponents until they sought safety in obscurity. If I may borrow Blake's phrase, what better way to frame the fearful asymmetry of this tiger than an edition of his letters, with full but not exclusive attention to his secret life?

It would probably have been harder to edit Washington's papers after completing the biography, because then the temptation would be hard to resist simply to select the document that illustrated the interpretation and themes of the biography. I published the first volume of the biography simultaneously with the appearance of the first two volumes of the papers, and I deliberately avoided in that first volume any effort to say the final word on Washington's character and personality. The editing project undoubtedly slowed the pace of the biography. Editing can be endless, laborious, and often downright boring work at times. My co-editor Ray Smock and I took turns reading aloud through the photocopies and typescript of every volume, and in the final reading of the galley proofs we had four people taking turns aloud. One pair of eyes was on the photocopy, one on the typescript, and two on the galleys. This may not have been mind-boggling, as I am sure many in the audience have done the same galley-slavery, but it was certainly mind-deadening. It was impossible to go home and write after a day of that.

So it took me ten years to write the first volume of the biography, and ten more years to write the second volume. It was easier to edit every day than to write every day, though neither is easy work, and it was also more necessary. The editing project was on released time and involved an obligation to staff members, to the university, and to the outside sponsoring agencies. I felt somehow more of an obligation to put out an edited volume every year than I felt about "doing my own thing." I must confess that throughout both enterprises I thought of the editing as a team effort and the biography as my own. This is not to deny the help of Ray Smock and others on the biography, but simply to explain my mental compartmentalization of the two scholarly enterprises. What the editing did for me as a biographer was allow me a leisurely second look at all the evidence, and a chance to see what each bit of evidence signified not only to me but to my fellow editors. Every interpretive theme could be tried out on an informed and critical audience before it found its way into print in my biography.

The biography also benefited in interpretation and general tone from its long contact with editing. In Washington's case it cannot be said that to comprehend all is to pardon all. His "dirty tricks" and his mealy-mouthed moderation in the face of racial injustice do not look any more attractive when thoroughly examined. But my original purpose was to write a much more detached, ironical, satirical biography. Sustained contact with the documents, and their fuller explanation of how Washington's experience dictated the course he took, changed that approach somewhat. A biographer cannot understand his subject if he keeps him forever at arm's length. The editing helped me to understand more and sit in judgment less. Now that it is all done, in spite of all my efforts I missed the quintessence of Booker T. Washington, the wizard of Tuskegee, but I believe that that is because he *had* no quintessence. His personality disappeared into the roles he played. So I end with a critical portrait of Washington, but I hope one that is more compassionate and understanding of a black leader born in slavery and flourishing during the age of segregation.

I think that obviously the work on the biography helped in the editing. I was always reading ahead, so to speak. At least, it helped me to win some arguments with Ray Smock about inclusion of one document or another, on the ground that the particular document was part of a chain of evidence on some facet of Washington's life that would assume greater importance later. Comprehensive knowledge of Washington's entire life was definitely a help in selection, the problem of which was magnified by the disparity between the million items in the collection and the less than ten thousand, or one percent, in the selection.

We have had no serious cause for regret about what we selected or what we omitted. It is true that one reviewer on two separate occasions faulted us for omission of favorite letters cited in my articles, arguing that "what 'author' Harlan finds significant enough to quote in his Washington monographs 'editor' Harlan should consider sufficiently significant to include in his Washington *Papers*." Another reviewer also reproved us for omitting a document. The biographer of another black man, George H. White the Reconstruction politician, complained that we had omitted a letter that proved that his subject had significantly differed with Booker T. Washington's conservative racial policies. What we found on rechecking the letter was that White agreed with Washington to the point of sycophancy, and we also concluded that we had been right to omit the letter as relatively insignificant.

Near the end of the project we decided to guard against errors of judgment in the selection process by going systematically through the scholarly books and articles touching on Booker T. Washington's life and citing his papers, to see if we might have omitted significant documents. We found that we had omitted several hundred so cited. But when we checked these, we found that our original judgment in omitting them had been correct, for cause. Most of the omitted documents contained nothing significant not already in some included document. Often they were simply links in a chain of correspondence in which we had selected the more informative or better stated letter. It is inevitable in a highly selective edition that only the meatiest of a series of letters will be published. In some thirty cases, on second or third thought, we have decided to include a formerly passed-over document. That is a good batting average, but it says more about the editorial process and Ray Smock's insistence that we double-check and our editorial team's ability to separate the wheat from the chaff than it says about a biographer being in the house.

The symbiosis of editing and writing on the Booker T. Washington project resulted in a lot more editorial self restraint than has been true on some other projects. That is not to say that editorial restraint is universally appropriate. Maybe if Julian Boyd were also a Jefferson biographer he would have dealt differently with annotation, but since he was not, maybe his methods were right for him and his circumstances and his subject. Editing is an art, not a science, and we ought to avoid universal rules about the amount and kind of annotation that is suitable. If Boyd was not our model, we did have the example before us of a distinguished biographer and editor, Arthur Link, and more often than we have admitted before, when faced with an editorial quandary we turned to his volumes for guidance. Needless to say, he is responsible only for our virtues, not our editorial sins.

We wanted the edition to have a separate existence, rather than merely illustrating the biography or proving by amplification of the evidence that the biographer was right on all counts. We hoped, for example, that the edited volumes could treat subjects beyond the range or depth of the biography—such themes as industrial education at Tuskegee, the relationship between town and gown and between black schools and white philanthropy, the black politics of the era, black tenant farm life, and the life and concerns of the black bourgeoisie. We wanted to deal with these subjects without tendentious annotation or overinterpretation that would take its tone from Washington's own social philosophy. Obviously, our selection process itself, taking one out of a hundred documents, was a form of interpretation, but we did not want to compound this by taking a monumental approach by which the documents would add up to a larger-than-life representation of Booker T. Washington. So we aimed at spare annotation, identifying or explaining the documents rather than exhausting the subject. As time passed, we found ourselves driven more than we intended toward the biographical by the very nature of the collection. Our resistance to this, however, our effort to study the labyrinth as well as follow the thread, we think helped us avoid an edition subservient to the biography. Of course, it helped also to be dealing with a historical figure who was often less than heroic.

I want to conclude by answering a few general questions that seem to arise out of the intertwining of biography and editing. Could another biographer come along now and do as well as I by looking only at our fourteen volumes? The answer is no, because any biographer worth reading has to try to know and understand all he can about his character, how he acted as a key to what he thought and felt as history washed him along. On the other hand, our edited volumes discovered facets of Washington's life that I did not know when I wrote the first volume of the biography, so the edition would be a good place to begin.

What are the audiences I see for the biography and the fourteen edited volumes, are they the same, different, or overlapping? To that I have to give the classic answer, that's a good question. Obviously, they are not the same. In the present-day book market, people buy biographies and libraries—a relatively small number of libraries—buy editions. Furthermore, monographs are almost exclusive as products of graduate-school workshops, and most of the scholarly books published every year are these monographs evolving from graduate study. There is a powerful vested interest in the monograph as the primary form of scholarship recognized and approved by the scholarly professions. We may deplore this and hope to change it, but it is a fact. In my opinion, letterpress editions are most valuable in providing broad information for the student and teacher rather than as specialized research materials. I have faith, that in the long run, this type of service to scholarship and learning will gain in recognition, as documentary history rather than as an aid to history.

A related question is, which will be useful longer, the biography or the edition? I hate to have to answer this, because I feel a greater proprietary claim on the biography. More of my own art went into fashioning its image of Booker T. Washington. It is mine, whereas the edition is ours. Nevertheless, I believe any biography is a thing of its season. It is impossible to write a definitive biography of any historical figure as protean and deliberately deceptive as Washington. On the other hand, more than one generation will find meanings in the published documents that even we the editors did not see. If we editors do our work well and with fidelity, our work will be readable and will be read decades from now, while the monographs of today will collect dust like the leaves of yesteryear, their provocative interpretations ignored or merely points of departure for twenty-first-century perspectives.

To turn to a final question, you have often heard the expression, "If you could walk a mile in my shoes, you would understand and approve of what I have done." My co-editor Ray Smock and I have often discussed the question—and let me take this opportunity to thank him for some of the better features of this paper. He may seek to hide behind his congressional immunity, but he cannot stop me from acknowledging his help. If we could have walked a mile in Washington's shoes, maybe we would have suspended criticism. But we could never go more than *half* a mile before our feet hurt and our critical faculties returned. We found many cases of Washington being traduced by his enemies, but also found him vilifying his critics. Many contemporaries and later scholars stereotyped Washington contrary to the evidence we found, but we also found him a power-hungry political boss and a self-contradictory actor who could publicly say one thing and secretly do the opposite. His character was such that we could explain him without feeling an undue temptation to defend him.

Index